W9-BYP-541

American Catholic Identity

Essays in an Age of Change

Edited by Dr. Francis J. Butler

Sheed & Ward

Sheed & Ward™ is a service of The National Catholic Reporter Publishing Company.

———————————◆———————————

Library of Congress Cataloguing-in-Publication Data
American Catholic identity : essays in an age of change/
   Francis J. Butler, ed.
      p.   cm.
   Includes bibliographical references.
   ISBN: 1-55612-707-3
   1. Catholic Church—United States—Membership.
  2. Identification (Religion)   I. Butler, Francis J.
  BX1406.2.A633   1994
  282'.73—dc20   94-25511
                                            CIP

———————————◆———————————

Published by: Sheed & Ward
                115 E. Armour Blvd.
                P.O. Box 419492
                Kansas City, MO 64141

To order, call: (800) 333-7373

Contents

Higher Education

Parish Life

Vocations

Youth Ministry and Catholic Schools

Evangelization

International

Foreword

"In a higher world it is otherwise; but here below to live is to change, and to be perfect is to have changed often."
— Cardinal John Henry Newman

Discovering new ways to reassert the religious mission and spiritual identity within Catholic institutional life has become an issue of imperative importance as the twentieth century comes to a close. A new environment for Catholicism, one with fewer numbers of clergy and religious, limited financial resources, and massive pastoral and educational demands, requires the kind of careful thought and discussion that is too rare in our deadline driven existence. Yet, for the past eighteen years, the Catholic foundation community has regularly set aside time to convene church leaders and scholars to help articulate how Catholicism should adjust to new circumstances and what will be required of membership in tomorrow's church.

Over forty national symposia have been conducted and transcribed. Together, these discussions provide a rich mosaic of contemporary Catholic life. What follows are but a few of the more powerful and insightful presentations in the series of exchanges. Although they are primarily aimed to guide philanthropists in their charitable programs, the relevance of these papers to both church professionals, educators, pastors and the wider believing community will be evident to all. Each of them speaks to a reality far more fundamental than charitable giving. Unfolding in these presentations is an understanding of what it means to be a member of the church today.

The editor wishes to thank the many contributors to this volume and especially members of Foundations and Donors Interested in Catholic Activities, Inc., the consortium whose commitment to the church remains a model for Catholic laity everywhere.

Appreciation is expressed to the Lilly Endowment, without whose effort many symposia would not have been held. Finally, special thanks is given to the Mary J. Donnelly Foundation, the Komes Foundation, and an additional member of FADICA who prefers anonymity, for encouragement and grant support they have given to this compendium project.

Francis J. Butler

Higher Education

1.

The Religious Impact of Catholic Higher Education: Is There a Gap Between What Catholic Universities Proclaim and What They Practice?

Edward A. Malloy, CSC

NOT LONG AGO I WAS READING A BIOGRAPHY OF JOHN HENRY Cardinal Newman. In one section the author describes Newman's experience at Oxford early in his university career. The young John Henry Newman wrote home to his mother describing his impressions of Oxford: "I think most of the students spend their time drinking, and then when they are finished drinking they drink some more. The thing they are best at is drinking."

One could conclude that this reflects a young person's naivete; he was not from an upper-class background like many of his colleagues at Oxford. But I think it does suggest that our picture of what goes on in universities and under university auspices can easily be romanticized. A former director of ours at Notre Dame, who is a specialist on the University of Paris during the thirteenth century, reminds us that the "town-gown" relationship was problematic even in those days. The students were thought by the townspeople to be problem-causing,

---

Rev. Edward A. Malloy, CSC is the sixteenth President of the University of Notre Dame.

1

spoiled brats who wasted their youth reading books and other such things. The less exposed the citizens could be to these young people, the better. And we remember that Socrates was put to death because he was thought to be undermining his students' morality and sense of perspective as well as the traditional way of looking at things.

Whether we go back to the origins of Western culture, concentrate on the Middle Ages, or look at our colleges and universities today, there is a wide variety of perspectives that we could bring to bear in our consideration of Catholic higher education.

I would like to begin by reflecting on context and then focus on structure. This approach may not answer the question of Catholic higher education's future, but I hope it leads us in that direction.

First, some thoughts about context. Through my participation in the International Federation of Catholic Universities (IFCU) and in the stages of discussion leading to *Ex Corde Ecclesiae*, I have learned a great deal about the relative merits and flaws of American higher education and, particularly, American Catholic higher education. IFCU is the closest we have to a Catholic umbrella organization, and it is one of the ways that we can interact with our colleagues who serve in some of the other continents of the world. The process leading to *Ex Corde Ecclesiae* was difficult. Several of us at this meeting have been through the wars, so to speak. Not that it was vitriolic, but firm points of view were reflected in some of the discussions. We had to pick up on the reality of Catholic higher education around the world in order to put together a document that did not simply reflect Western Europe or North America or the two combined.

What can we say about the context of Catholic higher education around the world? One, it is surely diverse, and some of the things that we presuppose here are not true elsewhere. Much of Catholic higher education, for example, is subsidized by the state or the national government. So the reality is not marked by a perpetual financial crisis and an ongoing solicitation of benefactors and foundations.

Another reality is somewhat more overwhelming. Quite simply, when the government provides the funds, you are beholden to it. If the state provides the majority of funds, there is a tendency for the school to allow a kind of hegemony over the nature of the curriculum, the faculty, the testing schedule, and similar elements. And so, the question about Catholic identity and mission has to take into account in all instances the relationship to government. In order to make it at all, you have to be sympathetic or at least not antagonistic toward the government. So when you put together a worldwide document on Catholic higher education, for example, and describe its contours and prospects, the various kinds of government supervision and control in other parts of the world form at least one reality that differs from the American experience.

A second factor is the culture in which Catholic higher education functions. What do we think is the state of Catholic faith and practice in much of Western Europe today? My limited exposure on trips would suggest that it is very different from that in the United States, including the attitude of young people toward their Catholic heritage and the vitality of practice. One can make a judgment about what the difference is, whether it is a good one, and whether we are doing better than the Europeans. I think it is important to note that the culture in many of the countries of Western Europe where Catholic higher education operates does not reflect all of our presuppositions, although some commentators suggest that we are just one generation away from being subjected to the same set of difficulties.

Catholic higher education in Asia is a whole other matter. Tokyo's Sofia University, a Jesuit school, and Nagoia's Nanzan University, a Divine Word school, can assume that between 1 and 5 percent of their student body and faculty, not counting the members of the religious communities, are Christian. It is a kind of witness in a culture largely non-Christian. We in the United States do not even think in such terms. Are they Catholic institutions? What about that surprising little section in *Ex Corde Ecclesiae* that said the majority of the faculty should be Catholic Christians? How do you implement something like that when you are talking about Japan, Taiwan, Hong Kong, or even India?

I made my first trip to India not long ago, and we gathered at a Catholic college in Kerala state. It was a very invigorating experience, but one of the difficulties in making a judgment about a complex culture and reality like India is that it all depends on which state you are in. Kerala is the most Christian part of India. When you drive around, you see shrines, Catholic colleges and hospitals, training programs, parishes, places of pilgrimage. It is almost like going to Ireland or Spain, but these do not reflect the reality of the country as a whole. Catholic higher education in India, which has many institutions, is not quite like Japan, but it is not like Canada or the United States either.

So a major obstacle to determining the true state of Catholic higher education in the world and what it should aspire to is its great variation from one culture to the next. I think we need to keep that in mind, especially when putting together a document for the universal church. The kind of judgment you make depends on your own concrete experience.

When we gathered together in Rome to put this document together, we had representatives from all parts of the world. A rector from a Catholic university in Beirut said, "As I got on the boat to come to this meeting, I saw the bombs landing on my university." What does that do to your perspective on your role? We talked to the rectors of several universities in Central America, and one said to me, "You know, the previous two rectors were murdered, and we have lost a lot of faculty to the violence that is endemic in our country." What can one expect in that sort of situation? And of course we remember the terrible tragedy in El Salvador.

Some sobering messages can be extracted from the complex reality of Catholic higher education elsewhere. No other country has such an extensive network of Catholic schools as exists in the United States. The Association of Catholic Colleges and Universities (ACCU), the umbrella organization for Catholic higher education in this country, estimates that there are approximately 230 Catholic colleges and universities here. Unfortunately a few of the smaller, less viable institutions have closed in the past few years.

Of those 230 schools, around twenty might be classified as research universities in one or the other sense of the term. This means that the remaining schools serve a different purpose and function and have a wide range of constituencies. Some are very small colleges, still run by the founding religious community or diocese. Some have emerged in the post–Vatican II period in response to perceived needs in the church. Others are historical institutions. Georgetown University, the first of the major universities, is 200 years old, and Notre Dame is 150 years old.

When we went to the meetings in Rome, one of the great concerns was the relationship between the Vatican (as the center of the Catholic organizational structure, particularly the Vatican agency that deals with higher education) and this wide variety of institutions of higher education. The tendency of almost all of the rectors of these institutions — around the world and not just in this country — was to argue for maximization of freedom, maintenance of the relative autonomy such as higher education enjoys in general in this country, and continuation of the role that boards play in supervision. But some others, not always episcopal figures, tended to see the threat of contemporary society and culture to the Catholic identity and mission of these institutions. They feared that, as Catholic colleges and universities became stronger academically, they would move away from their religious roots.

So we were reminded often of the American experience, with schools like Harvard, Princeton, Yale, Stanford, Duke, and so on. These schools began under religious auspices, and the religious component was an essential part of how they saw themselves in their early days. Eventually, usually reflecting faculty concerns, these universities gradually loosened their religious connections under the guise of either academic freedom or institutional integrity. The debate that preceded the final formulation of *Ex Corde Ecclesiae* concerned whether the kind of institutional autonomy that has prevailed in the West is a good thing and whether it is possible, in reality, to maintain one's religious mission and identity as a result. Of course, the answer is still unknown. One can exaggerate the control that presidents and boards exercise over institutions, but one can also be fear-struck in the face of all contemporary culture.

Is this the best of times or the worst of times? Was there a golden age? Is this a time of decline from some high standard of the past? My own inclination is to say that it is always the best of times and the worst of times. The optimists in our midst will point out what is good about it, and the pessimists and cynics will remind you of how things have gone to hell in a handbasket. I will try to provide here some unvarnished reflections. I really do not know your perspective on most of these questions, but I will give at least my version of what I think is happening. To some extent I will use my experience at Notre Dame, but I have had a chance to read about, look into, and talk with the leadership of some of these other institutions as well.

Students

I would first like to discuss the students who come to our institutions. One structural question is: Whom do we serve? Our outcomes, or outputs, are always going to be at least partially a function of who comes to us to study, whether at the undergraduate, the graduate, or the professional-school level.

We are only as good as those who come to us. What can we say about them? When I grew up, I went to St. Anthony's grade school; I had nuns for all eight grades. A couple of weeks ago Bill Byron was there. We had a Mass and dinner celebrating the hundredth anniversary of my parish, where I went to grade school and my sisters went to grade school and high school. Schools under church auspices were proliferating at that particular moment of American Catholic history.

Many of them were peopled by members of religion communities and very dedicated individuals like those who gave me a fine education at the earlier stages of my life and opened up a new set of possibilities for me. I went to a Catholic high school; I had a fairly high percentage of priests and brothers, Augustinians, as teachers. Then I went to Notre Dame. In many ways I was prepared when I got to Notre Dame because of my family background — both of my parents were Catholics and took it seriously though they had different versions of what that entailed — but also because of the people I was exposed to in my early stages of education. When I came to Notre Dame, I found nothing there inconsistent with what I had known already. It was just the next level of education. The rule structure, the expectations for moral performance or at least what could get you in trouble, were similar to those prevalent at other campuses. A kind of aura of Catholicity pervaded Notre Dame not unlike that at St. Anthony's and Carroll High School. That was true, I think, pretty much across the board. Whether people went to Catholic grade school or high school, there was a fairly easy continuity to maintain when they got to the university or college.

That simply is not true any more. A recent statistic said that about 45 percent of our Notre Dame students come from Catholic high schools. The majority of undergraduate students currently at Notre Dame therefore have not come from a Catholic high-school background. The number who went to Catholic grade school also varies from previous times. There are many families, as you know, who make a choice. If they are going to send their kids to Catholic school, some choose grade school and not high school; some choose high school and not grade school. In either case, the number of our students who come from a Catholic educational background at both levels is declining. We face a different kind of reality in what we can presuppose about students, with fewer Catholic schools and fewer students enrolling in them or able to afford Catholic educations.

The second component of change concerns the values and principles inculcated in students at Catholic schools. Even if students go to Catholic schools, notions proliferate about what should be taught and what should be the teaching methodology. The background of teachers has changed; more and more are laypeople. That is not a critique, but a recognition of the reality that the older, deeply embedded, pervasive Catholic culture is becoming more difficult to sustain, even in the Catholic school system, among the teachers who teach there. This development opens up the possibility for a greater degree of creativity, for embodying or personifying in the teachers the experience of marriage and family life — something that may not have been possible before — and many other things. But as far as maintenance of religious culture is concerned, I think that has changed significantly.

A third change has occurred in the family backgrounds of our students. Many more of them come from mixed religious backgrounds: one parent Catholic, the other one not. And the non-Catholic parent might be more religiously fervent than the Catholic parent.

Many more of our students come from divorced, single-parent, or divorced and remarried families. Even if someone has been granted an annulment and is remarried, there is still that kind of raw edge in terms of interpreting questions about process and attitudes. In my instruction of the graduating seniors, I have become more accustomed to thanking the parents, the extended family, and the surrogate parents of our graduates, because that more adequately reflects their experience. If you have a sophomore or junior parent weekend and both parents come, it is sometimes a traumatic moment for students because they have to deal with two sets of families. Personal circumstances have changed.

Another change is in the experience level. More of our students have been sexually active before they come to college. All the statistical profiles suggest that, even if they adhere to or acknowledge the significance of the Catholic value system with regard to sexuality, they have had some experience of sexual activity, including intercourse, at some time before they arrived at college. Drugs, which are, of course, available today — we speak of the drug culture — and alcohol, the most pervasive drug, often creep down into the middle stages of grade school. When we impose or suggest, particularly in on-campus living situations, a certain standard or expectation for young people, their experience before they get to college has an impact on whether they think these regulations are reasonable or realistic. It has become more difficult to predict whether students will abide by an institutional value system and the rules that flow from it or will instead rail against it in the student media and ultimately refuse to cooperate.

There are many positive experiences that students engage in before they come to college. A higher percentage, in my reading of it, have had outreach opportunities through service or social justice activities in grade school or high school. They often are much more sensitized to questions about homelessness, AIDS, ecology, and public policy practices. Many schools, and I am very happy to say many Catholic high schools, have required a period of service or volunteerism as part of getting their degrees. As I remember my own experience as an undergraduate, we were not in any way as socially conscious as many of the students today.

Finally, I will mention religious literacy. I live in a dorm and still teach one class a semester. I find that the students' religious literacy, for whatever set of reasons, including the factors that I have adverted to, has changed dramatically from the past. Students are very interested about the structure of worship — why we do certain things, what the symbols of worship mean. They are curious, but often they do not know what we call systematic or dogmatic theology, the linkage in the life of faith among the different things we proclaim as Catholic Christian people. They may have had bits and pieces of it, but the terminology is often unfamiliar. They have not had any holistic presentation of how these things come together and how they have been passed on from generation to generation and refracted through the experience of different eras of the Christian community.

Their sense of the sacramental practice of the community is often underdeveloped, and yet there is a great yearning. They seek the ability to pray and to seek what we call in spiritual terms the reality of God in their lives; there is a hunger there. I think many Catholic colleges and universities find that retreats, under whatever name, are oversubscribed. In the same way that students tend to be easy to motivate for service activity or outreach to the community at large, they are likewise very open to learning more about the rudiments of faith. This experience can come in a curricular way through theology courses, in extracurricular opportunities for reflection, and also in the form of a deep-rooted sense of need for spiritual development. So, even though their backgrounds are different, the absence of certain things has broken down the resistance to being tutored in the life of faith. And I would like to point out that Catholic colleges and universities take people as they are and do not simply lament that they are not like they were 20 or 50 years ago. There is an awful lot that can be done in a positive vein to build and to construct lives of faith.

A few final thoughts about the students. Many of our students are pious on campus and critical off campus. They go home to their home parishes and get turned off. It is difficult for a one-priest parish to offer the variety of liturgical opportunities that are often available at a Catholic college. And a typical home parish is much more heterogeneous in its range of ages and social and personal situations, so there is no easy resolution to the problem of "comfort" and "fit."

Andrew Greeley has made some very good points about the revival of religiosity among American Catholic young adults when they marry and start to raise a family. People in this age group face a difficult transition as they go from the campus out on their own and on to marriage. Our graduates usually live in areas with high concentrations of young adults as they begin their work career, or they go on to graduate or professional school, where the criticism of religion and religious practice is quite high. But there is a lot of evidence that when young adults begin to assume responsibility for their own minichurch, as we might call the family, they get much more involved in the church.

Another factor is that not only do students vary in how Catholic their background is, they come racially and ethnically from a much richer mix than they have in the past. For example, as we try to upgrade the percentage of black students on our campus, we can assume that the majority of them are not Catholic. They may have a certain image of what Catholics are like, particularly that Catholicism is a white person's church. They may not have had much experience of the black Catholic tradition as such. Further, we may too quickly presuppose that Hispanics are going to be active participants in a faith community, when, in fact, a certain percentage are very Pentecostal or immersed in Protestant groupings that stress small communities and a highly affective sense of membership. They may feel lost or alienated from the larger, more impersonal environments of the Catholic community.

And finally, the male-female factor is important. As you might expect, I find that as our students get immersed in the debate about gender and its significance in our culture, particularly attitudes about the church where women's ordination becomes a symbolic issue, a certain percentage are very harsh in their judgment of the institutional church. They think it ironic that in many communities the majority of those who worship and practice at the local level are female. Gender-based ecclesial issues are not going to go away. The bishops are struggling right now to put together a document, and whatever the final formulation says, we can predict it will meet a very difficult reception. I think that all of us face the challenge of bright, energetic, and thoughtful young women and men who relate to the church as an ongoing historical community.

Faculty

My second set of reflections concerns faculty. I believe that the Catholicity of our institutions will in the end be determined by the faculty. Administrators come and go, but faculty as a group have the decisive influence on the character of an institution. This issue, as I experience it, has a number of levels. The first is the issue of whom we hire and how we go about hiring them. I know there are a range of opinions about this. At Notre Dame, we ask everybody whom we are considering as a potential faculty member to answer the question regarding their religious affiliation. Some refuse to do it the first time around. Some only do it when somebody else fills it in for them. Some are Catholic and think it is not the kind of question we should ask. Some are not Catholic and think it is a question that will be held against them.

I guess our dilemma is that even when we ask the question about religious affiliation, and even when we make a very serious effort, it is very difficult to maintain a core group of dedicated Catholic faculty. And the higher your standards in a given discipline or college, the harder it is to find the pool that fits your needs. How can you make hiring decisions influenced by religious affiliation when you're trying to juggle the following variables: a chemical engineer who works in a highly refined area of chemical engineering; a biologist at the right age and rank with credentials fitting the needs of the department at this particular moment; a sociologist who is available and interested because she thinks that your campus offers something worth dedicating her life to and provides an environment conducive to her personal development and particular skills?

If there is anything that causes me anguish, it is hiring. We at Notre Dame claim that our faculty are somewhere between 60 and 70 percent Catholic. This is only an estimate. We do not have a squad of people go out and check into personal lives, nor do we ask faculty a series of questions about orthodoxy or their experience of the institutional church. So, even Catholic institutions like ours that ask the religious question are operating from only partial knowledge.

Let me phrase the question this way: What percentage of faculty ideally should be Catholics in the significant sense of the term — practicing Catholics for whom the faith is a personal, significant reality, a commitment, who perceive a connection between what they do, their notion of vocation, and their choice to work in a Catholic institution? How can we function as Catholic institutions in the absence of a core group of committed Catholic faculty? Some of our most dedicated faculty — dedicated to the school's religious identity — are not Catholic. Some of those least dedicated to the religious identity checked the box saying they were Catholic. Some faculty who were hired 20 years ago have been through two divorces and remarriages and are totally alienated from the church. Others have had bad experiences with clergy or with some public-policy issue or moral issue that they disagreed with. Their level of emotional involvement and connection to the school's mission and identity is very much truncated as a result, and they end up only being partially committed. If it came to a vote about maintaining the Catholic identity, how would our faculty vote?

We are now trying to inculcate a set of values and initiate new faculty into the reality of our particular institution — what it means to be a Catholic university. You cannot do it by preachiness, only with a great degree of sophistication and sensitivity. We feel that we have neglected this task in the past. We make videos and organize panels and presentations. As part of our 150th-year celebration, we have documented in depth the events in our history that are significant and explain how we got to where we are now. I find that many new faculty are very open to this experience.

A second dimension is the promotion of faculty members. We also say here that religious affiliation does not matter, that is, there is an equity in the judgment standards we apply. But one of my Holy Cross peers from the past used to talk about "factor X." When you are making a judgment on somebody, you can put all these standards on paper, but the question remains: Whom do you admit, hire, or promote when everybody looks the same? Factor X suggests that there is something about a person that fits the institution and what it is about. It is your refined sense of such individuals and the way they have acted, their level of participation and commitment to their task at the university.

I believe in factor X. It is an intuitive positive judgment that this person, when there is indecision about whether they should be promoted or not, ought to be promoted if they have this particular set of qualities, which may or may not be able to be put down on paper. Promotion, of course, takes place in highly convoluted processes, depending on how many faculty you have. By the time it gets to you, your hands are not exactly tied, but you do not want to exercise too much totalitarian privilege lest you be out the door next year. So promotion is a collective practice, and the Catholic dimension in promotion may be hard to quantify, but I am convinced that some people ought to be promoted because of factor X, beyond simply their overall academic performance.

A third dimension concerns what the faculty do. Is there a certain kind of research agenda? Can the life experience of the Catholic community be brought into their pedagogical style? I hope that at least a percentage of our faculty would want to explore the Catholic value system and tradition relative to some of the great issues of the day, like pollution control, medical support structures for the general population, or ways of thinking about prejudice and bigotry that can open up new sets of policies and attitudes. I think the American Catholic university has a special responsibility not only in the undergraduate curriculum but also in the kind of research in which its faculty are engaged. One of the ways that this responsibility is exercised in Catholic institutions is under the rubric of ethics. I think that ethics is a way of saying, "What is the relationship between our theory and our practice?" We produce an ethical profile of our own institution when we perform curriculum reviews, when we apply our disciplinary procedures to the misbehavior of faculty, staff, and students, and to some extent every time we hire or promote somebody.

The faculty is, in the end, the most crucial group when it comes to the Catholicity of the institution, but it is the most difficult aspect of contemporary institutional life to control, whether you are president, provost, dean, department head, or member of the advisory board or controlling board. For there is only so much that any of us can do in the face of the momentum and the well-conditioned practice of the academy in this country. We want to be respected by our peer institutions, religiously affiliated or not, and it is extremely important for us to maintain traditions that are accepted in the academy in general.

There are 3,500 institutions of higher learning in this country. I think last year the number of faculty "dismissed for cause" amounted to probably two or three. Others, of course, were encouraged to leave and did, or went through a process of review. The accusations made against faculty include all kinds of behavior that most people would consider totally unacceptable in general terms, and more so in a religiously affiliated school. But the willingness of faculty review groups to dismiss for cause a fellow faculty member is close to zero, because of the fear of litigation, of public scandal, of being put on the "hit list" of the American Association of University Professors (AAUP), and so on. It is not that we have to address widespread misperformance. It is just that the kind of self-protective mechanisms in place for faculty in higher education make it extremely difficult to confront unprofessional behavior and other conduct at odds with our Catholic character. I think it is one of the primary responsibilities of the presidents, boards, and other academic and university-wide officers to make sure that they are not simply intimidated in the face of this reality.

Governing Boards

The third and last structural component is the role of governing boards, whatever they may be called. Ours is called the Board of Trustees. The primary responsibility of most boards is to elect the president, chancellor, or whatever the CEO is called. The boards need to avoid micro-management, but in most Catholic institutions a fundamental responsibility of the boards is to protect the institution's mission and identity and to review the performance of the officers in this regard.

My experience of institutional boards at Catholic institutions suggests that board members recognize their responsibility and desire to fulfill it faithfully. But in the face of the things I mentioned about the student body and the faculty, what can the board do if they are unhappy about something except appoint a new president, or refuse to give money, or accept humbly the criticism of the local bishop or of parents? The board's role in the life of Catholic institutions is often based on anecdotal evidence describing what people are learning and how they are developing. They receive input from their children and from the students or faculty groups who come to the board to ask or complain about something. They do not have the first-hand experience of the daily goings-on and of the often very subtle changes that occur from day to day and from year to year.

But the board, which is designed as a protective mechanism, can exercise its role most effectively when the data flow is adequate to the task. The board needs to structure itself, to make sure that it is able and willing to ask questions, including uncomfortable ones, about how things are going, It has to ask for periodic review of aspects of the institution, particularly those related to the central core of its institutional identity and mission. How is Notre Dame doing? How is Loyola Marymount or Fordham or Mount St. Mary's doing? How are any other schools doing? The answer is probably mixed.

During my time at Notre Dame, I have become aware of a wide range of social and personal behaviors, some of which inflict severe harm on others, their property, or their reputations. This is the dark side of the picture. I am also aware of individuals who are bright, reflective, hardworking, generous, and loving; who marry each other;

who have great aspirations to establish a family and to raise them within the Catholic Christian tradition; who are involved in every form of work in our society and very much in the forefront trying to establish high standards of integrity; who are committed at the parish and diocesan level to leadership and service; who are active in every kind of civic organization; and who are willing to take on some of the great challenges, even at the risk of their own personal safety.

The challenges in Catholic higher education today are daunting. We are going against the trend. Do we have the wherewithal to make it? I think in the short term we surely do. Is there any guarantee that there will be a significant number of truly Catholic institutions of higher education 50 years from now? There is no guarantee at all. The great danger to Catholic universities is that they will take the route of Harvard, Princeton, and Yale, that they will shuck off their religious identity as they become more academically sophisticated and mature. If it happens, it will not be by way of a vote, but simply by default. Many of our Catholic colleges will be challenged to maintain their existence as private institutions as they become more expensive, as their traditional clientele shifts, and as people become less concerned or less committed to giving the opportunity of Catholic higher education to their daughters and sons. In the face of all this, we will also have a new demographic reality in terms of religious life and clergy. Only if lay people, in collaboration with clergy and members of religious communities, continue to maintain the commitment of the institution to Catholic principles and to take on all of the challenges related to our students, our faculty, and our boards, will we have a significant number of Catholic institutions 20 or 30 years from now.

Overall, I am optimistic. I think that we have a greater chance of sustaining a wide variety of Catholic higher educational institutions here in the United States than in any other part of the world. I think we benefit right now from a particular opportunity as much of higher education is subjected to a critique of purpose and identity. If we can remain distinctive, then I think we will get the support we need from benefactors, from foundations, and from other interested parties. But as soon as we lose our distinctiveness, we will lose our rationale for being, and that will be our death knell.

2.

Catholic Higher Education and Its Religious Impact: A Bishop's View

Bishop James W. Malone

MY TOPIC IS ONE OF SPECIAL SIGNIFICANCE FOR THE CATHOLIC Church in the United States at this time.

Higher education in general, and Catholic higher education in particular, were both extremely significant factors in the post–World War II transformation of the Catholic Church in the United States from a church of immigrants to a church whose members now are fully assimilated into the life and culture of our nation. And, for its part, Catholic higher education made a profound impact on the religious identity of its graduates.

I am amazed at how often Catholic lawyers, doctors, and business executives in their late fifties and older speak of what they learned in their college philosophy and theology classes. I also am edified that many graduates of Catholic colleges and universities participate in the life of the church as well as in other volunteer and philanthropic causes.

Today is a new moment for Catholic higher education. We are in what is variously described as a postmodern, postconciliar, post–cold war, post-Watergate, and

---

Bishop James W. Malone is the Bishop of Youngstown, Ohio, and a member of the Bishops and University Presidents' Committee of the National Conference of Catholic Bishops.

post-Irangate world and society. And many within the pastoral leadership of the church and within the ministry of Catholic higher education have become concerned about Catholic higher education. In simplistic terms, the question being raised is whether Catholic higher education has lost its Catholic character. Or to put it in more positive terms, what ought to be the nature and character of Catholic higher education as we move toward the beginning of the third millennium of Christianity?

As a pastoral leader, I believe that more is to be gained by answering a positive question than a negative one. Consequently, I would like to address the future. My thesis is simple. One of the most significant goals of Catholic higher education should be to provide its students the opportunity to be formed in a Catholic identity that is assertive but not sectarian. I am not questioning or demeaning other critical objectives that pertain to the mandate of higher education. They can and must be constitutive elements of Catholic higher education. In fact, one might argue that one of the unfinished agendas of Catholic higher education is the development of internationally recognized graduate-level programs that will place Catholics more at the forefront of science and the arts, as they already are in business and law.

For a Catholic school, excellence in scholarship is not enough. It is my opinion that if a school chooses to call itself a Catholic school or a school that participates in the Jesuit or Dominican tradition, then by that very fact it has chosen to associate itself with the life and mission of the community of faith that is the church. And one of the essential tasks or missions of the church is to provide those it encounters with the opportunity to be formed in a Catholic identity that is assertive but not sectarian.

Note the words I have chosen. First, opportunity. As a community, as a family of faith, we offer an opportunity, indeed a very special opportunity. We do not impose or coerce someone into faith or into religious practices. If we were to do so, then we would be testifying to our un-belief. We would be saying that we do not believe in the power of God's grace or the fact that faith is a gift that must be freely accepted or not. It is this sense of offering an opportunity that allows a Catholic institution to re-spect and honor the canons of liberal education while still being Catholic.

Second, identity. In the end, Christianity is a way of living. It is the Christ-way of living, a way of living that is capable of being integrated in an authentic fashion into the depths of an individual's personhood. For this reason it is appropriate to speak of identity — of the manner in which a person integrates the many dimensions of one's personhood and relates to one's self, to others, to the world around, and to the concern for ultimate meaning. And to be trite, we know that identity is not taught, but developed.

What does all this say to Catholic higher education? On the one hand, that courses in Catholic thinking or Catholic practice are not enough to make a school Catho-lic. On the other hand, that if there is not a distinctive and all-pervasive character to the life and ethos of a school, it will not be effectively Catholic. If the opportu-nity for a Catholic identity is to be experienced, then an institution must be truly comfortable with having a Catholic soul. Only in this way will students, faculty, and administration be able to experience the distinctive élan of Catholicism and the on-going interaction that contrib-utes to the development of a person's identity.

Next, an identity that is not sectarian but is asser-tive. One of the profound insights of the Second Vatican Council was its understanding of the relationship between the community of faith and the individual believer on the one side and, on the other, the world and society in which they are situated. The isolation of the Catholic past, which saw us over and against the world, has been replaced with a realistic sense of mission. The individual believer and, in particular, the lay person who participates in Catholic higher education, is called by baptism to be "like a leaven" that raises up and empowers what is good in the world and transforms what is evil. The identity in which our students are formed sends them forth from classroom and campus with their newfound learning to serve and to transform.

I realize that what I am proposing will not be easily achieved. The administration, faculty, and student body of some of our institutions of higher learning have become as pluralistic as the society in which we live. The individualism endemic to our culture, when combined with the skeptical criticism that is part and parcel of academic scholarship, serves as a powerful counterforce to the attainment of this identity. But as a pastor of a local church who shares responsibility for the pastoring of the universal church, I refuse to accept these limitations as definitive. For our schools have many in administration who believe in the distinctiveness of Catholic education, many teaching in classrooms who see their scholarship as an expression of their baptismal commitment, and many students who arrive with a sense of belief in which they seek to grow.

The church in the United States continues to need women and men, skilled in learning and committed in faith, who can become tomorrow's leaders to carry on the Christian mission. But how will this happen? I would suggest that we must become more focused on our objective. The failure of nerve and the religious insecurity of the past twenty years in some places must be replaced with an agenda that, while respecting individual conscience and honoring the distinctive autonomy of the secular sciences, nonetheless pursues and celebrates Catholic identity. To that end, Catholic colleges and universities should strive to incorporate into their life and activities three traditionally Catholic characteristics: a sacramental awareness, a sense of community, and a pursuit of the real truth.

A word on each of these characteristics. As regards sacramental awareness, we believe that all of life is shot through with the holy. So, the life of an institution such as a college or university is a continuous source of revelation. For this sacramentality to be experienced, however, it must be named, raised up, celebrated. This naming, this celebrating, is not just the responsibility of the office of campus ministry. It begins with the president's office and moves throughout campus life. That is how to celebrate a sacramental awareness.

Second, a sense of community. We know that ours is an age of individualism but also a time of great loneliness. As Catholics, we believe that salvation is experienced in the fellowship of faith, the *koinonia* that is the church. This profoundly Catholic instinct of community should be able to address the aloneness that so many experience. Though the challenge to a sense of community certainly would be more formidable in our commuter schools, could we not learn from the base-community experiences of Latin America how to transform our Catholic campuses?

Third, a pursuit of the real truth. The Word of God, the Logos, is the beginning and the end of all creation. The pursuit of human knowledge is a pursuit of the divine truth, a search, not for the rationalistic truth of the post-Enlightenment, but for truth that is open to mystery. Witnessing to such an integral understanding provides a needed bridge between the world of studies and the life of faith.

So, a pursuit of the real truth, a sacramental awareness, and a sense of community. The purpose of these rather pithy exhortations is to invite us to think collectively about how we can put some flesh to the bones of Catholic identity. By nature and conviction I am an optimist. And I am confident that if we marshal our resources and utilize the strengths of our tradition, we will be able to offer our students the greatest gift we have: the opportunity to develop a truly Christian and Catholic identity.

Parish Life

3.

Are Catholics Active Enough in Their Church? A Reflection on Membership and Catholic Identity

Margaret O'Brien Steinfels

ARE CATHOLICS ACTIVE ENOUGH IN THEIR CHURCH? I ASSUME that the question is not posed to me as a theological question; or to put it the other way around, I am not a theologian and, therefore, will not reflect primarily on questions of faith, grace, conversion, or the mystical body of Christ, which of course may be more relevant than my focus.

Are Catholics active enough in their church? Other questions inevitably arise. What does "active enough" mean? What do we mean by "church"? And in a reflection on membership and Catholic identity, what do we understand "membership" to be? And what is "Catholic identity"?

The question "Are Catholics active enough in their church?" can be answered in three ways. The first answer is "Yes, Catholics are active enough." The second answer is "Maybe"; "maybe" Catholics are as active as they can be, should be, or anyone wants them to be. And the third answer is "No, Catholics are not active enough."

Margaret O'Brien Steinfels is Editor of Commonweal *Magazine and a board member of the National Center for the Laity.*

Three contradictory answers — all of which may be true — point to the stress and tension Catholics see and feel about being a Catholic today. Which answer we give rests on how we define membership and, especially, Catholic identity.

Active Catholics

Yes, Catholics are active enough in their church. The Notre Dame study of parish life reported that Catholics in the parishes that were studied often had deep feelings of attachment to the parish and serious commitment to the core beliefs of Catholicism.

Andrew Greeley, in his studies of American Catholics, indicates that despite disagreement over *Humanae Vitae* and criticism of certain aspects of parish life, like preaching, Catholics remain remarkably loyal. They continue to call themselves and view themselves as Catholics, although they may not attend Mass as regularly as their parents did.

And then it must count for something that the number of Catholics in the United States continues to grow. There are between 55 and 59 million Catholics, about one-quarter of the American population. That percentage remains about the same because the general population is growing at a faster rate than the Catholic population. Still, there are a lot of us. And among these millions, each of us knows people deeply committed to the church — nuns, priests, laypeople — who have given their lives to preaching and teaching, to living out the demands of the Gospel in a very deeply committed way.

We may not care for all the expressions of this deep commitment, We may get nervous around charismatics, a little bored around theology professors, or annoyed at Catholics who claim that theirs is true-blue Catholicism — and that the pope agrees with them. Still, we must count all of these deeply committed people among the

most active members of the church, and through their efforts a good deal of the ordinary, everyday life of the
church is carried on.

Other active Catholics are not parish stalwarts but
rather people who consider that they live out the Gospel,
their religious beliefs, in their everyday lives, as lawyers,
as parents, as politicians. *Commonweal*'s series on "Faith
and Life" featured a number of such people: nurses, engi-
neers, lawyers, mothers, educators, computer program-
mers. The work of the Christian in the world is central to
their understanding of the Gospel. The National Center
for the Laity focuses on this group with what some regard
as a single-minded intensity.

Though active Catholics have many ways to express
their support, we can legitimately ask how many of them
put their money where their mouth is. We have the sense
— and some data supports it — that your average Catholic, who is almost certainly better off than his or her parents or grandparents, may not be as generous as they
were. Could St. Patrick's or any diocesan cathedral of that
size be built today? If not, why not? On the other hand,
Notre Dame University could be built today; it is being
built. They don't seem to have trouble raising money.
SOAR seems to generate enthusiasm among Catholics
who are ready to help support retired religious. Little
Flower, a child care agency in the diocese of Brooklyn
that I happen to know, always needs more money, but
their fund-raiser gives me the impression that they have
many generous supporters. *Commonweal* itself runs an
annual deficit, and the lack of money has undoubtedly
kept us from reaching broad numbers of well-educated
Catholics who would appreciate the magazine's outlook
and message.

Catholics, therefore, can be generous when asked to
support projects or institutions to which they are committed or for which they feel direct responsibility, perhaps
because no one else will provide the support. This is the
group I call active.

The "Maybe" Catholics

Then there is the group about which we want to say, "Maybe." "Maybe" Catholics are as active as their parish permits or encourages them to be. Some Catholics are not drawn to their parish or the church subculture around them. You know people who have moved to a new parish and feel it is alien to their deepest understandings of the church. Or people who are active when their children are young, then pull back or drop out of parish activities as the children grow up. It's as if there is nothing in the parish for them. Or sometimes they become disappointed with a new pastor.

About three years ago I spoke at a parish in Connecticut. The new pastor was much younger than the former pastor, who had been there since the days of Vatican II. This parish considered itself a community and seemed to have developed a great number of programs, projects, and relationships that worked and made the parish into a home. The new pastor did not see things that way. I was there about six months after he arrived, and could see the way in which this parish was beginning to dissolve under the discouragement that many people felt about the new pastor.

Some parishes are the provenance of the pastor, with activities circling around him; this is a kind of clerical parish, where parishioners agree with or accept the pastor's central role. My parents live in such a parish in Chicago, with its thick network of friends, clubs, and organizations. Sometimes those parishes can keep people out because they are so thick.

On the other hand, at least a few parishes are sensitive to the socially marginalized Catholic. You might say they recycle people: singles, divorced, young people. Or there are the new immigrants, Hispanic and Asian, whose cultural and religious traditions are not easily integrated into already established parishes and organizations.

Other "maybe" situations: Catholic kids go off to a Catholic college and are untouched by, unconnected to virtually any of its Catholic components, even when these are apparent and vital. They often feel peripheral or marginal to the church in that setting; some of them want to be peripheral. The church at hand does not speak to their understanding, their experience, their passions, or does not challenge and engage them. Not infrequently the Catholic college itself may be marginal to its own religious affiliation. I know a young woman who took her first and only theology course as a junior at a major Catholic college and was sorry she wasn't required to take more. And since she wasn't required, there was no room in her schedule for more. Kids who go off to non-Catholic colleges present real challenges for Newman clubs, Catholic centers, etc. I was somewhat surprised to find out from the chaplain at its Newman Center that, because it does not ask about religious affiliation, the University of Minnesota was no help to its Newman Center, Protestant Center, or Jewish Center in locating members of their religious faiths. The only way the Newman Center can come in contact with Catholics is to have them walk through the door.

The "maybe" category raises questions about links between family, parish, college, young adult life, and family and marriage. There are breaks in the connectors. Is there something we should do about this?

Catholics Who Are Not Active

Then there is the third answer: there are Catholics who are not active in their church — sometimes for understandable reasons, sometimes for reasons that elude us, and sometimes for bad reasons. Some feel unwelcome or think that they are not listened to. For others, their parish is just O.K., or the public church in their diocese may really put them off: the pope, the local ordinary, the social atmosphere of the local church is insular or odd; it does not speak to them. We Catholics pay too little attention, both at the diocesan and the national level, to this question of differences in the local churches — differences in history, religious elites, and established networks. Those local differences can be a boon to cohesiveness, but also a barrier to new people.

The new agenda encouraging bishops to use the media to teach was meant to have a positive impact on Catholics, and yet the belligerence that comes through or that is highlighted by the press and TV can put people off. A bishop's employment of the local media to teach is a real challenge and can have negative effects, particularly on those Catholics who get all of their information about the Catholic Church from TV and local newspapers, and not from *Commonweal* or the *National Catholic Register*, for example.

Questions of cultural affinity and social class enter here. The culture of the nineteenth-century immigrant church is largely gone; but a culture of middle-class, educated Catholics has not replaced it. The Notre Dame study of parish life shows that, where it still exists, ethnicity can be a strong binding element for a communal sense of parish. But recent immigrants, even though middle-class, such as Hispanics from Latin America, may not feel comfortable in an Anglo suburban parish in Minnesota. Even some Anglos may not feel comfortable in a suburban parish in Minnesota. In an interview with *Commonweal*, Anna Quindlen of the *New York Times* talked about not feeling comfortable in her parish in Hackensack and going off to Pennsylvania for church on Sundays. This raises a fundamental question: Can you have a religion without a culture? And if you can't, how can we create one?

And then there are so-called cultural Catholics, people who acknowledge their debt to the church and to Catholicism, but no longer consider themselves believers. They are not active in the church, but they are not necessarily unsympathetic to some of the questions I raise here. I know several people in this category, and they are an interesting resource for thinking about what it is that keeps them attached even though they do not consider themselves believers.

Some Catholics are not active for odd reasons, or reasons that are hard to fathom. Let me point to a couple of these reasons. First, the assimilationist tendencies of our society have made many Catholics comfortable in this American culture. But the church holds, at least in its best moments, countercultural values — the option for the poor, a certain level of asceticism, a critical stance toward consumerism, an understanding of the spiritual, and a consciousness of God's providential love. These religious values are hard for people to hear, at least in American culture, and many Catholics don't feel comfortable in a church that preaches at them, even when it preaches at them only half-heartedly.

And then there are those who would like to be members, except for some fatal flaw, usually having to do with something that's been lost: incense, Gregorian chant, that old discipline, the days when nuns were nuns and priests were priests and nothing was ambiguous. Jimmy Breslin, a columnist for *New York Newsday*, writes a column about once a month on this subject. Or consider my daughter's friend, who thinks that the Catholic Church is a racist and bigoted institution, and draws on her childhood parish school and the Catholic kids she grew up with for examples. She smiles when I say it isn't so. Her experience tells her something else.

Other people hold beliefs deeply compatible with Catholicism, but they've redefined themselves and their religion. They hold to what we might think of as Catholic and Christian values, but won't have anything to do with the "official church." I have a friend who works in a shelter, takes in stray teenagers, and has helped build low-income housing, but is repelled by Catholicism, the religion of her childhood, and attracted to that of an Indian guru.

We all know Catholics who have found in the Episcopal Church, the Orthodox Church, or other churches a home that more clearly meets their Catholic sensibility. Why? How has that happened?

Obviously, some of the ways in which we answer yes, maybe, or no to the question "Are Catholics active enough in their church?" concern the definition of terms. Local conditions, personal experience, our image and understanding of the parish, the pastor, a group of lay Catholics, or the bishop can influence the response.

What we do mean by the church? Is it the parish? The public church? The neighborhood? Old friends? The family? There are not only ecclesiastical but also sociological, theological, and psychological questions here. There are also questions about whether and how we should love the church. Is going to Mass on Sunday really the sole criterion? But what if we haven't been for twenty years? Are we still Catholics? These are questions that may be difficult to answer in this society, at this moment in time. We have gone through a period in which a certain latitudinarian attitude about Mass attendance, for example, has taken place, and I think we are seeing the effects of it. Even if we say that you are a Catholic although you do not go to Mass on Sunday and have not gone in twenty years, I still think we need to ask you if you are really a Catholic. That is what I would like to ask Jimmy Breslin if I ever meet him.

What does it mean to be a member? At the most basic level, you've signed up, you get envelopes, you show up on Sunday, and you support your parish. But we know affiliation does not necessarily bring generosity or commitment.

What does it mean to be active? Or active enough? Active as a parishioner means contributing money, time, talent. Active as a believing Catholic means good works, prayer, reading *Commonweal*. (That is part of my definition!) What goes into our social construction of reality? Are we active enough if we go to Mass every day, but treat

our employees with contempt? What have we set our
hearts upon? Being saints? Being well off? Do we really
want the conversion of heart and mind that we take to be
our ultimate sign of membership? This is an old question.
Jesus posed it to the rich young man, and I think many
of us give the same answer he did.

Catholic Identity

This brings us to the major question, the one at the
crux of our concern about the future of the church: What
do we mean by Catholic identity? If we turn to the dic-
tionary, we begin to see some of the ramifications of this
question.

First, identity is a set of characteristics by which a
thing is definitively recognizable or known. When you are
in New York City, you know you're there. It has definitive,
recognizable characteristics.

Second, it can be a set of behavioral or personal
characteristics by which an individual is recognizable as a
member of a group. It used to be easy to distinguish a
Catholic from a Protestant, and apparently, it is not hard
at the moment to tell a Croatian from a Serb.

Third, identity can refer to the personality of an individual regarded as a persisting entity. We remember who
we are and where we came from.

Altogether, we might take these three aspects of the
definition and see Catholics as individuals embodying definitive and recognizable characterizations — and recognizable over a lifetime. That is part of what might be
meant by the Catholic identity of an individual and of a
group.

Psychological, sociological, even political and ethnic
implications form part of the meaning of identity. Questions of national identity, so important in the history of
nineteenth-century Europe, are back with us today in
Georgia, Slovakia, Croatia, and the former Yugoslavia,

and they have religious underpinnings. Do we ourselves not retain a sense of identity with the Irish, the French, or the Germans because our ancestors came from Ireland, France, or Germany?

There is also a psychological meaning to identity. One of the first places I encountered the word was in Erik Erikson's book *Identity: Youth and Crisis*. The crisis of adolescence in our culture was and is the problem of moving from the secure identity accorded by parents, siblings, church, neighborhood, and school to the more ambiguous and insecure identity of a young adult. If you are not going to follow your mother or father in being a farmer, doctor, lawyer, housewife, or househusband, or in being a Catholic, and you are not going to live in the city or town where you grew up, then you have questions about who you are and where you are going. You have an identity crisis.

Identity becomes an issue when people lose a sense of wholeness, of integration into a larger community, or of continuity in their life course. We all need supports and props, links and connectors to remind us who we are. Isn't this why mixed marriages pose particular problems for religious groups, perhaps especially in an ecumenical age?

Identity questions — Who am I? To whom do I belong? Who are my people? — are a chronic and neuralgic point in modernity, and particularly so in our own culture, which is so heterogeneous and so individualistic. It would be surprising if the Catholic Church did not have to face up to some of these issues, at least in this culture.

Our problem is that we have not clearly defined the source or sources of our concerns; as a result, we are not clear what to do about it. Most of our parents would never have asked or worried about this question. Either you were a Catholic, or you were not. They did not pose questions about boundaries, about who's in and who's out, about authority, about who gets to say who's in and who's out. Who speaks to us of what is Catholic? Archbishop Romero and the four women killed in El Salvador? Anna Quindlen? Mother Teresa? Cardinal Ratzinger? Madonna? Bruce Springstein? Our pastor? Our spouse? Even our children? Perhaps all of them have something to tell us about our Catholic identity.

For a church that has historically seen itself and its beliefs as self-evidently true, this is problematic. The Catholic Church is two thousand years old; it traces itself back in an unbroken line to the life and words of Jesus. It is the one, true, holy, apostolic, and catholic church — "The Church," as Lenny Bruce said. How can Catholics have an identity crisis? Well, we do. It has hit us particularly hard over the last twenty-five years, and I think we are beginning to see all of the ramifications of these twenty-five years. I have four points I would use as examples:

1. The confluence of the sixties in the United States and of Vatican II in the Catholic Church led to an erosion of a traditional understanding of authority in our culture and in our church. This doesn't mean there's no authority; it means that leaders and teachers and parents can't just say, "It's true because I say so." Persuasion, example, compassion, understanding, insight, debate, teaching with conviction are among the virtues authority is now required to exercise, in the church as in the culture. And in both places they seem in short supply.

2. There is the success of the nineteenth-century immigrant Catholic Church in the United States: assimilation, education, wealth have made us insiders, not outsiders. Our religious cohesion no longer depends on others persecuting us or looking down upon us. Efforts to revive the sense of persecution are ill-considered. Cohesion depends on our own work, our own convictions, our own conversion of heart, and our willingness to stick together and to tell our story to others. When people say religious affiliation is now

voluntary, that is partly what they mean. We are not forced. We are not carried along without thinking. We must choose. And we must work at it.

3. The American Catholic Church is not, and has not been, at war with the culture of modernity, at least as it is expressed in this country. But Catholicism in Europe, if not now, was at war with modernity and, in some respects, is certainly still uneasy with it. The pope and Cardinal Ratzinger often express this uneasiness — an uneasiness that many American Catholics do not share. Our country and the American Catholic Church may have a lot of tensions, problems, and real conflicts. But I do not think they are the ones Rome is pursuing; nor am I sure that the solutions Rome proposes for the problems it sees are not counterproductive in our society.

4. Finally, who's responsible for the Catholic Church? Who owns the church? Who says what's Catholic? I don't mean doctrinally; I don't think we have a lot of difficulties there. I mean culturally, sociologically, religiously in the broad sense of the term. As long as we had our ethnic differences, as long as local churches and dioceses were isolated from the outside, we might have clung to idiosyncratic devotions, attitudes, and ideas in the name of our Catholicism. But for many white, educated American Catholics, these particularities have disappeared. Without the props of ethnicity or the support gained from living in the same parish all of our lives, we have to struggle harder to fathom and practice our Catholicism.

A Plan for Being Catholic

Of course, fundamentally we must find our identity in the way Catholics always have, in an understanding of what Jesus did and what he taught, in grasping what he meant when he said, "Do this in memory of me." That is, we find our most profound identity in the Eucharist, in our Sunday worship, and then live as if his teaching made a difference. But to understand this fully, to be drawn to it, and to bring others with us requires a culture — institutions, learning, books, catechetical strategies, magazines, role models, leaders, habits, prayers, ways to socialize children and teenagers, ways to maintain adult knowledge and commitment, mechanisms to sustain the morale and wisdom of our leaders. In other words, we need a serious plan for being Catholic and passing on Catholicism in our kind of culture, which though tolerant of religion is, in many ways, moving at cross-purposes to it.

I think some of the anxieties and difficulties we see and feel express our sense that the infrastructure in the church, like that in the country, is going. We are living off what we could call our patrimony or matrimony. For the past twenty-five years, we have lived on all the good things that people have done for two centuries, and I think we are simply unclear whether we are maintaining that kind of patrimony to pass on to the next generation. And that's why the identity question looms so large. It has been raised about Catholic colleges and universities, about Catholic hospitals, about grammar schools where non-Catholic children are educated. It is raised when we look at the declining number of priests and women religious, the decline in religious orders, the appointment of bishops seemingly committed to restoring a notion of authority that is not likely to be successful, at least in this country. All of these issues press in upon us; we have a sense of anxiety about the future, but as laypeople we also desire to take some responsibility for dealing with that future and contributing to it. Our anxiety is well founded, but our desire for responsibility is at some critical level still not welcomed, not nourished, not really understood by Rome, by some in the hierarchy, and even by many laypeople.

On the brink of a new century, we are in the midst of both a crisis and an opportunity. Some of our actions over the next decade will be pivotal in shaping our future response and our sense of whether in the next century there is going to be a living, breathing, vital Catholic Church.

4.

Our Sunday Worship Experience:
What It Is, What It Could Be

Bishop Kenneth E. Untener

IN THE CATHOLIC CHURCH, WE ARE NOT USED TO PAYING
professionals. We don't pay priests as professionals, and I
do not think we should. But we also did not pay religious
women, especially when they taught in schools, as professionals, and so now we have trouble with teacher salaries.
We did not pay musicians as professionals. When I grew
up in St. Charles parish on the east side of Detroit, Lena
played the organ for a dollar a mass. Now, you cannot get
good music without paying a professional salary, and we
are not used to that across the board.

What is happening with Sunday liturgy has to be put
in a larger context. Did you ever see a sign that said Road
Closed Ahead? In 1962 John XXIII told us that the road
we were on was not going to take us into the future.
Thanks to him, we are the only major religious denomination to anticipate the tremendous upheavals in the world,
to sense that something massive, a great shift, was about
to happen or was just beginning. Of course, we are in the
thick of it and nobody knows what it really is, but we
anticipated it by a massive shift in the church.

---

*Bishop Kenneth E. Untener is the Bishop of Saginaw and the
author of a number of books including* Sunday Liturgy Can Be
Better.

Now, I do not know what you do when you see a sign like that. I have a lot of back roads in the Saginaw eleven counties, and I say, "I'll bet I can get through." I try, and of course then find that the bridge is out five miles down the road, so I come back to where I started. There are a lot of Catholics saying, "I'll bet it wasn't closed" and wanting to get back on that old road.

Picture yourself in a car, and somebody in the car says, "I know a better way." You get off and start to work your way through back roads into dirt roads and dead ends. You know what it is like in the car when you are doing that. Remember the feeling? A little tension develops, and someone says, "Let's go back on the one we were on; at least we knew where we were going." This is where we are right now. I was ordained in the "old church" in 1963. Everything I did, everything I learned, the mass I said for a year, was completely unchanged for the last 400 years. And then I went onto the new road. At that time, I thought everything was all set, we were on a new course. But it was not true, and we are still finding our way. We have to acknowledge that we have not figured out how to do this new church. We haven't figured out parish councils, we haven't figured out when to do confirmation, how to celebrate the sacrament of reconciliation, how to do collegiality, how to do the liturgy.

Now this is an adventuresome, wonderful place to be, in a way, but it has its drawbacks. Some people are saying, "Let's go back to the other road," others are saying, "Over here" and "Over there." We all have different ideas on how to get there, and we haven't figured it out.

Another analogy is that of a shellfish. Yves Congar pointed out that in the pre–Vatican II church, especially since the Council of Trent, there was a comprehensive Catholic system, like a shell, that embraced all of life. Everything was worked out. You had a nice checklist to identify yourself as a good Catholic, and the path was charted neatly. Remember how it was for Lent? So many ounces of food. And so forth.

I did not bring that up to make fun of it; we needed that. There was a climate in which this shell was needed. And shellfish need their shell. The point of Yves Congar's analogy is that in the evolution of animal life, when the shell starts to dissolve, that is a step forward in the development of the species, because the animal then develops an inner skeleton. The shell is needed when there is no inner skeleton. When the shell dissolves and an inner skeleton develops, that is a good step. But while that is taking place, it is a very wobbly period.

We are in the middle of such a time. That comprehensive shell is gone now in the church. In Saginaw we perform an October count of the people at mass. We have only been doing it for about five years, and the number has gone down 10 percent. Statistically, it is disastrous to have that kind of a cut in Sunday mass attendance, but I think it is true around the country and perhaps around the world.

Maybe this decline is bad and maybe it is not. I do not mean that Catholics should not come to mass. I think that they should, that not coming to mass is mortal — mortal to the community, just as it is mortal to the family not to gather. It is a mortal blow if people who are part of a close family just haphazardly show up and do not come to Thanksgiving. But we are going through a stage. When I was growing up, I do not think I ever deliberately missed mass. And the options were quite clear, of course, in those difficult adolescent days, when you might be more tempted to do it than you are as a bishop (I confess I am not now seriously tempted): go to mass or go to hell. That has changed. We now have the outer constraint missing, and we are developing the inner skeleton. But it is a wobbly metamorphosis, probably a shift to a healthier thing but not fully developed yet. We need to preach the importance of Sunday liturgy, and the liturgy has to be good enough to draw people there, but I think they should come even if it is not the best, because ritual is not what you get out of it, it is what you put into it.

These are analogies describing where we are. I believe that we are on a good course, but we are by no means there yet, and we are in the middle of a lot of confusion. But that is all right. If you clean the garage, it always looks worse halfway through. For instance. we are still trying to figure out how to do religious education; I do not think the catechism is the way, because it answers questions nobody is asking. We need a new approach, but we have not yet found it.

The biggest shift is in Sunday mass. When I was ordained in '63, I was like a concert musician. You all gathered out there and all the music came from me, and you were there to receive it. There was interaction to the extent that you received it and responded to it, but I gave you what was there. I originally learned classical piano, then in high school shifted to playing by ear and learned to play the music I like. The recital or concert pianist is shifting now to the sing-along pianist.

The concert pianist brings the music to the people. But when someone says to me at a party, "Hey, Ken, let's liven this thing up. How about getting a sing-along going?" the first question I ask myself (it is not easy to get a sing-along going) is, How can I find the music in them? A sing-along pianist may teach them a song along the way, but he is trying to find the music in them.

This is a tremendous shift for the celebrant and also for the participants. The architecture of our churches, too, has shifted from the concert model, from the altar up here and the people out there as the recipients, to the sing-along model around the piano letting us join together in doing something. The leader now is trying to say, "How can I trigger, or activate, what is in them, so all of us do this together?" A massive shift, a comedown for some priests, as it would be for Van Cliburn if we said, "Van, we brought you here to give a concert, but we changed our minds. We've got some beer. How about a sing-along?" He would say, "I don't do that. I don't know how to do that." And he would get right back on the plane and go home. That is how a lot of priests felt and still feel. Many different skills are required to make it work. And the people, too, say, "Wait a minute. I just wanted to watch. I didn't want these sloppy people shaking my hand; I don't like sitting in chairs instead of pews where you could feel more secure, sitting in a half circle where you have to look at them. I want to be there for prayer, silence, reflection."

To put it in more theological terms, the key question about mass is: Who offers what? Now if I asked that question in 1963 and the same question today, all of the answers in '63 and some even today would say that the priest offers Jesus Christ. But that is traditionally and contemporaneously wrong. It is not and never has been our theology of what happens at mass. For the body of Christ — namely all of us together — offers the whole Christ. That is the difference.

One of the footnotes to this is that in Saginaw persons who are not ordained priests now pastor 10 parishes out of 115. And so, often during the week and sometimes on weekends, such a person will lead a word and communion service. The people call it mass. The pastoral administrators try till they are blue in the face to say that this is not mass. Sister Nancy, who has been in one parish seven years, told me she has given up fighting it. In the wintertime, during the week, if it was really cold, they would sometimes have the service downstairs in the basement, which is easier to heat for a small group. For seven years, when the people used to say, "Sister Nancy, is the mass upstairs or downstairs?" she would say, "It is not a mass, it is a communion service." She tells me, "Know what I say now? 'Mass is downstairs.'" The reason is that we have not yet succeeded in experiencing and realizing what really happens at mass. The priest is there to help transform the whole group into the body of Christ. I say over the bread and wine, "Send your Spirit upon these gifts of bread and wine that they may become the body and blood of Christ." This is the Spirit that came upon

Mary and she conceived the Lord Jesus. It is the Spirit that came upon Jesus in the Jordan River and he began his life-giving ministry. So I call for the descent of that transforming Spirit on the bread and wine. Over the group I also say, "Grant that we who are nourished by His Body and Blood may be filled with His Spirit, and become one body, one Spirit in Christ."

The whole community offers the sacrifice, offers the whole Christ — our work, our family. That is why we bring the gifts up the aisle. It would be a lot easier, American pragmatism, to say, "Why don't you just have a little table next to the altar, so you won't have to wait for all these people to bring up the bread and the wine? You know you are going to use it!" The answer is that it symbolizes. This moment is always a big part of the mass for me. I am saying, "Lord, I am putting on the altar all the things I didn't do and should have done. I'm putting down here the joys and the sorrows, and I am thinking about what they are, the people I like and don't like and the people that don't like me. I am offering everything of my life and of this world and of this country and of this diocese." When we put it all into the Lord's hands, we are like the disciples with the loaves and the fishes. Jesus said, "Take care of these people," and they said, "We can't." He said, "Bring me what you have." They did, and it was enough. And so at Eucharist we bring everything to the Lord, we offer the whole Christ, and with him, together, lift it up to God, in whose hands everything works out.

This is the Eucharist. This is traditional theology. It is the sing-along, the whole group doing something together, what the Eucharist could be and, in some instances, is. I assume all of us have attended a Eucharist that we felt was worth driving fifty miles for. I know I have, and some of them were grade-school masses where they simply engaged in the whole thing together. That is as the Eucharist is meant to be, what all the ritual surrounding it is meant to produce.

The Scriptures are another aspect we have not yet figured out how to do effectively. I once heard Ralph Kiefer say that Catholics have pious eyes (we are used to seeing things; reading the missal, for example) but don't have pious ears (we are not used to listening). That is why we have babies crying in church, why we often have second-rate music. Protestants have pious ears. You'll never hear a baby crying in a Protestant church, and you'll always hear good music. Could you imagine somebody bringing a person who has never been to mass? They go through the entrance rite, then sit down for the liturgy of the word, and the Catholic taps the person on the elbow and says, "Now get ready for this; this is dynamite!" I cannot picture anyone doing that. But it is meant to be dynamite.

The Sunday mass is not the only place where God said he would intervene and be significantly present. But it is the only place where God said he would *always* be present, active, saving and touching you. Each of us should come to the liturgy saying, "God is going to speak to me." Now, it might be a boring homily, it might be lousy music, but one of the words of a song, of a prayer, or, praise be God, of the homily will be for me. This is God, present, acting. That is what sacramental ritual is.

5.

The Pastor: His Diocese, and the Universal Church — How Much Support?

Frank J. McNulty

THE THEME OF THE PLAY WAS HIGHLY SERIOUS BECAUSE IT concerned a couple who had a retarded child, but it was billed as a comedy — a black comedy. It was very well done. The couple was on stage and, gradually, as the first act progressed, turned to the audience and talked to us about this horrible experience. Then they took different parts as they told the story. She was telling how the local vicar reacted to this retarded child, and the man playing her husband slipped into the part of the vicar. As a priest, I sat there squirming and feeling sorry for the poor guy as he tried to explain what cannot be explained, and he went on and on. She screamed out at him, "You're as bad as the doctors. All you try to do is give me answers, explanations. I don't want that." He looked at her with this awful frustration on his face and said to her, "What do you want of me?" And she looked him in the eye and said, "Magic."

If the average pastor turned to his people and said, "What do you want of me?" some of them might say,

---

Rev. Frank J. McNulty is a pastor in the Archdiocese of Newark where he serves as the Archbishop's Delegate to the Priest Personnel Policy Board.

"Magic." And some of the magic is not the spectacular kind, like healing a retarded child.

The other image that comes to mind when I think of pastors is from the old *Ed Sullivan Show*. I remember being fascinated by the juggler who would spin dishes on sticks. He would go all along the row and get the dishes spinning, and then have to run back to the beginning as the first dish started to wobble. He would start up the line again to keep all the dishes spinning. So he was running back and forth spinning dishes.

And as if that is not enough — being a magician and a juggler — every once in a while a comedian has to come on in a show to keep the crowd happy. Sometimes the pastor has to be the comedian, too.

The pastor also heads the complaint department. The complaint usually starts with "How come . . . ?" Three ladies caught me after mass one day and said, "How come Our Blessed Lady's statue isn't there now? You took it away to put in the Christmas crib, and this is the first year that has been done." When I inquired of my assistant if this was, in fact, the first year, he said, "No, it's about the eighth year it's been done."

The demands that come to the priest — the expectations — come not only from himself but also from others. The persons making the demands think that they are the only ones doing it. They forget that other people are as well. Someone spots you in the school hallway or the vestibule of the church and says, "Father, we only need you for about twenty minutes. Can you sit down and talk to us for twenty minutes?" You do it, but they forget that everybody else wants twenty minutes, or a half hour, or whatever. And so the pastor feels overwhelmed: keep the keys, grant or get the permissions, organize the meetings, preach well, raise the salaries, remove the snow, turn up the heat, turn down the heat, and of course, have a great school. Think of all those demands on the local scene; and then think of those from the larger Church, the diocese and the universal Church.

The diocese also has expectations and needs to be fulfilled, and so it calls upon the pastor to be a magician. The religious ed departments send questionnaires to be completed. The Family Life Department calls and asks the pastor to do pre-Cana — only two Sunday afternoons in the spring. Continuing Education asks that he attend a two-day workshop. The Liturgical Committee decides that he and his staff must spend a week learning about RCIA. Then the people from the bishop's drive want to talk to him about aims, goals, and objectives. They send a packet of material and tell him what to say in the pulpit, how to collect the money, where to bring it, and all the rest. And then, every once in a while, the dean sends a notice that he is coming to look at the marriage records and check all the books — in two weeks. Serra calls to ask that you bring the altar boys to a very important afternoon where they will get awards. The right-to-life people are having another march, so you should plan to hire a bus and get to the cathedral and pray with them. "We are running a series of concerts in the cathedral, and here are the tickets. Can you sell them, send the money in, and bring your people?" The black auxiliary bishop is running a big day on Martin Luther King, and the bishop who just retired is going to be honored at a dinner, and would you please bring a table of parishioners? And so on.

Everybody in the diocesan structure, it appears, is trying to justify their jobs, so they keep asking the pastor to cooperate with their departments. The pastor gets a little overwhelmed by it and says, "Will you please leave me alone and let me be a pastor? And stop telling me how to do it. Instead of meeting with me all the time to figure out how to do it, would you please just let me do it?"

This is the average pastor's response to the diocesan structure. But sometimes it goes the opposite way, and the diocese provides much needed guidance. Shortly after I became a pastor, a permanent deacon came from the diocese and spent two hours explaining the diocesan financial regulations and how to handle them properly. He is the only one I can remember who gave me the impression that he was there to serve me. More often the pastor comes to look upon a diocesan office as an organization that piles on more demands.

His relationship to the bishop is, of course, of great importance to the average priest. I have a quote: "Because of this common sharing in the same priesthood and ministry, bishops ought to regard their priests as brothers and friends and ought to take the greatest interest they are capable of in their welfare."

Things have gotten better in recent years. Much more bonding occurs between bishops and pastors and their priests — much more of calling priests by their first names, of knowing priests personally, of spending money and effort in rehabilitating priests who are in trouble, of being sensitive toward men who are leaving active ministry. As a vicar of priests, I noticed how often sensitivity was shown. I would deal with a priest who had struggled with his decision. He would go to see the bishop, and if he was treated well, I would hear it from his whole circle of friends. That kind of treatment helps priests stay.

But geographical areas differ on this relationship between a priest and his bishop. I find the priests in our area (New Jersey) or in a similarly big diocese don't expect personal visitations from the bishop, but priests in rural areas are very disappointed if the bishop doesn't call them up, drop in for supper, sit down with them for a couple of hours, have a drink with them. If the bishop in one of our big dioceses suggested doing that, the priest would get very afraid, sure that he was in deep trouble.

In thinking about the pastor's relationship with the universal Church, I like the image of the hourglass. Teachings, especially moral teachings, come down upon the pastor, and he is supposed to bring them to his people. The best image that comes to mind about the polarities that exist today among priests and the Church is scripture scholar Ray Brown's. He says that in our Church today we all stand on a very wide spectrum. At one extreme of the spectrum are those having what he would call the "blueprint" mentality — people who feel that Jesus drew a blueprint and that we who are Church today only need to look at that blueprint and follow all of its lines. At the other end of the spectrum are those with the "erector set" mentality, who say, "Let's knock the Church down and start all over again." Of course, many people are right in the middle of that spectrum, but there are also many on both ends. Others, and priests especially, lie at a great variety of spots in between, and it doesn't have much to do with age any more. For some young priests lean very much toward the blueprint mentality while some older priests lean toward the erector set mentality. And they are doing ministry together and trying to sort out what is coming to them from the universal Church — in the teachings of the Church, especially the moral teachings.

There has been a tremendous change in the teaching style of the Church. Before Vatican II, the teaching Church and the learning Church were separate. The hierarchy taught and the rest of us learned. Authority was stressed much more than reason, and the Church was pretty much like the father or mother who says to a child, "Why? Because I told you so." The best image for this Church was that of the pyramid: pope, bishops, priests, and laity.

After the council, the Church came up with an entirely different definition of what Church is, and it was no longer a pyramid. The learning process became a part of the teaching process. And this is when we started to talk very beautifully about the fact that there is one Spirit but many charisms, that the Holy Spirit influences the whole Church, and that we are all called to be Church. In that kind of an ecclesiology, the Spirit is speaking to all of us. The pope and bishops have a doctrinal and pastoral charism; they are the authoritative teachers. And this is an integral, necessary, and irreplaceable element in the Church. But that task is not just custodial. Besides that charism, however, since Vatican II we have been speaking much more of other charisms, of the prophetic charism first of all. Vatican II recognized that all the faithful — clerical and lay — express their minds humbly and courageously about those matters in which they enjoy competence. Now the pastor has a high level of competence; he hears confessions, along with his other priests, and runs communal penance services, and so the pastor has a prophetic charism. He has a wisdom, and an obligation to share that charism with the Church.

Another charism is the scientific charism. This is the charism of the theologian, who has a duty not simply to preserve and explain the teaching of the Church but also to contribute to its advancement and improvement, to deepen the understanding. So, the theologian in the post–Vatican II Church is not just a question answerer but a question asker. The Church needs theologians to keep asking the important questions. I have a wonderful little cartoon in my file. It's one person saying to another, "I used to ask serious and important questions. I really did. My answers never seemed to fit. Know what? I'm happier now. I don't ask questions that will upset my answers!" The theologian, however, is called upon, and has a charism, to ask questions that will upset his answers.

So, in light of the impacts of those charisms and of the universal Church on the teaching of the pastor, just think of the tensions he feels. The pastor is in the trenches, wiping away the tears of people, listening to all those hearts that are breaking, struggling to minister with compassion to all kinds of people, to people who are on the fringe, who are not making it, who are failing, who are confused and don't understand the teaching. And he is torn all the time between ethical response and pastoral compassion. He is torn all the time about the teaching authority of the Church. Although the Church has a right and a duty to teach morality, it has always taught that people must follow their own consciences. It is much easier to write a document than to sit in the front office of a rectory and help a person make a moral decision. The pastor is torn between the word that comes to him from "up there" — coming down the hourglass — and everything happening at the grass roots. There is a lot of wisdom in those grass roots, and the pastor wants to turn the hourglass over and let the teaching Church be affected by the collective wisdom of all the people who are trying to live out the will of Jesus.

The Church — the official part of the Church, those with that doctoral and pastoral charism — has a crying need to listen to the rest of the Church.

A television program several years ago highlighted Cardinal Wright and Msgr. Fox in New York and the contrasts in doing ministry. While showing Cardinal Wright, who was taking someone through the offices in Rome, the camera zoomed in on a group of people who were deciding the age of first confession. They were all bishops and cardinals, and none of them looked younger than seventy. I was watching it with a priest who asked, "When do you think those guys sat in a confessional box and heard little seven-year-olds' confessions?"

The pastor is more than willing to go along with the teaching of the Church once he knows that people are hearing what he is saying and that his wisdom is contributing. But he finds it very frustrating that the people who seem to be making the decisions about many pastoral practices, such as communal celebrations of reconciliation and the age for receiving the sacraments, are not there on the scene.

Just how much support, then, is this pastor getting from the diocese and the universal Church? As I prepared these reflections, I called a pastor friend of mine and posed this question to him. He said, "Support? You've got to be kidding!"

You see, the average pastor never thinks of the diocese and the universal Church as giving out support to him. Grief, yes; but not support.

6.

Preaching in American Words and in American Symbols

Walter J. Burghardt, SJ

A RECENT BOOK BY THE PRESIDENT OF THE UNIVERSITY OF Rochester has an engaging title: *God and the New Haven Railway and Why Neither One Is Doing Very Well.* At one point George Dennis O'Brien is disturbed about the split between proclamation and ongoing life. He notes that most people at the train station are not likely to see church service as "one of the livelier, more salvational times of the week." Their appraisal is more likely to be "Saturday Night Live, Sunday Morning Deadly." Not long ago, a university professor of literature suggested that the time had come to speak truthfully to the Church about the quality of its rhetoric. "Discourse in the Church," the lady lamented, "is so dull. In sermons, in social-action statements, in all the communication we hear within the Church, the guiding principle seems to be blandness."

Twas not always thus in America. In the middle of the 19th century, not only novelists and poets but preachers as well were often exciting and creative. Why? Because "discourse in the antebellum period" was "rooted in a religious tradition and built upon popular language."

Rev. Walter J. Burghhardt, SJ is Director of the Preaching the Just Word project of the Woodstock Center for Theology and the former editor of Theological Studies.

Nor are American sermons always dull in our decades. Black preachers from Martin Luther King, Jr., to Jesse Jackson stir spontaneous amens from the sophisticated and the simple, from college teachers and the untutored. Why? Because their sermons are not only "rooted in a religious tradition" but "built upon popular language."

I shall not ask whether American Catholic preaching is "rooted in a religious tradition," despite my apprehension that our homilists are increasingly ignorant of our doctrinal and spiritual resources, to the impoverishment of our people. My focus is rather on "built upon popular language," for that phrase is synonymous with the title delivered unto me, "Preaching in American Words and in American Symbols."

In harmony with my trinitarian bias, my song and dance has three movements. First, a work of recognition, analogous to the anagnorisis in Greek drama: I want you to perceive the precise problem at issue here and isolate it from other, related issues. Second, a work of reconstruction, analogous to a drama's denouement: I want to suggest how our homiletic doldrums might be lifted. Third, a work of rejuvenation, analogous to the comic in drama: I want to lighten the heavy weight of theory, illustrate my ideology, by revealing how preaching "built upon popular language" can delight, excite, thrill, even convert a congregation and restore a preacher's youth. Recognition, reconstruction, rejuvenation.

Recognition

My initial movement is a work of recognition. What is the precise issue here? What am I not talking about, what am I talking about, and why am I talking about it?

First, my theme is how, not what. What I preach, the content of my homily, is always and everywhere the gospel, god-spell, the good news of Jesus Christ, as understood within the Church. I assume, therefore, that what issues from the pulpit is an effort to express what God has said and is saying to us, from the burning bush at Midian and the gas ovens of Auschwitz, from the cross that imprisoned Christ and the cross erected over history, through the travail of theologians and the rapture of mystics, through Roman encyclicals and Christian experience. I assume that the homilist is passionately in love with Scripture, does not shun Scripture because (to plagiarize Magdalene at the tomb) the exegetes "have taken away my Lord and I know not where they have laid him" (Jn 20:13). I assume that the parish priest did not close his last theology tome when a bishop oiled his hands, because theology is the ceaseless struggle of God's people to touch the hem of God's garment, to penetrate Paul's "mystery hidden for ages in God" (Eph 3:9), to "know . . . the only true God, and Jesus Christ whom [God has] sent" (Jn 17:3). This I assume—perhaps naively, because so much evidence contradicts it. But I must assume it, else my address is senseless. There is no point to a homiletic "how" without a wisdom-seasoned "what."

Second, my "how" is not the husk of homiletics, the skeleton, the bare bones. What concerns me is the "how" that is part and parcel of the gospel—where the medium is the message. I am talking about style, what the Earl of Chesterfield called "the dress of thoughts." *Webster's Second International, Unabridged,* put it into an elegant definition thirty years ago: style is "the quality which gives distinctive excellence in artistic expression, consisting especially in the appropriateness and choiceness of relation between subject, medium, and form, and individualized by the temperamental characteristics of the artist." More simply, I am speaking of a fine art.

Third, why am I talking about style? Because if any word demands to be proclaimed "with style," it is God's word. Because without style in the sense described, the gospel threatens to fall on deaf ears, risks disaster. Because the view from the pew is dismaying: we are dull as dishwater, our words are woven of timeless abstractions,

our language does not excite, thrill, inflame. When I was
a boy in St. John the Evangelist parish in New York City,
each Sunday Mass had its quota of what we called
"sharpshooters," men on one knee in the back, just wait-
ing for the sermon—the signal to sneak out for a smoke.
The tradition has been lost, but I often wonder how many
of the faithful would remain if the homily followed the
final blessing, how many would choose rather to "go in
peace."

Reconstruction

The problem calls for a solution. How do you develop
a style—a style of speech that catches the hearer, "grabs"
an audience, keeps people pleading for more, makes them
sorry it's over? Basically, my response, my "reconstruction," is discoverable in my title, "American Words and
American Symbols." (Here note that I shall not be speaking sheerly of symbols in a strict sense—signs pregnant
with a depth of meaning evoked rather than explicitly
stated. Under the broad umbrella of symbols I am pre-
suming to include images and metaphors as well; they are
indispensable if I am to deal realistically with popular
language.) But how do you put homiletic meat on those
bare bones, "American words and American symbols"?

First, a radical realization. I mean Karl Rahner's in-
sistence twenty years ago that to preach is to translate:
the form of preaching in a particular age must be "translated" into another form of preaching to make the message understood, particularly if the meaning of the message must remain the same. This preservation of identity
cannot be achieved by the mere repetition of old expressions if the mentality and concepts change in secular society through a historical development that is not under
the Church's control.

The point is, the Judeo-Christian revelation, for all
its divine authorship, comes to us through "human words

that were already current and loaded with overtones from the surrounding world." "Lamb of God" made a strong impression on the earliest Christians not only because the paschal lamb was a venerable religious symbol but also because that symbol hit them where they lived. Jesus was born and bred among people for whom the lamb was a primary source of food and clothing, a fundamental factor in their economy. Transfer that symbol to Papua, where the sacred animal is the pig, where women may nurse piglets at their breast if no sow is around, and the preacher has a problem. And a lamb is a more likely symbol in New Zealand than in the District of Columbia, where the lamb is simply a political wimp who had best not lie with either the elephant or the mule.

Nor is it only that sacred symbols—lamb, shepherd, Son of man, suffering servant, bread of life, kingdom, yeast, vine and branches, fountain of living water, the fish and the plow and the star, the bark of Peter—can lose significance as the Church moves from age to age, from culture to culture. Ordinary words call for translation. Can you be content with Matthew's "eternal fire prepared for the devil and his angels" (Mt 25:41) when your congregation "thinks of fire as a combustion process with oxygen"?

Well then, move from Scripture to theology. After all, isn't theology itself an effort at translation, a ceaseless struggle to make contemporary sense of God's word? It is indeed. But good as it is, crucial for Christianity, indispensable for preaching the word, theology is not yet homiletics. When revelation is translated into dogma or interpreted by theology, it is not yet the preacher's word. It has its own jargon, its technical vocabulary, its classical lingo from Nicaea through Chalcedon to Vatican II, from Augustine and Aquinas to Lonergan and Rahner. Dogma and theology must themselves undergo translation, build upon popular language, tell God's story in today's idiom. Neither the rhetoric of Roman encyclicals nor the dry bones of eschatology, the apocalyptic, or the supernatural existential are calculated to turn our people on.

All well and good: effective preaching demands translation—a concerted movement from an alien culture, from a dogmatic dress, from a scholarly abstractness to words and symbols that speak to the heart of our age, to the experience of our people. But how do you do this in the concrete?

I do not suggest that we empty our rhetoric of all the classical Hebrew and early Christian symbols, that today's symbol for Christ be not the lamb but the pit bull, that the divinity undergo a sex change, that God the Father be replaced by George Burns with a cigar. Deep within many ancient images and symbols are powerful forces that need only be intelligently grasped by the preacher and imaginatively presented to set hearts aflame.

Mull over just two examples. First, a key theme in the New Testament: the kingdom of God. Do you avoid kingdom language because "king" brings to mind a butcher named Herod, mad King Ludwig with his crazy castles, Old King Cole calling for his pipe, his bowl, his fiddlers three—perhaps the Burger King? Because kings are anachronisms or dictators or figureheads? I say no. A delightful, insightful French film titled *The King of Hearts* had no trouble fascinating millions of film fans here and abroad — teenagers, yuppies, senior citizens. It simply took imagination.

The magic word: imagination. The imagination that turned a turn-of-the-century French Cyrano de Bergerac into today's totally American Steve Martin, without betraying Rostand's romantic intuition. The fresh, childlike approach to fantasy that Steven Spielberg brought to an utterly believable *ET*. The sheer spectacularism of Andrew Lloyd Webber's musical *The Phantom of the Opera*—like bringing the elephants into *Aïda*. I mean *The Yellow Christ* of Gauguin, the pure color that induces a particular feeling, the stark symbolism of the Vietnam Memorial—58,156 names etched into black granite.

Take a second scriptural symbol, at superficial glance the contrary of the king: the suffering servant. A wedding of words not particularly appealing to the American psyche. Servant? That conjures up low income and menial labor, Topsy in *Uncle Tom's Cabin* or the old-time maid in apron and minicap, the indentured servant in the colonies. Suffering? Try redemptive suffering, as I did, in a Jewish synagogue still harrowed by the Holocaust. Try it on blacks struggling to live a decent human existence, to simply live. Try it on Christians who've got it made, for whom living is the survival of the fittest, and the devil take the hindmost.

Do you sacrifice the symbol? I say no. It's too deeply identified with Christ, with Christianity, with the Christian. You wrestle with it. Not, by some semantic alchemy, to transmute the base metal of servant into the gold of master. Not, by some spiritual sedative, to deaden the pain of suffering. Quite the contrary. By wedding theology and imagination you contemporize two inescapable Christian realities: belief shorn of service is lifeless, and the cross is for ever erected over history.

And still it remains true, symbols come and symbols go. The Sacred Heart was a symbol of love that pervaded my youth and my early priesthood; now it is scarcely alive in the consciousness of Catholics. The Beatles are far from dead, but Beatlemania is not the idolatry it once was. Even "The Star-Spangled Banner" is reserved for sports events and sung by professional singers; American hearts are rarely clutched by "bombs bursting in air."

What, then, are our contemporary symbols? Quite obvious are a few patriotic symbols. The Statue of Liberty still beckons compassionately from New York Harbor. The American flag still spangles over public monuments and private homes. "America the Beautiful" tugs at untold hearts. And doves as well as hawks weep silent tears before the Vietnam Memorial.

But it is cultural symbols that are riding an unprecedented wave. Where do you start and where do you end?

Some fit well together, others are contradictory. Most are secular, some are explicitly or potentially religious. You have heavy metal and MTV; the computer, car phones, and crack; stretch limos or a Volvo with a baby seat; country, pop, and rock; Michael Jackson and Jesse Jackson; freedom and human rights; Madonna or Mother Teresa; Rambo and Dirty Harry's "Make my day"; the comic strip "Peanuts" and a President's jelly beans; yuppie or Alzheimer; Walkman and the boob tube; Sandra Day O'Connor or *Playgirl*; sushi and Mexican beer; Super Bowl and Big Mac; prochoice or prolife; Mike Tyson and Steffi Graf; a wasted *Challenger* or a Mars-bound *Discovery*; Wall Street and Haagen-Dazs; the "Army: Be All You Can Be" or the Community for Creative Non-Violence; the recreational hobo or the homeless on D.C.'s winter grates; black power and ERA; Star Wars and strawberry daiquiris; Marcel Lefebvre or John Paul II; Bill Cosby or *The Young and the Restless*; God as mother, God as lover, God as friend of the earth; AIDS and the compassionate Christ . . . Fifty-five and counting. There is more, ever so much more—symbols my shortsightedness stops me from seeing, symbols the younger and still more restless than I can surely spy.

Precisely how any given preacher shapes a sermon within this welter of symbols I dare not tackle here. But this I do submit: unless your preaching is molded in large measure by this context, you will be whistling down the wind—Shakespeare's "sound and fury" perhaps, but "signifying nothing." Preach as part and parcel of this concrete world, aware of its paradoxes and contradictions, attuned to its limitless potential for good, saddened or enraged by so much folly and insensitivity, alive to the grace of God with whom nothing on earth is impossible, and the "American words" will come. Don't start with the words; start with the reality, the real-life symbols that surround you, the symbols within which, sense it or not, your own life is shaping.

Rejuvenation

Now, finally, a work of rejuvenation, an effort to illustrate my ideology by revealing how preaching "built upon popular language," upon America's words and symbols, can delight, excite, thrill, even convert a congregation and restore a preacher's youth. Examples from real life. First, August 28, 1963. Almost a quarter-million Americans have marched on Washington to demand that Congress pass effective civil-rights legislation. In the shadow of Abraham Lincoln a black minister is begging his brothers and sisters not to "wallow in the valley of despair." At that moment the gospel singer Mahalia Jackson calls out, "Martin, tell them about your dream." Departing from his text, Martin Luther King, Jr., hurls to the world one of history's most stirring visions.

> *I have a dream that one day this nation will rise up and live out the true meaning of its creed: We hold these truths to be self-evident, that all men are created equal.*

> *I have a dream that one day out in the red hills of Georgia the sons of former slaves and the sons of former slave owners will be able to sit down together at the table of brotherhood.*

> *I have a dream that one day even the state of Mississippi, a state sweltering with the heat of oppression, will be transformed into an oasis of freedom and justice.*

> *I have a dream that my four little children will one day live in a nation where they will not be judged by the color of their skin but by their character. . . .*

> *I have a dream that one day down in Alabama, with its vicious racists, with its governor having his lips dripping with the words of interposition and nullification; that one day right down in Alabama little black boys and black girls will be able to join hands with little white boys and white girls as sisters and brothers. . . .*

> *I have a dream that one day every valley shall be engulfed, every hill shall be exalted and every mountain*

> *shall be made low, the rough places will be made plains and the crooked places will be made straight, and the glory of the Lord shall be revealed and all flesh shall see it together. . . .*
>
> *When we let freedom ring, when we let it ring from every tenement and every hamlet, we will be able to speed up that day when all of God's children, black men and white men, Jews and Gentiles, Protestants and Catholics, will be able to join hands and sing in the words of the old spiritual,*
>
>
>
> *"Free at last,*
> *free at last!*
> *Thank God Almighty we are free at last!"*
>
>

Not a sermon, you say? Then, say I, show me a better sermon on racial justice, a more powerful American symbol in popular language. A symbol that did not die, but rose again like Christ, when Martin Luther King was killed five years later by a hidden rifleman as he stood on the balcony of a motel in Memphis.

A second example, a Presbyterian clergyman and convert from agnosticism. Frederick Buechner weds two arts as a first-rate preacher and seasoned novelist. Rarely do you find combined "such fresh language, such poetic vision, such unexpected twists and such a deeply personal witness to Christ." Listen to him retelling an Old Testament story in imaginative popular language. The place to start [the gospel as comedy] is with a woman laughing.

> *She is an old woman, and, after a lifetime in the desert, her face is cracked and rutted like a six-month drought. She hunches her shoulders around her ears and starts to shake. She squinnies her eyes shut, and her laughter is all China teeth and wheeze and tears running down as she rocks back and forth in her kitchen chair. She is laughing because she is pushing ninety-one hard and has just been told she is going to have a baby. Even though it*

*was an angel who told her, she can't control herself, and
her husband can't control himself either. He keeps a
straight face a few seconds longer than she does, but he
ends by cracking up, too. Even the angel is not unaf-
fected. He hides his mouth behind his golden scapular,
but you can still see his eyes. They are larkspur blue
and brimming with something of which the laughter of
the old woman and her husband is at best only a rough
translation.*

*The old woman's name is Sarah, of course, and the old
man's name is Abraham, and they are laughing at the
idea of a baby's being born in the geriatric ward and
Medicare's picking up the tab. They are laughing because
the angel not only seems to believe it but seems to expect
them to believe it too. They are laughing because with
part of themselves they do believe it. They are laughing
because with another part of themselves they know it
would take a fool to believe it. They are laughing because
laughing is better than crying and maybe not even all
that different. They are laughing because if by some
crazy chance it should just happen to come true, they
then would really have something to laugh about. They
are laughing at God and with God, and they are laughing
at themselves too because laughter has that in common
with weeping. No matter what the immediate occasion is
of either your laughter or your tears, the object of both
ends up being yourself and your own life.*

Third, take the unexpected example of a systematic
theologian. Karl Rahner is hardly bedtime reading, but his
sermons may surprise you. Preaching one Ash Wednes-
day, he took for his topic a graphic symbol Scripture uses
to declare our essence:

*Dust—truly a splendid symbol. Dust, this is the image of
the commonplace. There is always more than enough of
it. One fleck is as good as the next. Dust is the image of
anonymity: one fleck is like the next, and all are name-
less.*

It is the symbol of indifference: what does it matter whether it is this dust or that dust? It is all the same. Dust is the symbol of nothingness: because it lies around so loosely, it is easily stirred up, it blows around blindly, is stepped upon and crushed—and nobody notices. It is a nothing that is just enough to be—a nothing. Dust is the symbol of coming to nothing: it has no content, no form, no shape; it blows away, the empty, indifferent, colorless, aimless, unstable booty of senseless change, to be found everywhere, and nowhere at home.

I am all dust, never cease to be all dust, only become more than dust when I admit it, accept it, endure through it. The new thing is that the Son of God became dust. In an outrageous reversal we can say to God's Son what God told us in Paradise: "You are dust, and to dust you shall return" (Gen 3:19). Ever since then, "flesh designates . . . also the pivot and hinge of a movement that passes through dust's nothingness into life, into eternity, into God."

Rahner and Buechner and King—all well and good, you say, but why not move from Germany to the U.S., from the Presbyterian scene to the Catholic, from the '60s to the '80s? How does Burghardt himself operate in the concrete—he whom the *London Tablet* recently dubbed (a dubious compliment) "the grand old man of American homilists?" A legitimate question.

First, for American symbols I am profoundly indebted to film. On a March evening twenty years ago, at the Lotos Club in Manhattan, I was privileged to address the Second Annual Joint Award Reception of the Broadcasting and Film Commission of the National Council of Churches and the National Catholic Office for Motion Pictures. In the audience were such neon-light figures as Warren Beatty and Maureen O'Sullivan. My address, "To Films, with Love," said in part:

*I am here as one who lives with symbols (word, sacra-
ment, Church), who plays with mystery (spirit and matter, divine and human, God and man). And, as a theologian, I am here to thank you for tackling more powerfully
and profoundly than I the common task that is ours: human experience and its meaning — "What's it all about?"
. . . What makes you so unparalleled an expression of
experience is that you are now consciously all the arts in
one art: you alone are sculpture and architecture, paint-
ing and poetry, music and the dance, dramatic art. . . .*

*This evening I am happy, because I can unofficially wel-
come you to the fraternity of theologians, those who live
with symbols and play with mystery.*

Some of my most effective homilies have had film for
their springboard. I have crafted a sermon from *Chariots
of Fire*, using three succinct sentences of Eric Liddell, the
1924 Olympic runner: (1) "God made me fast." (2) "The
power is within." (3) "When I run, I feel His pleasure." I
have shaped a sermon from *Amadeus*, with its portrayal
of two men with diverse fatal flaws: the genius Mozart, an
"obscene child" who never grows up, a self-centered adolescent aware of naught save his music and his pleasure;
and the moderately talented Salieri, eaten by envy, unable
to understand how God can make him mute and gift with
genius "this foul-mouthed, bottom-pinching boor," this
boy "vulgar and vain, with the social graces of Caligula." I
have honed a homily from *The Gods Must Be Crazy*, with
its empty Coke bottle that falls from a plane among Bush-
men in South Africa's Kalahari desert, the Coke that
changes their lives, the single bottle through which Eden
becomes Babel and primitive innocence discovers the
ways of civilization.

For other American symbols I search through songs.
The decibels indeed drive me to distraction, but I must
remember that even the decibels are a contemporary symbol. And there is a message, a powerful message—heavy
or haunting, loving or lustful, tender or raw—in American

words and American symbols. Listen as Amy Grant sings
"Love of Another Kind":

They say love is cruel
They say love is rather fragile
But I've found in You
A love of another kind

They say love brings hurt
I say love brings healing
Understanding first
It's a love of another kind

The love I know
Is a love so few discover
They need to know
Jesus' love is like no other

They say love won't last
I say love is never ending
'Cause in You I have
A love of another kind

They would change their tune
They would add another measure
If they only knew
This love of another kind
Love of another kind

And if Amy is dated, try Grammy winner Randy
Travis. *Time* calls him "the soft-spoken, tall-sitting, sweet-
singing eye of a most congenial storm." What is his music
all about? "People," he reflects, "think country music is
related to a bunch of rednecks drinking beer and fighting.
They think it's all songs about drinking and cheating. But
it covers a lot bigger area than that, you know. Covers
everything." And if that fails to tug at your homiletic
heartstrings, perhaps purse strings will. Do you know
how many musical dollars were plunked down in the U.S.
in 1987? Some 5.6 billion.

Third, I find American words, American symbols, in
everyday experience. Earlier, without heroic effort, I listed

fifty-five American symbols, images, metaphors. They surround me, invade my privacy, circulate in my blood-
stream. An enigma: How do homilists manage to ban
them from the pulpit? All around me—on D.C. streets and
in Atlanta's Omni, in *Newsweek* and *Rolling Stone*, in
M*A*S*H and the Top 40 tunes, in Steven Spielberg's
films and Whoopi Goldberg's sizzling social commentary,
from AIDS and Arafat, in the scores of men and women I
touch each day—all around me, every hour, I hear language that burns or soothes, wounds or heals, frightens
or amuses, delights or challenges, murmurs in rapture or
cries out in pain. By what sleight of hand do they disap-
pear from our podiums? The American priesthood is an
incomparable storehouse of stories. Not all can be repeated in the pulpit; but by what unwritten canon have
all of them become classified information, top secret, or
sacred to sacerdotal socials? I am reminded of Ralph
Waldo Emerson's famous iconoclastic address at the Harvard Divinity School 150 years ago, when he railed at the
junior pastor of his grandfather Ripley's church in Con-
cord:

> *I once heard a preacher who sorely tempted me to say I
> would go to church no more. . . . He had lived in vain. He
> had no word intimating that he had laughed or wept,
> was married or in love, had been commended, or
> cheated, or chagrined. If he had ever lived or acted, we
> were none the wiser for it. The capital secret of his pro-
> fession, namely, to convert life into truth, he had not
> learned. Not one fact in all his experience, had he yet
> imported into his doctrine. . . . Not a line did he draw out
> of real history. The true preacher can always be known
> by this, that he deals out to the people his life—life
> passed through the fire of thought.*

There is a peril in the first person singular, a delicate
line between the "I" that stirs others to think and tell
their own story, and the "I" that embarrasses, that makes
others mumble uncomfortably, "I'm sorry for your trou-

bles, Father." But the risk must be dared, for in the last analysis my homily is . . . I.

The wine of the gospel never grows old; it is always and everywhere new. Don't put this "new wine into old wineskins. . . . New wine must be put into fresh wineskins" (Lk 5:37–38). Here, for a preacher, for me, is the risk and the joy. The risk is expressed in the Italian maxim *traduttóre traditóre*—to translate is always, in some sense, to traduce, to misrepresent, to play traitor, especially where human frailty tries to decipher what is divine. At least the danger is ever there. The joy? Why, the exciting effort to do for God's people in my time what preachers like Jeremiah and Joel, Peter and Paul, did for God's people in their time: to express God's inexpressible word in syllables that wed fidelity to felicity, syllables that flare and flame, syllables that capture minds and rapture hearts, syllables charged with the power of God.

Such preaching, my sisters and brothers, is not an option within Catholicism; not a "nice" thing if you have the time for it, a gift for it, if you can hack it; not unimportant because supposedly *the* saving event is the Eucharist, the consecratory word, "This is my body. . . . This is my blood." Surrender the homiletic word and you must confront the sobering affirmation of that remarkable theologian in a wheelchair, Yves Congar: "I could quote a whole series of ancient texts, all saying more or less that if in one country Mass was celebrated for 30 years without preaching and in another there was preaching for 30 years without the Mass, people would be more Christian in the country where there was preaching."

If this be homiletic heresy, here I stand and I can do no other.

7.

The American Catholic Parish

David C. Leege

ASKING WHAT AMERICAN CATHOLICS LOOK LIKE TODAY IS like asking a geologist to describe the Earth's features. American Catholics are very heterogeneous, but the majority have now entered the American mainstream and the educated middle class. Catholics are found decreasingly in ethnic enclaves. The immigrant parish with its emphases on devotional pieties, parochial education for the children, passive liturgies, a plentitude of vocations, and hierarchical leadership is giving way to the post–Vatican II parish with biblically oriented adult education, participatory liturgies, a scarcity of priests and religious, and ministries and governance shared by the laity. When the Church began to view itself as the people of God following the Second Vatican Council, it found an American Catholic laity with many of the advantages of education and with middle-class attitudes that made them ready to assume responsibility.

The greatest leaps upward in education came between the Second World War and the mid-1970s. By any criterion of educational mobility, Catholics outpaced every other religious group during that period. But when you begin well behind the starting blocks, you have a longer

Dr. David C. Leege is a political scientist and a research scholar in religion, church, and society. He is on the faculty of the University of Notre Dame.

race to run. And the competition does not stand still. Thus, although the mobility data from the 1960s and 1970s hinted that non-Hispanic Catholics would soon become the most well-educated sector of the American populace, the average educational attainment of adult Catholics in the mid-1980s, while above that of Methodists, Lutherans, and Baptists, was still slightly below that of Jews, Episcopalians, and Presbyterians. This phenomenon is partly regional; more Catholics are in the Northeast, more Protestants are in the South.

Important Trends

So much attention has been paid to mobility, however, that analysts have not emphasized the implications of two other features in the educational-attainment data. First, the second- and even third-generation college student is now becoming the norm in many non-Hispanic Catholic families. In the 1950s and early 1960s American colleges and universities took in many young Catholics who were among the first generation of their families to attend college. Prior to that time, most Catholic young people had to go to work or to war after high school—if they finished at all. They took on adult responsibilities for wage earning and parenting at an early age. Since they moved into a relatively fixed class system, their parish connections remained stable. Now that Catholic families are into the second and third college generation, however, we must recognize that the period of economic dependency on parents is longer, even though children may become geographically separated from their parents earlier. Their old parish connections are often first interrupted for college and then virtually severed as young people move into the first job and apartment and, much later, take on marital responsibilities. The normal age for first marriage is pushed back because it takes longer to finish college and perhaps professional school and to get settled in the right white-collar or professional position. Given these widespread destabilizing forces, the remarkable phenomenon is not the decline in Mass attendance among educated young Catholics, but the relatively high attendance level.

The second factor hidden by the emphasis on educational mobility is a simple matter of baby booms and birth rates. Contrary to stereotypes, American Catholics of child-bearing age have not always and do not presently have the largest families. The post–World War II baby boom hit Protestant families sooner than it did Catholics, and the average number of children in families of Protestants now in their 60s is actually slightly higher than in the families of Catholics of the same age. But Catholics now in their 40s and 50s had much larger families than Protestants. That baby boom has created a bulge in the Catholic population, so that 4% more of the Catholic population are between 18 and 29 than is the case with the Protestant population.

Therein lies one of the reasons why Catholics are currently disproportionately represented in the enrollment figures of American colleges and universities. One report says that Catholics, while 25% of the U.S. population, make up 40% of those enrolled in college. Another reason is that mothers of the baby boom generation with children out of the nest feel they have to catch up with other college-educated women they know. They are among the growing nontraditional-age student population.

Regardless of what interpretation one accepts, the results are the same. American Catholics are far more educated than they ever were. Women are pursuing education, just as are men, in all fields. Both men and women have greater skills to offer their parishes. Their expectations of parish ministries and programs have probably increased. Finally, they have often experienced many years without stable roots in a parish because of residential mobility.

The implications of these social characteristics for the Church's ordained leadership at the parish level and above are obvious. Many lay members, male and female, have as much or more education than do priests or bishops. The legitimacy accorded Church authority is no longer traditional, but increasingly rational. Catholics have known both education and life away from ancestral parishes; they are accustomed in their jobs and daily life to means-ends calculations and often have to be won to the reasonableness of Church policy. They live in a society, and have been socialized through an American educational system, that seldom accord absolute authority to any human being. They are accustomed to owing loyalty to an institution while still questioning specific policies of its leaders. They find no great inconsistency in accepting the central mysteries of the Church and rejecting some of its more recent teachings. Finally, they often possess as varied skills for parish service as do priests or religious.

The American emphasis on voluntarism tells today's Catholics that those skills should be used and that they should be consulted on program planning at the parish level. They are also very pragmatic when it comes to policy. Either having never known a submissive life of devotional piety or having replaced it with active post–Vatican II Trinitarian theology and people of God imagery, they are sufficiently confident of their own faculties and the presence of the spirit of Christ to confront crises with basic policy changes. We have seen evidence of that in Project 1990 in Chicago, where lay leaders appear quite willing, after study of the matter, to accept married priests.

One aspect of American Catholic demographics is easily misunderstood. We have found from analysis of GSS data that around the late 1970s a significant change in family size was occurring. The National Center for Health Statistics has found that birth rates have changed, so that white Catholics are now having fewer children than white Protestants. We do not know whether Catholics are simply marrying later and will eventually equal or surpass Protestants in family size, but their birth rate is lower at the present time.

There is a risk of misinterpreting this finding. Some people automatically assume that fewer children per family will lead to a decline in the size of the next generation of Catholics. Not at all. Since there are more young Catholics of child-bearing age nowadays as a result of the earlier baby boom, the total number of Catholics will either continue to grow or remain about the same, even if they have smaller families than Protestants. Thus, any notion that there will be less need for parochial schools, CCD, youth ministries, family-counseling services, and so on one decade hence must be quickly dismissed. The children and their families will be there to be served, even if birth rates decline among the products of the earlier baby boom.

Analyses of income and social-class data from GSS for the 1960s and 1970s argued that after Jews, non-Hispanic Catholics had attained the highest average annual family income among American church groups. That was quite a surprise to many ethnic Catholics, who for years had operated with an underdog psychology. The GSS data for the 1980s, however, suggest that non-Hispanic Catholics are closer to the middle of the pack. Jews, Presbyterians, and Episcopalians still have higher family incomes than Catholics; Methodists, Lutherans, and Baptists are lower. However, this finding appears to be primarily the result of the bulge of the Catholic population in the 18-to-29 age bracket. These people have a decade or two to go before reaching their maximum earning potential.

In contrast to young Protestants, young non-Hispanic Catholics are staying in school a bit longer, appear to be pursuing higher paying jobs earlier, and are settling into marriage and parenthood later. Unless the boardroom is somehow barred to Catholics, we can anticipate that as the baby bulge works its way through the life cycle, non-Hispanic Catholics will indeed be at the top of the economic ladder within a decade or two.

Diversity

The political consequences of these demographic developments are evident, within both the Church and the larger society. Many Catholics have grasped economic power and learned political savvy. While the plurality of non-Hispanic Catholics still call themselves Democrats, their ideology has tilted decidedly to the right. In fact, the entire country has shifted to the right during the last decade. Catholics still trail this shift by about seven percentage points, but it is gathering momentum, particularly in the baby-bulge generation, those 18 to 29 years old. There are apt to be pronounced differences among the New Deal liberalism of Catholics over 50, the ideological liberalism of Catholics in their 30s and 40s, and the acquisitive conservatism of Catholics under 30. On major public policy issues, Catholics have about as many different viewpoints as France has wines. When leaders of the Church speak to public issues, other Catholics can commandeer the bully pulpits and find receptive audiences for contrary opinions. We have seen it in the response to recent pastoral letters. Lay Catholics have the same potential for reacting against the economic teachings of pope and bishops in the 1980s as lay Protestants had for reacting against the civil-rights efforts of their leaders in the 1960s.

There are three aspects of American Catholicism that we tend to overlook. First, about 30% of American Catholics do not reside in the great urban centers, where culture and the public agenda are shaped. They live in small towns, in unincorporated areas, on farms. We think of Baptists and Methodists as rural and small-town people and of Catholics as urban. But the total Catholic rural and small-town population is as large as the total membership of the Baptist or Methodist churches, and larger than the combined Lutheran churches. This population covers the spectrum from foreclosed farmers to rich ranchers, from minimum-wage laborers to well-paid professionals. A description that portrays only the immigrant Church of the cities and the middle-class Church of the suburbs misses a large part of the American Catholic community.

We must also pay attention to the Hispanics and the Asians. The ancestors of many Hispanics were within the Church in the United States well before most of us other Catholics were. Most Hispanics today, however, are recent immigrants. While they share a single language, they are many peoples with great cultural diversity. They are as different from one another as the Chicago physician who migrated from Cuba and comes from a ruling-caste Spanish family is from the migrant Mexican-American farm worker who descends from American Indians, or the black Dominican taxi driver whose ancestors were African slaves. Our Church is also their Church. The Hispanics are beginning to come of age in America. Consider the forecast that before the turn of the century, over half of all Catholics in Chicago will be Hispanic or nonwhite. Asians, as ethnically and culturally varied as the Hispanics, are also increasingly evident in parishes all over the country. In the five-county Los Angeles metropolitan area, one estimate says that 40% of the adults are foreign born. Most of these people are Hispanic or Asian, and at least 80% of them are thought to be Catholic. Just at a time when the dominant element in American Catholicism is white, well educated, and middle class, we become aware that large parts of this Church are not white, not well educated, and not middle class.

Finally, we often forget that many Catholics over the age of 35 remain rooted in the old immigrant experience. They were either partially or completely socialized by that constellation of values and practices associated with the immigrant parish. In the rush of change we sometimes forget the persistence of memory, both personal and communal. Just as my father clung to the certainty that the language of heaven is German, so the 60-year-old parishioner feels deep bewilderment at the failure of her parish to practice a corporate devotion to its patron saint. It would be difficult to convince this faithful Catholic that there is a greater sense of community in the congregational hymns, responses, and other forms of liturgical participation than there was in the silent devotion practiced in her youth. Is it any wonder that the road to liturgical change has been rocky?

So that is what we are: white, urban, educated, middle class, participatory, powerful, pragmatic; and at the same time, tan, black, yellow, rural, working in necessary but demeaning tasks, on the outside looking in, nostalgic for devotions past. If these are American Catholics, can you think of any more complicated task than planning for the American parish? But the very genius of a church, as opposed to a denomination or a sect, is that it learns how to celebrate and sanctify cultural diversities and social differences. Let us briefly examine the interplay of some of these characteristics of American Catholics and study the characteristics of their parishes.

The American Catholic Parish

Catholic parishes are very large. The average parish serves about 2,300 people, and about 15% serve 5,000 or more. Interestingly enough, the average number of Catholics in a parish has increased over the past five years, and so has attendance at Mass. When contrasted with parishes in Catholic countries elsewhere, American parishes are still rather small. But the average Catholic will compare his parish with nearby Protestant congregations, and the Catholic parish is almost always larger.

Most Catholics now realize there is a serious shortage of priests and religious. Slightly over one-half of American parishes are served by one full-time priest; a little over one-quarter of the parishes have two full-time priests; about one in seven has three full-time priests. About one-third of the parishes have access to a part-time priest. The average age of priests continues to push up-ward, yet there is no bulge of young candidates for the priesthood to match the bulge in the young Catholic population. If the average number of Catholics per parish is over 2,300, it is sobering to note that the average num-ber of full-time priests per parish is 1.7. This is a better ratio of priests to laity than is found in most Catholic countries, but it is well under the ratio of Protestant pas-tors to laity in the United States. But participation in Mass and parish programs is much higher here than in Belgium, France, or Italy, where as much as 85% of the people simply don't practice their religion.

Vocations to religious orders have also declined pre-cipitously. Our data attest to the unavailability and the increasing age of sisters and brothers.

Someone has to pick up the slack. The laity are try-ing. In parish after parish we find a cadre of laypersons who volunteer nearly as many hours to parish service as the pastor or paid staff is contributing. These volunteers, whether they be in ministries of nurture or mercy, liturgy or governance, are disproportionately women. Since American Catholics are educated and are products of cul-tural values that encourage pragmatism, voluntarism, participation, and responsibility, the laity do not feel the need for special charisms to fill roles formerly filled by priests or religious. When asked about the essential fea-ture of the priest's role, by a wide margin parishioners said it is bound up in the celebration of Mass and the sacraments. It appears that they would be comfortable sharing (or taking over) virtually all other aspects of his work. When asked to rank the trait they most value in a pastor, parishioners named sensitivity to the needs of oth-ers by a wide margin over holiness, learning, good preach-ing skills, good organizing skills, or anything else. They want a pastor who understands them, who consults them, who respects them as contributors to the common life of the parish.

A large proportion of core Catholics—about 85%—seem comfortable with the idea that they will attend the parish within whose boundaries they reside, although they will occasionally participate in a Mass elsewhere. (Core Catholics are those with definite parish connections.) Interestingly, the reason people cite most often for attending a given parish, beyond geographical location, is not its style of liturgy or acceptance of Vatican II reforms, but the quality of pastoral care. Pastoral care refers not just to the actions of a priest, but often to those of an entire team made up of priest, religious, and laity; "pastor" is becoming a corporate term in this country. This is perhaps another reason that people look for a sensitive priest. They want someone who can work with a leadership team of staff and volunteers and at the same time appreciate the needs and gifts of ordinary parishioners.

About 85% of the core parishioners express the view that their parish satisfies their religious needs, while only 45% feel that it meets their social needs. The suburban parish—typically the largest parish in our sample—was least likely to meet social needs. Yet that does not seem to matter to many suburban Catholics. Those most satisfied with the parish as a social unit are the highly active people who volunteer for a wide variety of ministries and programs. Those who claim the parish fails to meet their social needs do not assign great priority to improving the social life of their parish, because they feel its primary purpose is religious enrichment. In the functionally specialized suburbs, then, many Catholics want little more out of the Church than a satisfying religious life; they conduct their social life elsewhere. It is quite the opposite in the small towns, where parishioners place heavy social demands on their parishes. Curiously, despite the size of parishes, only one in eight has made a conscious effort to organize parish subdivisions or smaller communities within the parish.

In some ways, parishes are failing to keep pace with the changing needs of their parishioners. Although about

25% of adult Catholics who have ever married have experienced divorce or separation, only 20% of the parishes have programs for divorced Catholics. On a wide variety of survey indicators, core Catholics told us that the Church needs to understand better the nature of contemporary American life. In fact, there is a decidedly this-worldly, rather than otherworldly, cast to the programmatic priorities of core Catholics. For example, not only would they like their parishes to offer more effective service when marriages are in trouble; they would also like to get better help on some of the things that make marriages go on the rocks—alcoholism and other substance abuse, economic problems, and so on.

Almost all respondents give high priority to religious-formation programs for children and teens; virtually all parishes have such programs. On the other hand, while a sizeable proportion want more attention paid to adult religious education, only a little over 60% of the parishes have some kind of adult-education program. It should come as no surprise that educated Catholic laypeople will want to continue their religious education, just as they have their regular education. They will seek Bible-study groups, prayer groups, or religious discussions in nearby Protestant churches or ecumenical neighborhood groups if they can't find such opportunities in the parish. Finally, despite the obvious need to increase lay responsibility for parish ministries, only about one-fourth of the parishes have organized lay-leadership training programs. By and large, diocesan programs do not yet penetrate to the parish level. One sign of hope is that about one-third of all parishes have followed some version of a formal parish-renewal program. Often the need for lay-leadership training is recognized during renewal.

Many patterns of leadership are emerging. Some involve parish councils, but often the council is not the most important component of the leadership network. While 76% of parishes have a council, parishes have also evolved other strategies for policy planning and review:

congregational assemblies, elected executive committees, functionally specialized boards, surveys, and so on. Our studies clearly show that laypersons expect to participate in governance, regardless of its structure. No parishes are in deeper trouble, based on measures of identification and loyalty, than those where lay involvement in formal liturgical roles and in parish governance is suppressed. It is not that laity want to dominate. They simply want to be heard and to be affirmed as responsible members of a community.

Our studies of influence within the parish community generally show that those performing a ministry have the greatest voice in parish planning and policy. Disproportionately, it is women who are conducting the ministries and thereby gaining influence. Moreover, influence is becoming less centralized and formal. Position and structure alone no longer tell the story of parish governance.

One other suggestion emerges from the data. There is a tendency toward recognizing lay responsibility by providing credentials to graduates of training programs. Thus, there is a credentialed liturgist or a credentialed minister of adult education or a credentialed minister to the sick. Some pastors and leaders are seeing, however, that these programs give individuals such a distinctive set of skills that they intimidate other parishioners, creating new splits in the parish. Just as the priest has had to learn how to be sensitive, so the credentialed lay minister must remember that the parish is a people of God that must be encouraged and affirmed. Otherwise, we have merely traded a hierarchical dominance based on ordination for one based on training credentials.

Pastors wonder, "Where is this mythical parish where so many laypersons want to serve? In my experience, it is always the same old people." Nothing is clearer from the patterns of recruitment in our leadership sample than that people may want to serve but are shy in offering their services. Our data for volunteer leaders show that 68% had to be asked to participate. But once asked, once encouraged, once affirmed, once shown "how to," they take on responsibility after responsibility. One of the challenges in pastoring is that of taking the time to recruit, form, and nurture leadership talent.

Foundational Beliefs

The Roman Catholic Church has historically been a sacramental church. It offers community rites that collectively lift its people's eyes vertically toward God. The post–Vatican II Church has stressed that it is also a community in which people relate horizontally to each other and to the world they live in. Both the traditional and the contemporary themes emphasize objective community. On the other hand, a central problem of the Protestant denominations emerging from the Reformation was that they lacked the symbols of community. They stressed the individual's nakedness before God and moral values that called for personal responsibility rather than societal responsibility.

The ethos of the United States derived largely from ascetic Protestant traditions. Liberal individualism guided the prevailing political and economic ideologies; education stressed the development of the individual; popular psychology made the feelings of the individual the measure of worth; and consumer advertising accented me—my gusto, my image, my consumption. American Catholics are American, and it is bound to show both in their most deeply held religious values and in their corporate worship. Individualism poses one of the most serious challenges to liturgical life and faith.

Our questionnaires contain an important measure of foundational beliefs, those beliefs and outlooks that probably are more fundamental than dogmatic symbols. This measure has several dimensions. For some, religion is individualistic; it focuses on me and my problems. For others, religion is communal; it identifies the common needs of people in their social state. Sometimes religion is vertical, directed upward to or downward from God; at other times religion may be horizontal, directed outward to other people. The messages some hear in their religious values are restricting, while for others they may be releasing. Some see religion as a source of comfort, while others find in it a challenge. Individualism and social concern are identified especially in the individualistic-communal distinction.

We coded all parishioners by whether their religiosity is exclusively me-centered, whether it is exclusively social in orientation, or whether it combines the individualistic and communal themes. The paradox of American liberal individualism in a Catholic setting shows clearly in our data. Of core Catholics, 39% are individualistic; they are concerned about their own shortcomings, about how they act on God or God acts on them, and about the reward they will receive either in this life or in the afterlife. Another 18% are communal; they define the central religious problem as alienation and social disharmony, and they look for a peaceful and just social order. Some 21% define their religious values through both themes, while 22% represent anomalous patterns or cannot think about religion in these terms.

It is sobering to note the dominance of individualistic themes in a Church that stresses community symbols. American individualism is a pervasive value that affects not only how people approach God, but how they deal with each other. From liturgy to politics, an individualism-preserving religion feels most comfortable with an individualism-preserving social ethic, while a community-building religion seeks a community-oriented social ethic.

Devotional Life and Liturgy

Perhaps just as troubling as the dominance of individualistic religiosity among American core Catholics is the absence of the sacramental option from the blueprint of their foundational beliefs. Only 15% of core Catholics fit reliance on the Church's sacraments into their salvation scheme. Despite the fact that Mass attendance and Communion participation are again on the upsurge, it is unclear whether the Eucharist truly has a deep meaning for Catholics.

What is clear is that Catholics, like other mainstream Americans, are more oriented in their prayer life to a Trinitarian God than to devotional pieties involving saints. The Christocentric emphasis of Vatican II is reflected in the fact that 63% of core Catholics pray to Jesus. About 28% address God the Father, and 15% pray to the Holy Spirit. At the same time, 46% of core Catholics address prayers to Mary.

Since the same parishioner may have many objects of prayer, it is interesting to examine the extent to which Catholic prayer life is exclusively directed to the Godhead or includes prayers to the Blessed Mother and the saints. Among core Catholic parishioners, 36% of the sample address prayers exclusively to one or more members of the Trinity; 23% pray to the Trinity and the Blessed Mother; 21% pray to the Trinity, the Blessed Mother, and the saints; 7% do not pray to the Triune God, but address their prayers to Mary and various saints; and the remaining 13% have no recognizable objects of their prayer or do not pray. The Trinitarian Godhead is even more dominant in the prayer life of parish leaders: 47% pray exclusively to a member of the Godhead; 22% pray to the Trinity and the Blessed Mother; 21% pray to the Trinity, the Blessed Mother, and the saints; 7% do not pray to God, but address prayers to Mary and various saints; and only 3% have no recognizable prayer life.

In no place in our data are the differences between the devotional life of the immigrant Church and that of post–Vatican II Catholics more vividly seen than regarding the objects of prayer. For rank-and-file core Catholics under 30 years of age, 57% pray exclusively to a member of

the Godhead; 25% address prayers to both the Triune
God and Mary; 18% pray to the Triune God, Mary, and
various saints. The figures for those between ages 30 and
40 are similar. But the Trinitarian emphasis drops pre-
cipitously among those over 40. Among the elderly, 23%
are exclusively Trinitarian; 25% pray to the Triune God
and Mary; 30% pray to God, Mary, and various saints;
and 14% do not pray to God at all, but only address
prayers to Mary and saints. Roughly 7% more of parish
leaders have a Trinitarian orientation within each age
group; in fact, nearly two-thirds of parish leaders under
50 pray only to members of the Godhead. Women are
more likely to engage in devotions to saints than men;
only one-third of core Catholic women are exclusively
Trinitarian.

We are uncertain whether the emphasis on persons
of the Trinity is a result of prevailing American religious
values or whether it derives from Vatican II theology. The
outcome is the same: the wide variety of devotional pieties
found in the immigrant Church is no longer prevalent,
even in the private prayer life of core Catholics. Such pieties survive mostly among older Catholics, women, and
those not in the leadership ranks. Moreover, they are less
often found in public worship. What visibly separated the
prayer life of Catholics from that of other American Christians in times gone by is less likely to be a source of
separation nowadays. In simplest man-in-the-street terms,
American Protestants and Catholics may now say, "We
pray to the same God."

One further feature of contemporary Catholic religiosity is found in the curious mosaic of ecumenism. Prayers
to the Holy Spirit, the charismatic renewal, gospel and
folk songs, neighborhood Bible study—all attest the cross-
fertilization of other Christian bodies with American Catholicism. Many of these cross-fertilizations have tugged
Catholics in the direction of me-centered religion. Certainly the Pelagian themes of much of the folk music in
our parishes derive more from the Baptist tradition than

from Catholic liturgical emphases. But in the ecumenical movement, there is also a counterthrust toward finding community in an objective God, in a sacramentally mediating church, and in a shared community-building liturgy with responses and hymnody. The common efforts of Catholic, Lutheran, and Episcopal liturgists are instructive in this respect.

Regardless of one's taste in music, I suspect that a sense of sacramental community does not derive from me-centered words and moods. Nor does this sense just happen where liturgical planning remains uncoordinated. Those two desiderata—preparation that lets the people sense God's presence in the community, and coordination that shows all share his presence in the celebration of the community—regrettably are often lacking in our parishes. Further, data on staff and leadership indicate that the parish music leader, responsible in part for shaping the corporate worship of the community, is isolated from the parish power structure and, not infrequently, has limited contact with others who have responsibilities for preparing liturgical celebrations.

We can learn much from Lutheran and Episcopalian liturgical practice on how to educate the faithful to move beyond liturgical individualism. Change can come in hymnbooks and service folders, in parochial schools and adult education, in the teaching objectives of the liturgist/music minister and the example of the choir member. Despite his theological individualism, Luther used hymnody and liturgical response to teach the fundamental values of a sacramental community. And absent any core collection of confessions, Anglicans carry the entire communion—the community—in a book of common prayer and hymnody. Our 36-parish observational data show that few hymnbooks, psalms, or liturgical settings are in people's hands. They also show limited effort to coordinate the hymns and responses for the day with the lesson for the day. Finally, there is little evidence of the use of schools, adult education, or the liturgies themselves to instill in the people a normative tradition of liturgical life.

Lacking such normative traditions, American Catholics are faced with the deterioration of ethnic pluralism into a consensusless liturgical individualism. Happily, some parishes in our sample shape community expression and carefully coordinate the leadership of that expression. But this is a heavy burden for the parish to bear alone. While some dioceses recognize the need to implant a normative tradition, others display too little understanding of the linkage between theology and liturgy to exercise discrimination in the selection of materials. Staff often rely on bishops for cues, and there is a short supply of trained liturgists in the bishops' ranks. Some well-meaning bishops who truly want the Church to be a participatory people of God have sanctioned liturgical materials that render it simply a collection of people.

Women

Where do women fit into the local parish? The answer to that question is simple and straightforward: not at the top, but very close to the top. Leaving the pastor aside, women are heading the important ministries of the parish, are slightly more likely than men to be rated high in influence, and are found in visible liturgical and governance roles almost as readily as men.

Besides the decline in priestly vocations, perhaps the most consequential events in American parish life in recent decades have been the shift of women religious from traditional to nontraditional roles and the increase of laywomen in positions of leadership. Women do not run the parish. No one would be so naive as to say that the pastor is no longer in charge; in all but about 10% of the cases, the pastor clearly is the leader of the parish team. But that team, whether formal or informal, is heavily populated by women. Further, when women religious serve on it, they often act as pastoral associates, functionally equivalent to the associate pastors in the multipriest parishes of bygone days. Nearly one-third of all parishes have one or more women religious on the pastoral ministry staff.

Married male deacons also handle many liturgical and pastoral functions that were formerly restricted to priests. Laymen are found in the pastoral ministries of about 30% of American parishes. While we do not know the exact proportion, it appears that most of these are married laymen.

The natural inclination is to ask how these data bear on the question of the ordination of women and married men to the priesthood. This issue needs more in-depth study. But among our core Catholic parishioners—a sample that is slightly biased to older, female, and conservative Catholics—a substantial majority feel that married men should be allowed to become priests and a little over one-third feel that women should be allowed to become priests. Nearly two-thirds of their parish leaders support the idea of married male priests, and a little over one-third support the ordination of women. Future analysis will reveal the kinds of Catholics who hold these positions and will determine whether their thinking flows as a natural progression from the heavy responsibilities laypersons, especially women, have assumed for parish life. For the moment, all we have is an isolated finding that requires further examination.

8.

Future Trends in Religious Giving

George Gallup, Jr.

IN RECENT YEARS, CATHOLICS IN AMERICA HAVE ACHIEVED a stunning momentum economically, politically, and spiritually, but this momentum could easily be stalled if current trends toward decreased giving continue.

I would like, first of all, to look at Catholics briefly from a demographic point of view, because demographics are very important in terms of giving patterns. And in this respect, we note that American Catholics generally tend to be young, well educated, upbeat, and upscale in the United States.

More specifically, the proportion of Catholics in upper income and education levels matches the proportion of Protestants in these groups. In addition, a higher percentage of Catholics are currently found in college than in the general population, suggesting that Catholics are poised for even further gains in income and in education.

One of the most striking things about Catholics is their youth. Twenty-nine percent are under thirty, and 36 percent are between thirty and forty-nine; by contrast, 24 percent of Protestants are under the age of thirty, and 41 percent are over fifty.

American Catholics have long been an immigrant people, and that tradition is continuing today. One in five

George Gallup, Jr. is a nationally known opinion pollster and Executive Director of the Princeton Religious Research Center.

Catholics now belongs to a minority group. Hispanics make up 16 percent of American Catholics, more than eleven million people. Three percent of Catholics, two million people, are black. Another 3 percent of Catholics describe themselves as nonwhites. Since very few Hispanics identify themselves as nonwhite, this suggests that the influx of Catholic immigrants from Southeast Asia is starting to show up in national surveys.

I have presented these figures because demographics are, as you know, important in analyzing trends in giving. If you look at the Catholic population as a whole, you would have every reason to think that the levels of Catholic giving match those of the rest of the nation, which of course is largely Protestant.

First of all, Catholics are as upscale as Protestants, as an increasing number are in leadership positions in government, business, education, and elsewhere. Catholics are also as economically bullish as Protestants. In a recent Gallup poll we found that similar proportions of Catholics and Protestants say that they are better off now financially than they were twelve months ago, and similar proportions say they will be better off twelve months hence. Furthermore, similar proportions of Protestants and Catholics fall into the category of "superoptimists"— that is, persons who say they are better off now than twelve months ago and also will be better off in the future. This is a very important group, because these people are purchasers of big-ticket discretionary items such as cars and appliances. So the country as a whole is bullish at the present time, with Protestants and Catholics equally bullish about their financial situation — an important finding.

Let's look at actual giving amounts. In the survey we conducted for the *National Catholic Reporter*, we probed the yearly contributions of Catholics to the church aside from those for parochial school education.

The survey found 7 percent do not contribute, 7 percent contribute from $1 to $100, 13 percent contribute from $101 to $250, 18 percent contribute from $251 to $500, and 16 percent contribute more than $500. The rest said they did not know, or refused to say.

Ironically, although Catholics give less than their counterparts in American society, one of their chief complaints about their church is that "the church is always asking for money." In a survey conducted for the Paulist National Catholic Evangelization Association, we discovered that the third highest reason unchurched Americans give for not joining or rejoining the Catholic Church — and this is from a list of forty-five items — is the perception that "the church is always asking for money." Whether this is, to some degree, a rationalization, it is still important to keep this complaint in mind.

Another factor that may have contributed, at least slightly, to reducing the amount of giving and the percentage of givers among Catholics is negative reaction to the sexual and financial scandals of TV evangelists in 1987. The percentage of Catholics who said that it was more important to give to religious than to other causes declined, along with the percentage of Protestants and the populace as a whole. Only 10 percent of Catholics agreed with the statement. The figure among Protestants was 17 percent.

In this regard, it is interesting to note that as many as one-third of Catholics said they had watched religious television during a twelve-month test period. Among Protestants the figure was 61 percent.

Why do Catholics give a smaller proportion of their income to their churches and religious organizations than their counterparts in the U.S.? Some strong clues may emerge from the survey we are now conducting for the Independent Sector.

First of all, when we look at reasons why there are twice as many big givers — people who give a thousand dollars or more — among Protestants as Catholics, we discover that Protestants are twice as likely to point to close involvement with an organization, that is, loyalty to an organization and personal experience.

In addition, a significantly higher proportion of Protestants than Catholics cite spiritual reasons. Indeed, in an earlier survey, a fairly high proportion of people who are unchurched said it is important to them that the Catholic Church put more stress on a personal relationship with Jesus Christ. Now this may relate to spontaneity of giving or it may not, but it is worth considering.

Let's move on to some possible steps to rectify the situation. These are, of course, merely suggestions, but I think that the survey results lend some basis for them.

First, identify the purpose of money to be spent by a church. For example, seven in ten Catholics believe that one can be a good Catholic without contributing money to the annual collection for the pope. Yet fewer than half, 44 percent, believe that one can be a good Catholic without donating time or money to help the poor. So certainly a clear indication of where the money is going is very important.

Second, help Catholics feel they have a share in the allocation of funds. Eight in ten Catholics, according to the survey for the *National Catholic Reporter,* said that the Catholic laity should have the right to participate in deciding how parish income should be spent. Only one in seven said they should not.

Third, reinforce the message among Catholic givers and potential givers that the money given to one's church is very cost effective.

Fourth, bear in mind that the public favors full disclosure and accountability on the part of religious leaders who seek funds, whether on the local or the national level. It is therefore important to set up watchdog groups to monitor for possible abuses.

Fifth, link giving with direct, physical involvement. One-fifth in a 1988 Gallup survey said there were times during the past year when they did not have enough money to buy the food, clothes, and medical supplies they needed. Given the serious level of poverty in this nation, we need to encourage a kind of crisis intervention, with the more privileged sectors of society working directly with the less privileged. As columnist Andy Rooney put it, "If you have your health, some happiness, some money in the bank, you don't need help; the chances are, you ought to be helping somebody who does need help."

The first step, of course, is to care in a deep way. If we truly care about the plight of others, we will do something, we will be compelled to action. It is very difficult, however, to care unless one comes face-to-face with the people in dire need, and I would suggest that most Americans have not really had this experience.

Thoreau once said, "If you give money, spend yourself with it." If those of us who serve on boards or committees dealing with human needs matched every hour spent sitting in the boardroom with an hour of direct involvement with the less fortunate, society would feel the impact and our committee work would be given new life.

Such personal contact would have an important payoff in terms of increased contributions to churches and religious organizations. An analysis based on a *Christianity Today* survey showed that those who perform volunteer work for churches or religious organizations are four times as likely to give 10 percent of their money to these organizations as are persons who do not.

These survey results would certainly seem to indicate that campaigns for money should, when possible, be tied to personal involvement on the part of the giver.

Sixth, encourage a sense of stewardship among the Christian community, a sense that appears to be missing in some degree. Financial giving, many believe, should be seen in the total context of stewardship.

Reverend David Sheldon writes: "One of the first things that we have to keep in mind is that stewardship is a spiritual venture and not just some fund-raising scheme, though the increase in revenue will ordinarily be a by-product of stewardship. Stewardship is not so much a venture in money for the parish as it is an adventure in faith, in unswerving trust in Divine Providence, in love of God on the part of parishioners." Rev. Sheldon offers a description of stewardship:

> What is Stewardship? Stewardship is simply one's recognition that God is the creator of everything.
>
> As creator, God is owner and Lord of all creation and therefore as human beings and as dependent children of God we do not have absolute ownership of anything we have. We are merely the stewards or managers of our lives and the things we possess. As stewards we must render to God an account of how we have managed our lives and the things of this world, our time, talent and treasure within the framework of God's will and his law, especially within the confines of the supreme law of love of God and neighbor.

The key to a successful stewardship program is, of course, careful planning. As religious observers have noted, growth in church membership is intentional. It does not just happen. Planning should include initial in-depth interviews of a small number of parishioners to probe such questions as: Why do people give? What is their potential level of giving? What would encourage them to give more?

I think surveys are a very important step, and I suggest undertaking them at the local level. They need not be large, projectable samples of a community; comprehensive interviews with a broad spectrum of parishioners, and not necessarily in great numbers, would yield valuable clues.

Effort should be directed towards determining the modus behind giving. Various surveys to date have indicated that among the most important motivations for giving are (1) a sense of religious commitment, including gratitude to God, and (2) a recognition of specific needs.

Giving that arises spontaneously from deep and total spiritual commitment is more likely to sustain churches than is a sense of duty. Some churches have had remarkable success in gaining financial support from their parishioners, not with the traditional methods such as pledge systems or a business approach to getting money, but by simply relating it to total commitment.

For instance, at St. Paul's Episcopal Church in Darien, Connecticut, the leaders and parishioners went through the traditional process, a very businesslike approach with committees and subcommittees and the like, with little success. Then the Reverend Terry Fullan tied financial contributions to the giving of one's total self, with spectacular results.

He told his parishioners that God does not want your money unless you are giving yourself, your life to it, that you can't tip God, you can't bribe God, you can't bargain or give him conscience money. The senior warden wrote:

> The congregation began to shuffle nervously. The senior warden trembled. I know. I was he.

> Then it came crashing like thunder: "I cannot have you believe," he (Fullan) said, "that your pleasures are pleasing to God if you have not committed your life to God." Several parishioners at the time tore up their pledge cards. For many of us the basic principal of stewardship came clear right then. Fullan said: "I appeal to you therefore brethren, by the mercies of God to present yourself as the living sacrifice wholly and acceptable to God, witness your spiritual worship."

Well, the result was tremendous financial support. There are, in fact, some churches that don't know what people give, yet receive heavy financial support.

I think the most important message is this: when a church brings people into a sense of total commitment, and into a personal relationship with Jesus Christ, this giving of one's total self ultimately will yield the financial support so many churches desperately need.

Vocations

9.

What Is a Priest?

M. Edmund Hussey

"WHAT IS A PRIEST?" IT IS IMPORTANT AT THE OUTSET TO remind you that there is no simple answer to that question. As Karl Rahner frequently pointed out, the priesthood has been and continues to be a very complex phenomenon in the Church. What I intend is a personal theological reflection on the priesthood. I shall reflect on the theological tradition of the Church as I have studied it and as I have attempted to teach it, and also on the priestly ministry in the Church as I have experienced it.

I begin my reflections with Sr. Ann Simeon, who taught me in the seventh grade. Our diocesan paper said that she was ninety-five years old when she died. She was an excellent teacher—one of the very best—and a very lovely person. She had an enormous influence on most of her students, myself included.

Sr. Ann Simeon was a great promoter of vocations to the priesthood, as were most nuns of that era. She knew exactly what the priesthood meant and was very clear about the identity of the priest. The priest was truly another Christ, an *alter Christus* who spoke in the name of Christ. As Christ on earth, the priest said to infants, "I baptize you," and to sinners, "I absolve you." Above all, at Mass the priest stood in the person of Christ and said

---

Rev. M. Edmund Hussey, a pastor in the Archdiocese of Cincinnati, is a former Fulbright Scholar and seminary professor.

over the bread and the wine, "This is my body; this is the cup of my blood."

I remember Sister telling us that the priest could call God down from heaven to the altar, that only the priest could do this, that no one else in the world had the power to do this. Many of us naturally were quite impressed and thought seriously about the possibility of becoming priests.

But Sister Ann Simeon was a realist, not a starry-eyed visionary, and she told us plainly that there were also costs—great costs—if we were to enter the seminary. We had to be good students, willing to study for many years. We would have to live a very disciplined life. We should not expect to become wealthy. We would not even have a home of our own and would have to go wherever the bishop sent us. Above all, we would have to give up marriage and a family of our own. Sister's vivid and dramatic presentation of the priesthood was, in fact, a very sound, reasonable, and orthodox one. It was based solidly on the Tridentine theology of the priesthood, which emphasized the priesthood as the principal ministry in the Church and whose starting point was the sacramental powers that belong to the priest alone and set him apart from the laity. The principal sacramental power, of course, was the power to change the bread and wine into the body and blood of Christ. To quote a medieval Latin formula, the priest had the *potestas in Corpus Christi eucharisticum*, the power over the eucharistic body of Christ.

The Tridentine era of the Church died in October 1958, less than five months after my own ordination to the priesthood. On October 9 of that year, Eugenio Pacelli, known to the world as Pope Pius XII, died at Castel Gandolfo. And on October 29, Angelo Guiseppi Roncalli was elected Pope John XXIII in the Sistine Chapel. John XXIII called a council that would take a new look — and, as it turned out, a non-Tridentine look — at the Church and the world.

This new council, the Second Vatican Council, did not emphasize the priesthood as the principal ordained ministry in the Church. The council documents clearly state that the priest participates in the ministry of the bishop, that the priest takes the place of the bishop in the parish and the priest depends on the bishop in the exercise of his ministry. The priest is now imaged as a stand-in for the bishop. The *alter Christus* has become an *alter episcopus.*

This new perspective is an important one. It inevitably makes dramatically new demands on the relationship between the bishop and the priest. In the Tridentine Church, where the priest was imaged as an *alter Christus,* the relationship between the priest and the bishop was not nearly as crucial as it is today. Even an erratic and unreasonable bishop—and there were one or two of those—could generally be avoided and could even serve as a source of much amusement at clerical gatherings. After all, an *alter Christus,* one who is another Christ, could quite easily survive estrangement from a mere bishop. But an *alter episcopus* cannot.

As important as the Second Vatican Council's emphasis on the bishop was, its emphasis on the whole Church, on the people as the Church, was even more important. Instead of beginning the discussion of the Church with the hierarchy, *Lumen Gentium* begins by emphasizing that the Church is fundamentally and basically the entire community of believers. Although this emphasis sounds almost trite when so baldly stated, its implications have been of great importance to us priests. I shall mention only two of them. First, if the Church is the entire community of believers, then the liturgy of the Church could no longer be a spectator sport, at which the people watched someone else do something for them. The liturgy had to become once again the public work of all the people. In other words, no longer could I be a priest so that others did not have to be priests, but I had to be a priest so that others could be priests. I had to be a priest to enable the entire community to be a priestly people, a worshiping Church, a eucharistic community. No longer could I say Mass that others heard. No longer could I even celebrate Mass at which others assisted. Rather, the entire community must now celebrate a liturgy at which I would preside.

Second, if the Church is the entire community, then the work of the Church was not my responsibility as a priest, but was the responsibility of the people of God, of all of the baptized. No longer could I feel that I was entrusted with the mission of the Church in a special way and that the people had to support me in my work. I now had to realize that the mission of the Church is the responsibility of all who are baptized and that I have been ordained to assist them in that work.

I suppose, looking back at it, that is perhaps the most dramatic change in my ministry in thirty years. I was ordained to do the work of the Church, and the rest of you were supposed to support me in that. I hope that the young priests today have a better sense that all are baptized to do the work of the Church, and they are ordained to support you in that. It's a very dramatic change in focus.

Therefore, the Second Vatican Council called us priests, not to envision ourselves as a priestly caste endowed with special powers, but to see ourselves primarily as baptized Christians, and only secondarily as those who have been ordained to serve the community of believers.

The Council of Trent had summarized its teaching on the priesthood by characterizing it as the power of consecrating the true body and blood of Christ and of remitting or retaining sins. But the Second Vatican Council, in its *Decree on the Ministry and Life of Priests (Prebyterorum Ordinis)*, does not even mention the priestly power of consecrating the bread and wine. Instead, it begins with a discussion of the priesthood of the faithful and then speaks about all ministry in the Church as a means of enabling the Church to be the one body of Christ. *Preby-*

terorum Ordinis affirms that the basic ministry in the Church belongs to the bishop, whose "ministerial role has been handed down to priests in a limited degree." This document teaches that the bishop fully possesses the priesthood of Christ (in the sacramental order), while the priest participates in that priesthood in a derived and dependent manner. The bishop is the sign of Christ to his flock, while the priest is a sign of the bishop.

Now, it is important to remember that *Prebyterorum Ordinis* is not one of the great documents of Vatican II. The major documents are the documents on the Church, on the liturgy, on the pastoral office of the bishops, on ecumenism, and on religious liberty. The *Decree on the Ministry and Life of Priests* is definitely among the minor ones. While it does say some fine things about the priesthood, it does not develop a contemporary theology of the priesthood. In fact, the council fathers took the priesthood somewhat for granted and did not feel that there was much need to discuss the matter at great length.

But, indirectly and unwittingly, the council fathers severely undermined the traditional role and significance of the priest in the Church. First, by insisting that the bishop is the primary minister in the Church and that the priest is the helper of the bishop, the council demoted the priest from an *alter Christus* to an *alter episcopus*, from another Christ to another bishop. Second, by emphasizing the priesthood of the laity and de-emphasizing the sacred power, which set the priest apart from the laity, the council deprived the priest of his traditional identity and clear self-image.

In hindsight—and it is only in hindsight—the recent decline in the number of priests and the present straits to which we are reduced are the natural and, perhaps even inevitable, result of the documents of the Second Vatican Council. Now, I want to make it clear that the Second Vatican Council's emphases on the Church as the entire community, on the priesthood of all the baptized, and on the pastoral ministry of the bishop in the Church are all theologically sound and are all valuable corrections to the off-balance view that has prevailed for centuries. The fact that these emphases have created a great turmoil in our priestly ministry should in no way suggest that they are unhealthy and unsound developments. In fact, I am convinced that they are positive and enormously valuable steps forward. But the fact remains that they also raised important questions not only for priests but for the entire Church, questions that have not yet been answered sufficiently and satisfactorily.

There is no question that the priestly office and the priest's own understanding of his office are in a period of great transition. The Tridentine image still survives, of course, but it is no longer taken for granted and, indeed, is even challenged by many. Yet no new image has acquired clear enough outlines to take its place.

As I have mentioned before, Karl Rahner has insisted that the priestly office in the Church has been and continues to be an extremely complex reality. He cautions against any attempts to reduce this full reality to only one of its basic elements or characteristics. In fact, it is my impression that if there was a flaw in the Tridentine theology of the priesthood, it lay in reducing this very complex reality to one of its components and then seeing that as the entire reality.

So, rather than make a futile attempt to present a neatly packaged theology of the priesthood, I would like merely to suggest two theological principles and five concrete characteristics of our priesthood as we actually live it. I will not, of course, develop them fully but only present them briefly.

Two Theological Principles

My first theological principle concerns the relationship between the ordained priesthood and the priesthood of the faithful. In order to avoid a simplistic identification of the priesthood of the baptized and the priesthood of the ordained, Church documents, ordination homilies, and theological articles frequently appeal to paragraph 10 of *Lumen Gentium*—the Second Vatican Council's document on the Church—to affirm that they differ from one another not only in degree but also in essence. But I want to point out to you that the sentence from *Lumen Gentium* that is cited to support this essential difference actually affirms a close connection between the two and merely presumes the essential difference. In the English translation of the council documents edited by Walter M. Abbott, SJ, the sentence reads: "Though they"—that is, the priesthood of the faithful and the priesthood of the ordained— "differ from one another in essence and not only in degree, the common priesthood of the faithful and the ministerial or hierarchical priesthood are nonetheless interrelated."

Consequently, although we must not deny the difference between the two, the difference ought not to be overemphasized and used as the starting point for developing a theology of the priesthood. In fact, I believe that a search for the essential difference between the two as a starting point for understanding the ordained priesthood simply complicates the matter unnecessarily. I would suggest that the principal affirmation of that sentence in *Lumen Gentium*, the interrelatedness of the priesthood of the faithful and the hierarchical priesthood, might be a better starting point. It might then be easier to see that the ordained priesthood does not intrude between God and the priesthood common to all the faithful but, rather, enables the priesthood of the faithful to be fulfilled and effective.

My second theological principle concerns the relationship between the priest and the bishop. It is somewhat similar to my first principle. Just as an overemphasis on the essential difference between the priesthood of the faithful and the priesthood of the ordained creates unnecessary difficulties, so also, I believe, an overstated attempt

to separate the bishop and the priest will create other unnecessary difficulties.

In fact, throughout much of our history the exact relationship between the episcopacy and the priesthood has
been a matter of some dispute. In the Tridentine era of
the Church, the bishop was seen essentially as the priest,
but with two additional sacramental powers: the power to
ordain and the power to confirm. The post–Vatican II
Church no longer tends to see the bishop in terms of the
priest; rather it tends to see the priest in terms of the
bishop. In the Tridentine Church the bishop was a "priest
plus"; in the post–Vatican II Church, the priest is a
"bishop minus." And that has been the difference in focus.

While leaving aside right now a complete development of this point, I do want to state the fairly generally
accepted theological principle that the priesthood is not
radically separate from the episcopacy. In fact, my next
theological points will confirm that principle. For I want
to list now five concrete characteristics of our priesthood
as those of us who are ordained priests actually live it.
These characteristics, which also have application to the
episcopacy, are absolutely essential for understanding the
priesthood.

Concrete Characteristics of Our Priesthood

First of all, by virtue of our ordination, we priests
have a presidential role in the Church. We preside at the
assemblies of the Church and we are the presidents of
local churches in a very real sense, especially if we are
pastors of parishes. The bishop, too, is the president of a
local church — a local church that we call a diocese
rather than a parish.

It is important to remember that in the early Church,
there was no distinction between a parish and a diocese.
Most cities of the ancient world were small towns by our

standards. Thessalonica, Ephesus, and Corinth were more like our midwestern county seats than the large cities where our bishops live. The Christians in those ancient cities belonged to one local church, to one ecclesial community, presided over by an *episkopos* (bishop) who was assisted by a council of *presbyteroi* (priests) and served by one or more deacons. The gradual development of parishes and the consequent distinction between parishes and dioceses is one of the most important and least studied developments in our structures.

At any rate, the local church of the New Testament and the subapostolic era has no exact counterpart in today's Church. Legally, or canonically, the local church today is the diocese, and only the bishop is empowered to ordain and thus provide for the continuing life of that local church. However, the parish is the real local church for most people today, for the parish is where they gather to celebrate the Eucharist, where they are baptized, where they are married, and where their funeral liturgies are celebrated. In the parish they learn the tradition of Christianity, and from the parish they derive spiritual nourishment for their lives and their work.

Second, by virtue of our ordination, we priests have an important sacramental and cultic role in the Church. In the past, there was a tendency to suggest that the full significance of the priesthood could be found in its cultic or sacramental function. The post–Vatican II Church has rightly insisted that the priesthood also includes very important prophetic, educational, social, and counseling tasks. The cultic function of the priest, however, must not be belittled. The symbols, the rituals, the sacraments, and the liturgy of the Church are entrusted to us who are ordained priests, in a very special way. When I preside at the eucharistic liturgy, when I baptize, when I anoint the sick, when I bless marriages, when I place ashes on the foreheads of the people at the beginning of Lent, and on similar occasions, I exercise the priesthood most visibly and most profoundly.

Third, by reason of our ordination, we priests are ecclesial persons: we are authorized to act in the name of
the Church. There are, of course, other ecclesial persons;
bishops, deacons, religious sisters, professed brothers,
and monks all are ecclesial persons in various ways.

But within this group, our place is especially visible
and recognizable, for we are authorized and delegated by
the Church, by the community of believers, to preside at
liturgical gatherings, administer ecclesial sacraments, and
preach the ecclesial tradition. Other persons are authorized to perform some of these same functions, but except
for the bishop, the priest has the most comprehensive
and unqualified authorization and delegation to act in the
name of the Church. And our exercise of this delegation is
more familiar and frequent than the bishop's in the daily
life of the Church.

Fourth, by virtue of our ordination, we priests are
established in especially close and publicly recognized relationships with other members of the Church. Whether I
like it or not, because I am a priest, other members of the
Church feel that I belong to them in a special way, that I
have a commitment to be interested in them and to care
for them. They feel that they have a claim on my time and
my energy, and if they are harshly rebuffed, they are very
hurt and even feel betrayed.

Fifth and finally, again by virtue of our ordination,
we priests are symbolic centers of the Church, icons of
the Church, a sort of embodiment of the faith, the values,
and the traditions of the Church. Now, certainly, the
bishop is an even stronger symbolic center than the
priest, and without doubt, the president of the college of
bishops—the bishop of Rome—is a still stronger symbolic
center and sacred icon of the Church.

The fact remains, however, that when people meet ordained priests, they do feel that they meet the Church
and all that it stands for in a special way. This is a very
precious and valuable asset for us, because it enables us
to have far greater influence and effectiveness than we

could ever have by ourselves. But it also carries a far greater risk, for it will inevitably magnify the opprobrium and the stigma of our sins and our failures.

These five closely related characteristics of our lives as priests are certainly necessary elements in any comprehensive treatment of the priesthood. They are obviously only some of the aspects of a very complex reality, and I have not treated them in any depth. But I am confident that further reflection on these points can help us better understand our priesthood and exercise it more effectively in these changing times.

Selecting Bishops and Finding Priests

I would like to mention two other items that powerfully affect our lives as priests and, I believe, need to be addressed by the Church in a new and creative way. One is the process for selecting bishops. I do not hold a brief for a particular method of choosing bishops, and certainly not for the popular election of bishops. But I believe, because of the very close personal relationship between the priest and the bishop and between the bishop and the whole local church, that the local church should have an open, clear, and effective role in the selection of its bishops. I also strongly believe that American bishops should be chosen by the American church in a well-defined manner and then confirmed by Rome, rather than appointed by Rome and then accepted by the American church.

My suggestion is not prompted by any illusion that we will get better bishops in this way. In fact, my impression is that our bishops are generally above average in intelligence, in talents, and in dedication. My suggestion is prompted by a recognition of the increased importance today of the relationship between the bishop and the priests, and the bishops and the local church.

My second item is the recruitment and education of priests. I believe that we need to search for other ways of enabling persons to become priests besides those of the present system. I am not arguing for the abolishment of the present seminary system, in which men make application to study for the priesthood and then, after evaluation and acceptance, are given the theological, pastoral, and spiritual formation necessary for their future work. All of us who are priests were trained in that system, which has served the Church fairly well since the Council of Trent. And I believe that our seminaries, on the whole, still give very good training.

But the present method of recruiting and training priests is obviously no longer meeting our needs. The continuing decline in the number of priests in the United States is reaching an alarming level. On the other hand, the increasing number of certified or commissioned lay pastoral ministers and ordained deacons certainly indicates that there is a large supply of generous and dedicated leaders willing to serve the community in a variety of ways.

It seems to me that we ought to look for dedicated and talented Christians who are already recognized as effective leaders within the Church and who might be called to ordination in ways that do not require going through the whole seminary system. Now, of course, that raises all kinds of concerns. Many of the proven leaders in our Church today are women and married men. Consequently, the questions of clerical celibacy and the ordination of women come to the fore. Premature and abrupt changes in these areas would cause more division and turmoil than improvement and advantage. On the other hand, it seems quite clear that both of these issues will continue to haunt us until they are confronted realistically.

I have packed many undeveloped and controversial assertions into my presentation. But, in essence, I have suggested that two theological principles should govern the development of contemporary theology of the priesthood. First, the ordained priesthood should be seen as the servant of the priesthood of the faithful. Second, there should not be a radical separation between the priesthood and the episcopacy.

I have further suggested five concrete characteristics of our priesthood as necessary ingredients of a theological reflection on the priesthood: the priest's presidential role; the priest's cultic role, perhaps flowing from the first; the priest's role as an ecclesial person; the priest's very special relationship with other members of the Church; and the priest's role as a somewhat symbolic center or icon of the Church.

And, finally, two additional processes need to be addressed in a creative way: the selection of bishops and the recruitment and training of future priests. Not everyone will find all of my reflections sound or realistic, but I hope that they are at least thought-provoking.

10.

2001: A Priest's Odyssey

John A. Coleman, SJ

I CANNOT BEGIN TO TELL YOU HOW DIFFICULT IT HAS BEEN FOR me to compose this address. To be sure, I have had my fair share of writer's block before, but over the years I have coaxed out stratagems and devices which usually break through the impasse. It took me a long while to realize why I had such a hard time getting into the topic. I learned that we lack a central and controlling metaphor for the priesthood today as powerful as the earlier metaphors of the priest as an *alter Christus* (another Christ) and as a mediator between God and humanity. We also lack consensus about the obvious next step: programs to renew priestly ministry for the third millennium.

Just before the 1990 World Synod of Bishops in Rome, which addressed the formation of priests today, Archbishop Jan Schotte, the general secretary for the synod, stated that many groups of bishops from around the world called for "a clear and complete definition of the identity and mission of the priest today." Although many of the episcopal delegates at that synod spoke eloquently to the issue, no one pretends they got us much further than a very initial and tentative conversation about that definition. Why should I individually or my hearers collectively fare any better? I will, then, refrain from trying to formulate such a clear and complete definition as prema-

Rev. John A. Coleman, SJ is a Professor of Religion and Society at the Graduate Theological Union at Berkeley.

ture. More modestly, we can seek for a new guiding image or metaphor for the priest today.

Generally, I have two simple strategies when I brainstorm for a lecture or written article. First, I read widely in the current literature on the topic, and second, I informally interview knowledgeable insider experts to get the lay of the land, the state of the question, the needed areas for exploration. I spent several months on today's topic. So, I have titled this contribution "2001, A Priest's Odyssey."

Maybe I was also stopped in my tracks because of the universal response from the about twenty priests and laypeople I interviewed for this presentation. All were thoughtful, prayerful, hopeful, and deeply pastoral people, obviously joyous and competent in their own ministry in the church. I explained to them carefully the ground rules for the meeting at which I gave this presentation: We are not trying to be Pollyannaish or to be in a state of denial. We know very well Richard Schoenherr's research about the demographics connected with a dire priest shortage, as well as the 1988 report of the U.S. bishops' Committee on Priestly Life and Ministry about severe morale problems in the clergy. But for a change, instead of looking at these crises, we want to be more positive: What is a new cadre of priests doing to prepare us for a renewed image and ministry for priests a decade from now? Of the people I interviewed, many served as spiritual directors of priests or of seminarians in formation or were buoyant and successful pastors or active members of priests' senates. All affirmed either their own priesthood or the ideal of priesthood for others. None were really young, but all represented tested, mature, and even holy ministers, the best and the brightest. Imagine my chagrin at a near unanimous litany of "Good luck — what will you say after the first minute?" All seemed to sense that the problem was likely to get worse before it got better.

One respondent, a deeply respected spiritual director to many priests in the Northwest, both young and middle aged, put it this way:

> Look, the direction in which the church has been moving does not suggest any callow optimism or easy fixes on this question. Certain possible solutions—such as a married clergy or new roles for women in ministry—cannot even be discussed. People feel that in the institutional church at present honest and credible discourse has been ruled out. There is a litmus test put on the kind of bishop who gets appointed which only solidifies this veto over an open, prayerful discernment for the future of the priesthood. The world church seems to be moving from centralism toward the right, a restoration of a more authoritarian way of proceeding. In this climate, you have to ask hard questions about who gets attracted to priesthood, who stays, and who gets promoted within the system. We have all seen the data: we are not attracting the best and the brightest, not getting self-starters in the ministry. Moreover, a new and unheard of anti-clericalism is on the increase among the thoughtful laity. Many who are active in ministry see priests as more competitors than collaborators. Some even resent celibacy and do not see the celibate priesthood as a path to holiness but more as a symbol of clerical privilege, unhealthy sexual adjustment and avoidance. You cannot postulate a more hopeful future for the priesthood until these issues are faced.

Another informant, a director of formation in a religious order of priests, noted the percentage of candidates in his group who come from dysfunctional families. He said he probed deeply with his novices two important questions: (1) Have you dealt with your own family history in such a way that in ministry you are not just repeating earlier family dynamics (i.e., being the nice guy or the caregiver in a dysfunctional family)? (2) At the present time in your life, from what sources do you receive deep emotional support and a kind of intimacy? As he put it, "Who do you hang out with whom you can't fix? Whom do you let minister to you?" This informant argued that the issue of intimacy for celibate priests is the key developmental issue for a renewed priesthood.

Still a third interviewee, a very thoughtful, youngish (late thirties) pastor and member of a priests' senate in a midwest diocese, worried about his fellow clergy's (including bishops') ability to deal creatively with conflict. "They usually deal with conflict by avoidance and passive aggression," he commented.

Actually, in retrospect, I am rather hopeful because these informants in general did not run away from the unpleasant or difficult realities facing the priesthood today. They asked hard questions. Nor, interestingly, did they an any way want to water down the high ideal of the priesthood as a corps of spiritual, relatively mature and free ministers. On the other hand, they refused to entertain cheap illusions or idealizations by putting priests on pedestals. Rather, they probed deeply for spiritual bedrock, since they assumed a renewed priesthood could only be premised both on honest confrontation with sin or mediocrity in its structures and on the only truth that brings wholeness, a relation in trust to Christ. The presence of such people on the staffs of seminaries explains why, by and large, our seminary programs and formation programs for future priests are in pretty good shape in America today. I will argue for placing emphasis less on the improvement of seminaries than on programs for already ordained priests in active ministry, since their wholeness and competence in ministry will determine future candidates and vocations. Put bluntly, we need to put energy and imagination into retaining and nourishing our current priests if we want to improve the number and quality of future recruits.

My second strategy, that of widespread dipping into the current literature, showed me that there is no dearth of articles, books, and new scholarship probing topics from a history of priesthood to burnout in ministry. I found, for example, in *Origins,* the weekly documentary service of the United States Catholic Conference, an average of ten to fifteen articles or documents per year during the last five years or so treating the identity and ministry of priests. No one can reasonably claim that we are not talking a great deal about this topic in the American church, discerning, praying, hoping, trying to imagine in new ways. This, too, is a hopeful sign for me, although none of the twenty or more speeches or documents I read in *Origins* convinced me — with an "aha!" recognition — that any of these thoughtful writers, however wise and balanced their treatment, had found a formula that clearly fits the renewal of priestly identity and mission today.

I want to structure my remarks around three simple topic sentences: 1) What we need today for the renewal of priesthood is less some new theology of priesthood than a new image or metaphor for the priest in our time. 2) We have some helpful clues about how to enact the next steps in a renewal of priesthood in our time. Assuming that the present structure of a celibate male priesthood will continue for the next decade or so, what can we do now to renew the presbyterate, given the real problems we face? 3) Where, finally, do we place our hope for a renewed sense of priestly identity and mission by the year 2001—a date for a priest's odyssey rather than a space odyssey?

Needed: A New Metaphor for the Priest

We will never really think our way or theologize ourselves to a renewal of priesthood. New theology about priests is more likely to flow from new ways of embodying the presbyterate than vice versa. It has almost always gone this way. Yet we probably need new ways of *imagining* or *imaging* the priest. I am not, of course, talking about some slick packaging or surface polishing of an outer picture of the priesthood, as if it were some fast food we were marketing.

Again and again, recent sources on the priesthood talk about a blurred image of the priest. Thus, for example, in their report to the 1990 bishops' synod, the bishops of England and Wales note that "a less clearly defined position and role seems to make the priesthood less attractive." In his contribution, Father M. Edmund Hussey states: "There is no question that the priestly office and the priest's own understanding of his office are in a period of great transition. The Tridentine image still survives, of course, but it is no longer taken for granted and, indeed, is even challenged by many. Yet no new image has acquired clear enough outlines to take its place." And Archbishop William Borders in his seminal 1988 pastoral letter on ministry, *You Are a Royal Priesthood*, could claim, "In slightly over two decades since the council, the image and role of the priestly ministry in the minds of many have gone from being clear, solid and esteemed to being less clear, uncertain and controversial."

Although I agree with and admire most of the points Father Hussey makes in his truly insightful contribution, I took exception to his title as it appeared when his address was reprinted in *Origins:* "Needed: A Theology of Priesthood."

I do not think we need a new theology of priesthood, for several reasons. First, there already exists a vast recent literature on priesthood in the early apostolic age and in its historic manifestations. Recent scholarship, for example, Kenan Osborne's thorough 1988 study, *Priesthood: The History of the Ordained Ministry in the Roman Catholic Church* (Paulist Press), situates the priest as co-worker and consultant to the bishop, who enjoys the fullness of priesthood. Yet as Archbishop Borders points out, with the Second Vatican Council "the priest is not simply a surrogate or shadow of the bishop." As the council stated, priests are themselves consecrated true priests of the New Testament *(Christus Dominus*, 15) and by ordination "are so configured to Christ the priest that they can act in the person of Christ the head." *(Presbyterorum Ordinis*, 2, 13). So priests may be an *alter episcopus* (another bishop), but they remain also an *alter Christus* (another Christ).

Priests are called to continue the mission and ministry of Jesus: to preach the gospel as the good news of God's kingdom, to heal brokenness and sanctify by leading people to the life of God, to teach in Jesus' name. The priest shares directly (as, of course, do all the baptized in another way) in the mission of Jesus. Like Christ, he is called and commissioned by God himself to further the kingdom.

Historical scholarship has established that in the emergence of the presbyterate, ministerial leadership in general served as the basis for eucharistic leadership in particular. The one who presides as leader and pastor in the community also presides at the Eucharist. Priests have a pastoral presiding, or presidential, role in local communities of the faithful. Thus, as Bishop James Malone put it a few years ago in talking about the future of seminaries: "The priest is not just a sacramental machine that does what lay ministers cannot do. The pastor is not just a convener of staff meetings." Malone foresaw a danger, if this reality got lost, "that the priest will become a manager and not a minister. It is essential that the pastor be with his people. This presence does not require the exclusion of lay persons but rather brings to their ministry the support of the priest who walks with them."

And as Osborne notes: "The collegiality of Christian ministry remains a constant factor in the history of priesthood. Thus, priests belong to a corps, the order of the presbyterate, as co-workers and a college of consultants for the diocese."

Vatican II seems to have clarified several earlier unclear or distorted points in the theology of priesthood. Thus, unlike the Council of Trent, it clearly situates the ordained priesthood in the ministry and mission of Jesus himself. It sees the episcopacy as the fullness of the priesthood. It eschews an earlier one-sided emphasis on the cultic character of the Catholic priesthood to locate it in the threefold offices of Christ: priest, prophet, and king. The priest must embody aspects of all three in his role as teacher and leader. Finally, Vatican II situated the ordained ministry as unique and distinct from, yet linked to, the universal priesthood of all believers.

With all the recent scholarship on a priestly theology, haven't we already a powerful theology of the priest? Is it likely that a radically alternative picture will emerge different from that of Edward Schillebeeckx, Bernard Cooke, or Kenan Osborne? What we need is less a new or even renewed theology for priesthood than a new way of imagining or imaging the priest—a new metaphor for our contemporary understanding of priests.

One of the very best theological works on Christian ministry, Thomas O'Meara's *Theology of Ministry* (Paulist Press, 1983), includes an intriguing chapter entitled "The Metamorphoses of Ministry." O'Meara inspects varying operative and dominant images of the priest from apostolic times to the present, which he labels evangelist, priest, monk, Herr Pastor, curé. His argument runs: "Beneath the Visigothic, Romanesque or Baroque, there is not one lasting Christian priesthood merely changing its vestments. Cultures bring their own material to the ministry; rather than diluting it, cultural forms free ministry to live."

Each of these metamorphoses took up a prime new metaphor, social role, or aspect of priestly ministry and made it dominant. Thus, for example, the role of monasticism in the early Middle Ages made the image of the monk-priest dominant. Monk-popes imposed monastic spirituality onto priests, making them, as it were, monks in the world or in the parishes. They mandated, for example, the Divine Office as the appropriate prayer of priests. No one, of course, questions that priests be men of prayer. But does their daily prayer have to reflect the prayer of monks? The monastic period saw the bishop as a kind of Father Abbot to his priests. The nineteenth century, in its turn, romanticized the spiritual director and interiorized him as the curé, exemplified in the Curé d'Ars or Bernanos' classic novel, *The Diary of a Country Priest.* As I have mentioned, the two metaphors of the priest as an *alter Christus* and as a mediator between God and humanity have dominated since the Counter-Reformation period, often with the unfortunate result of downgrading the priesthood of all believers.

So a telling question to ask ourselves is: What metaphor would you choose to typify ordained ministry today in order to differentiate it to some extent from other ministries in the church? Several possibilities suggest themselves:

1) Servant Leader

The priestly role remains essentially one of pastoral direction and leadership in a local community such that ministry at the Eucharist presupposes a wider ministerial presence to the people being served. Some commentators have suggested that we need to underscore the servant character of this leadership. As Archbishop Borders put it in his pastoral on ministry: "The ordained ministry does not exist for itself but only in and for the church. It exists to offer the service of leadership and sacramental nourishment through which it acts as a catalyst to enable and empower the whole community in the church to realize its mission in the world." In this meaning, the priest must, in some sense, engage in the four main ministries in the church: worship, proclamation of the word, community building, and service. He need not monopolize these four but serves as a catalyst for the emergence of multiple ministries around these four basic ministries. We see a natural transition from this image of the priest as servant leader to our second image.

2) Catalyst

This image is meant to stress the strong need for collaborative ministry, collegiality in a parish setting, team ministry with the pastor as catalyst rather than controller of ministry. The pastor is the one who evokes and calls forth lay ministry. Undoubtedly, with the wonderful explosion of lay ministry since Vatican II, collegial and collaborative ministry has become the most important form of ministerial presence in the church.

3) Leader of the sing-along, not a concert pianist

I take this image from Bishop Kenneth Untener of Saginaw, Michigan. As an image of the priest in his function as community builder, he contrasts to the solo performer of piano concertos the piano player who needs to pick up clues from his congregation and play what they can all sing together.

4) Teller of the story of Jesus

One of those I interviewed is a very successful pastor in an inner-city parish in the Northwest with an active program of liturgy, outreach to the homeless, a parish L'Arche community, and parish-based spiritual direction and prayer. He told me that he has learned that his role is not to control all meetings or produce all ministry, but to serve in many meetings, subgroups, and so forth in order to insist that parish action, decisions, etc. be related to the ground story of Jesus: how he acted and made decisions, and what values he brought to human behavior. I see this as a variation of the priest's essential ministry of the word.

5) Man of God

The image of the priest as a man of God, that is, a prayerful mediator between God and the needs of his people, has been a perennial theme in church history. The nineteenth-century curé and the Bernanos novel treat this theme. But so do more modern novels such as M.J. Mojbetai's lovely story of a Texas priest in her *Ordinary Time* or J.F. Powers' novels. A colleague of mine who conducts a seminar on priesthood for seminarians insists that these novels are as helpful as formal theology for eliciting images of priests.

I recently read, sometimes with tears, Paul Wilkes' story *In Mysterious Ways: The Death and Life of a Parish Priest.* Wilkes followed the daily pastoring of Father Joseph Greer of Natick, Massachusetts. No question that Greer represents a credible image of the man of God in our time. His advice to young priest interns in his parish ran: "You have to be nuts to go into the priesthood. It's an awful job. The pay is terrible, the hours are worse. People not only do not look up to you. They look down. You have to love God, and if you don't, it will grind you up. Remember no trumpets will sound. And you are going to spend more time being a carpenter than a priest."

Greer insisted on common prayer together in his rectory: "Despite our weaknesses and regardless of any personal tensions or animosities, it unifies us as priests and specifies what we do. It's a time to forgive each other. We are a small community within a larger community, and we need to ask the Lord's blessing for the day. Often it is the only time we get together."

In a hardheaded way, Wilkes faces the future of the priesthood: "Not only has the once-admired profession of the priesthood been badly battered, but the work priests have always done still has to go on, with or without the approbation and automatic respect that once attended it."

This book moved me deeply, emotionally, spiritually. Here was a priest to be proud of, doing the best of pastoral work, religious, educational, caritative. One way to get at the proper image or metaphor of a priest for our time might be to consider what brings tears to our eyes. I am reminded of an account of the burial of a much beloved priest in Seattle, Father Leo Eckstein, for almost thirty years a pastor or pastoral associate at St. Joseph's Church. I knew and admired Leo Eckstein and had reason to be grateful to him. I was told that, at his funeral, the church was packed not only with the people of the parish but with priests, and that they openly wept because he modeled what a priest should be. Maybe from literature and our experience of crying over the passing of a good priest we will get better images for the future of the priesthood than from academic theology. What kind of pastor would bring tears to your eyes today at his passing?

Some Next Steps Forward

I do not think we are bereft of clues about what some of the next steps must and might be for renewing the image and mission of the priest. I took it very seriously when there appeared the 1988 document of the U.S. bishops' Committee on Priestly Life and Ministry, "Reflections on the Morale of Priests" (*Origins* 18, January 12, 1989). I took it seriously because it was the product of the best and most pastoral priests in the United States today. It was not always pleasant reading, but it helps us put our pulse on some of the sore spots in the priesthood and address them. First, listen again to some of the comments about priestly morale:

> Role expectations among clergy leave many feeling trapped, overworked, frustrated and with the sense of little time for themselves. . . . The lack of a unified, coherent vision of what we are all about is a burden. For some recently ordained priests, the sense of professionalism and planning which they bring to ministry clashes with administration and service which they perceive as haphazard and without priorities. . . . Diminishing numbers dim any hope for gentler years ahead and graceful retirement.

> The need for intimacy, the distance sometimes created by the role of the priest and the integrity demanded between priests' feeling and public life need greater attention. . . . Differing ecclesiologies lead to a polarized presbyterate.

> Some priests feel at times that they are passing on to parishioners, who clearly disagree, pastoral decisions

which they sense their bishops do not fully endorse and which they themselves personally question. "Caught in the middle" is an apt description. They fear that their youthful hopes and dreams will never be achieved, that the vision they had seems at times to be slipping away or unimportant now; that there is no possibility of the rewards and recognitions they once dreamed of; that they will not be replaced; that they will be left quite alone; and perhaps most significant of all, they feel that they have little or no control over their lives and future, be it in terms of ministry, assignment, policy development or church direction.

The report pinpoints areas of concern: rectory living (balancing privacy and community), terms of office in the pastorate, personal contact with the bishop, personnel boards. Five of its suggestions call for our attention:

1) Mentor programs for the recently ordained

The report emphasizes the new need to prepare the recently ordained for what may turn out to be precipitous pastoral responsibility soon after ordination. No longer given the luxury of a leisurely apprenticeship, many will be pastors very shortly after ordination. But notoriously, mentor programs do as much for the mentors as for those being inducted into the apprenticeship. This suggestion speaks strongly to building up a vivid sense of the presbyterate as a collective order, a corps of priests who can experience a strong esprit de corps. In the past, mentoring took place in an informal manner. Now it must be more intentional. We need to program it and to study the various (and sometimes conflicting) models for mentoring in different dioceses.

2) Sabbatical programs for priests

These are more necessary now than a decade ago, to avoid burnout, to achieve new integrations intellectually and spiritually, and to give priests the leisure after a rich experience of ministry to integrate new images. Bishops will be more reluctant in a time of priest shortage to allow sabbatical programs. Pressure (and financing where it is necessary) will be most useful for assuring that we do not sacrifice long-term service for short-term gains.

3) Strong personal prayer life

In a moving address, "If We Begin to Think of Ourselves as a Vanishing Breed," Columbus, Ohio's Bishop James Griffin has reminded his priests that priests' ability to be creative long term depends on a strong personal prayer life: "In your pastoral work, do not neglect what St. Charles Borromeo called 'the parish of your own soul.' You cannot help people know God unless you first know him yourself. You cannot increase their love for him unless you first love him with your whole heart and soul and mind and strength." But who is funding and developing programs that help priests find a form of prayer appropriate to their pastoral ministry and pay for spiritual directors? However useful and essential spiritual directors for priests may be, most do not receive any salary for the task, and this makes religious orders and other groups reluctant to release people for this ministry. It may be worth noting, also, that mentors or spiritual directors for priests do not always have to be priests themselves. Many dioceses have begun to discover through houses of prayer and available spiritual direction new leases on life for their priests. Often, it is better if the spiritual directors are not directly responsible to the bishop (not opposed to him, of course) and so can more credibly position themselves as agents of and for the priests rather than as agents of administration. This raises again the question of funding for these positions in dioceses.

4) Priest support groups

Priests continue to complain of the loneliness of their life, and increasingly so as more of them live in rectories without assistants. Facilitating support networks for priests, where they can experience the deepest intimacy of friendship, would be high on my list of priorities, were I a bishop. In my own diocese it almost leaps at you when you correlate the senior pastors who stand out for leadership, maturity, and emotional health with membership in the priestly religious association, Jesu Caritas. Members of this group meet regularly for prayer, support, and uncensored discussion of the realities of their life, with its triumphs and warts.

5) Diocesan workshops for entire staffs, not clergy alone

It is a truism that many priests simply do not yet know how to embody, imagine, and work out collaborative ministry. It is also a truism that only such a ministry has a future in a church that, in Archbishop Borders's phrase, is totally a royal priesthood. The priest may buy into the image of the priest as catalyst for ministry but lack skills to function in that role. Resources for parish teams that will bring together entire staffs and the clergy to facilitate the skills needed for collaborative ministry should be a priority for funding and research.

Where We Place Our Hope

We can accomplish these five steps in short order if we find a way to imagine them and fund them. Although not panaceas, they would help to renew even now the image and ministry of priests. Let me end by reiterating where I place my hope for the future. I have no doubt that there will be priests in the year 2001, for I take seriously the words of Thomas O'Meara: "The life of the spirit in the church never ceases. The corporate service of Jesus the Christ in his body continues." And in the twenty-first century, there will be good priests (celibate or married) whom we will want to weep for when they die.

11.

American Seminaries as Research Finds Them

Katarina Schuth, OSF

IN THE PAST TWENTY YEARS, MANY POSITIVE DEVELOPMENTS and accomplishments have happened in Catholic seminary education: excellent programs have developed; the personnel is of the highest quality; and the needs of the Church are being met in very significant ways. I will address all those achievements, but I will also mention some challenges and opportunities for the future, because not everything is settled in the Church today as far as seminaries are concerned. These include vocations, enrollment problems, staffing needs, difficulties in meeting the needs of the Church, and planning.

I would like to begin with a little bit of history (based on unpublished research by Joseph M. White). It is always good to put ourselves in context and to know that we have come a very long way. In 1563, the Council of Trent first decreed that there should be seminary education. It is difficult to imagine that the Church survived for almost sixteen centuries without seminaries. People in those days, however, did not respond to the directives of the Church quite as rapidly as today. Not until the seventeenth century were there many seminaries at all, and then they were usually associated with cathedrals — many in France.

Sr. Katarina Schuth, OSF is Chair of the Department for the Social Scientific Study of Religion at the St. Paul School of Divinity at the University of St. Thomas.

The first seminary in the United States was established almost two hundred years ago, in 1791. It was St. Mary's in Baltimore, run by five Sulpician Fathers, with only 4 students enrolled. They had problems in those early days, too. By 1799, there were still five faculty members, but only 1 student. The situation improved, though, and by 1843, some twenty-two seminaries were open, with 277 students — 13 per school. However, that wasn't the end of problems. Many of those seminaries closed, and the reasons sound like today: the lack of local youth attracted to priesthood; an uneven supply of immigrant seminarians; the lack of clerical personnel to serve as staff; and the lack of regular funding. So those middle years — that half-century after the founding of the first seminary — must have been very difficult. And this continued until, toward the end of the nineteenth century, the Third Plenary Council of Baltimore was held and a serious effort to renew the seminaries of this country began.

John Talbot Smith, in *Our American Seminaries,* noted that "an ideal American diocesan priest should be an educated gentleman fitted for public life, physically sound, acquainted and in sympathy with his environment" — isn't that what we would like today? — "and imbued with the true missionary spirit." This clerical model was a reaction against an older ideal of the priest as "narrowly schooled, whose mind was exclusively on the supernatural, and whose aestheticism and unexercised body rendered him sickly and useless, and whose European background caused him to disdain American values and to lack the flexibility for the very demands of ministry in America." So if we have a few problems with our seminarians not adapting to parish life today, imagine how difficult it was to provide transition in those years.

In the early twentieth century, the issue of modernism dominated, with resulting setbacks for seminaries. Seminarians were forbidden to read periodicals, and some directives contained these remarkable words: "It is important to control enthusiasm for learning." Serious discussion of theological issues just didn't happen, and scholarship was greatly inhibited.

In the 1930s, some professional organizations, such as biblical societies, began to be formed, and these groups brought people together and helped renew interest in scholarship. This pattern continued into the 1950s, when considerable reform took place. Around that time the National Catholic Educational Association was established, and it became an important horizontal contact among seminaries, a way they could exchange ideas and learn from each other.

In the early 1960s, seminary enrollment reached its peak. In 1961, counting all seminaries — high school, college, and theologate — there were more than forty-two thousand students in over four hundred seminaries, with seminarians in the theologates numbering over eight thousand. In 1988, we had just over fifty theologates serving just under four thousand seminarians, with an additional three thousand other students.

There have been enormous changes since Vatican II, including a dramatic series of relocations and reorganizations of houses of study, schools of theology, and seminaries sponsored by both religious orders and dioceses.

Theologates are the institutions that provide professional education for ministry, generally, the last four years of training for priesthood; seminaries can also be at the high school or college levels. I am speaking only about theologates.

In 1986–1987, fifty-four theologates were identified as members of the NCEA Seminary Division. Most of these schools are divided into three categories; a few don't fit into any category.

The majority — thirty in all — are what we call Freestanding Seminaries, that is, schools that have all aspects of the formation program: personal, spiritual, academic, and pastoral formation. Even among these, you see many different categories, and their missions are also quite different — some are for diocesan seminarians, some are for seminarians of religious orders, and some include lay students. This last fact points to the emergence of laypeople in seminary education. In the early 1960s, as you see in the figures on the number of students, virtually no lay students were enrolled in theology schools. Now, counting both full-time and part-time students, well over three thousand lay students are studying with the four thousand seminarians in at least three-fourths of the schools.

The second group, consisting of theologates usually related to universities, is called the Supplemental Model. In these ten schools the academic component is provided in a university, while the personal and spiritual formation is taken care of in a house of formation.

Those named Collaborative Schools have a variety of expressions. The so-called Union Model schools — the Catholic Theological Union in Chicago and the Washington Theological Union in Silver Spring, Maryland — are the largest in total numbers of students, each with over three hundred. By contrast, about half of the rest have fewer than fifty seminarians each. So, one can see how precarious the state of those very small schools is. Another kind of collaborative school is called the Federation Model, where several institutions work together. An unusual combination of three small schools in Washington who relate to each other is termed a Mixed Model.

In the "Other" category, there are the Melkite, Byzantine, and two Cistercian religious seminaries.

Mission and Management

I would like to move now into a short discussion of the seminary models and the changes that have taken place.

Some seminary educators hold that it is best for seminarians to be separated from others while they are being educated for the priesthood. They have some very good reasons for this. They believe that it is preferable during those years to focus exclusively on the meaning of priesthood per se, not simply the teaching of a theology of ministry — which a lay minister might do — but rather priestly ministry. In addition, they feel it is also better for the seminarians to be separated into a more reflective environment.

Those who have chosen to change the model and have made the seminary — the theologate — open to a variety of students feel that it is in the best interest of the seminarians, and of the Church, that they be educated in a setting that more closely represents the population in general. The Church today requires that priests address issues from various perspectives, including that of the laity. And that means that if, during their education, they can interact and sometimes even argue with their lay counterparts in the classroom, it can help them later on when they become priests.

So, we have these two very different viewpoints. As you might expect, the first report from the recent papal visitations tends to favor the first model: seminarians only, with limited lay contact. One of the consequences of that stance is that seminaries have not felt — with a few exceptions — free really to engage in dialoguing about how to educate lay ministers, a question facing the Church today. As a matter of fact, many seminaries would find it difficult to stay open if they depended only on the enrollment of seminarians. So, if these seminaries are to continue enrolling lay students, those educating laypeople need to discuss more the ways to do it more effectively. Both ordained and other professional ministers need to learn how to work in a collaborative setting where the authority of the Church is respected. A number of seminaries have taken on the major task of working toward achieving that model, but I would say that we don't have a good model at this point.

In one questionnaire, fifty-three out of fifty-four rectors and presidents responded when I asked them to list three changes that have taken place in their seminaries in the last twenty years. I didn't ask for positive ones or negative ones, but all except five or six were positive changes. They said that they made the changes because of the needs of the Church and because of the theology of the Second Vatican Council. When asked what the impact of change has been, they said that the quality of education for the priesthood and of theological education has improved. So the impact, from their point of view, is an extremely positive one: these have been good changes for seminaries, and the seminaries are better than they were twenty years ago.

Continuing on the question of mission and management, I will say a few words about governance and finances. My recent research has looked at who serves on the boards of trustees of our seminaries. Not counting the university boards, there are forty-one separate boards of trustees that serve at the first level of authority. An additional twenty-two advisory boards also exist, so that makes a total of sixty-three boards that serve our seminaries not associated with universities. On those boards, there are 820 people. Two-thirds of them are clerics, one-third laypeople.

I have met many of these board members, who are of outstanding quality. Today, however, they need to have a better sense of what is they should be doing, that is, getting more involved with decision making and, often, with fund raising. In their view, the Church needs to learn how to share power and control and authority. This is a real challenge for the Church. It is very difficult to give up authority because it entails great risk.

One of the reasons that boards have expanded, certainly, is to search for financing. Seminaries have always been the "favored children," in a sense, of the Church and sometimes of the bishops who are funding them. But these days, as resources decline, it is becoming more difficult to finance seminaries. About thirty seminaries are sponsored by religious orders of men, which pour millions of dollars into these enterprises, with very little recognition of their contribution. It is not at all uncommon for an order to be donating three hundred to five hundred thousand dollars to seminary education so that the tuition can be kept low.

Over 40 percent of seminary teachers are male religious. That pool became available when many of their own schools closed in the early and mid-1960s and the two large Unions were formed. Thirty or forty orders gave up small seminaries to join the two Unions. Many of the former teachers in these small seminaries are interspersed throughout dioceses and throughout the seminary system. Since this pool will soon be diminished and will have to be replenished by lay people who need regular salaries — not big salaries but at least somewhat commensurate salaries — the costs will escalate and finances will become more and more difficult.

Of particular concern is the inability of the Catholic schools to give scholarships comparable to those given by institutions such as Yale and Harvard. Weston Jesuit School of Theology is located in Cambridge, Mass., very close to Harvard Divinity School, which has many Catholic lay students, in part because it can give more scholarships than Catholic schools. More and more, our future Catholic leaders are being trained in the Protestant divinity schools because that is where they find funding, and bishops are concerned about this problem. And until the finances of our schools can be assured with endowments or scholarship funds, the probability of attracting many more Catholic students is reduced.

It is not as if the seminaries are standing by doing nothing. Development programs are being established in many of the schools. Over half of them now have well-organized programs, many started through a Lilly project.

Personnel and Students

Let us now move to the personnel of seminaries. The number of administrators in seminaries has increased considerably along with the complexity of the programs. This has happened because, with the introduction of lay students, it was necessary to establish separate personal and spiritual formation programs for them, to expand the number of classes, and to have a variety of student services available. Moreover, the formation program — spiritual and personal formation — and pastoral programs for seminarians also have become more specialized and, therefore, more people are needed to staff them. We have moved from a simple system of perhaps two or three administrators — the rector-president and the dean — to ten or twelve administrators, with particular growth in the areas of student services and finance and development.

The turnover of rectors and presidents is very high. This is a concern for the future, because the continuity and the sense of history is lost. It is also more difficult to ensure that there will be good planning. Those who serve in these offices have roles that now involve considerable external work and responsibilities: fund raising, recruiting, maintaining the reputation of the school, belonging to national and professional organizations. Coping with those responsibilities, plus trying to keep the school going, has meant that there is tremendous pressure, and these officials simply don't stay in office for long. The same kind of turnover, for different reasons, is true of the position of dean.

Noting the structures and observing how seminaries have expanded, we need to analyze and redesign administration in light of the new complexity in the seminaries today. The schools have to look critically at what they are doing and then plan in new and different ways for their needs.

About nine hundred faculty members teach in the fifty seminaries. About three-fourths are priests and about one-fourth are laymen, laywomen, and women religious. This proportion is, of course, a shift from the years when priests composed virtually the entire staff. The quality of those who serve in seminaries, I believe, is extremely high. Just over two-thirds have a doctoral degree, and about one-third have a master's degree.

Faculty, like administrators, tend to feel overworked and overextended. They are expected to fulfill a dual role that includes not only teaching but also responsibility for personal and spiritual formation. It is not enough for faculty simply to know their discipline, they have to be persons who can relate to students on a whole other level of spiritual development. If we are to have young men who are able to relate to people in parishes, a tremendous amount of personal effort is needed on the part of seminary faculty.

And so, as seminaries look toward the future — a future where the number of teachers who are male religious and priests is declining, and where women are underutilized in various capacities — there will be real problems finding faculty without some planning now.

The personnel at seminaries consists also of the students. I have already mentioned some facts about the numbers and the different types of students. If there is any one area in which rectors and presidents would like to see improvement, I think it would be in the numbers of students available to them. Seminaries compete for the small pool of people who want to become either priests or lay ministers in the Church. Unless that number increases, we will soon suffer from a lack of trained people to serve the Church as ordained or lay professional ministers.

Students are very interested in service to the Church. Their motivation is definitely to serve other people. There are concerns, however, on the part of vocation directors and recruiters about the quality of students being recruited. They report that those students falling into the top 10 percent academically are no longer entering seminaries. In other words, that upper cut is, for the most part, gone. The rest of the students in seminaries are about the same academically, so there is not a significant drop in quality. However, with the upper group smaller than it ever has been, there is concern about leadership and about future educators in the Church. A very important question, then, is: How do we encourage vocations? Also, how do we encourage those who might enter lay ministry?

Programs

A third dimension is the programs of seminaries. I mentioned that there are three aspects of these programs: (1) spiritual and personal formation, (2) academic formation, and (3) pastoral formation.

Students consider spiritual and personal formation to be most central to their preparation for a future ministry as priests or as lay ministers in the Church. The programs have improved greatly over the last ten to fifteen years. We have learned so much about the kind of psychological impact that secular society has on students: what kinds of changes need to take place in them; what kind of ministry they are entering; and, therefore, what kind of person each needs to be. This personal and spiritual formation is developing well, but the training of those who are conducting the programs is probably not as good as it could be. Only in the last few years has there been specialized training, and more will be needed in the future if we are to avoid potentially major problems.

The academic formation has improved tremendously in the last two decades. About twenty years ago, Catholic theologates joined the Association of Theological Schools, and I think that has made a great deal of difference in the quality of academic education. Students, by and large, really enter into these programs — all-important to their formation.

One persistent question: Can faculty teach everything that needs to be taught in the few years that students have? The answer: It is very difficult. I think the schools do well in scripture, moral theology, and systematic theology. They are beginning to do more on pastoral preparation. But areas in which the young men will need some training — such as how to work collaboratively with lay ministers, and particularly women, in parishes and how to deal with conflict — are not routinely part of the curriculum.

Training in administration and management is very limited, simply because of the short time frame. But young men are becoming pastors at a much earlier age than in the past. In Kansas, Minnesota, and Montana, for instance, a young man is made a pastor after one or two years. That is tremendous pressure for a young person with little experience. We remember what it was like at the age of twenty-seven or twenty-eight; it was not easy to be in charge of anything. And the young men realize they don't have this kind of preparation. I think that has to have an impact on the vocations question as well.

Field education in pastoral formation has been given great emphasis since the Second Vatican Council. This is an aspect of training in which the young people who are entering into ministry "practice," so to speak. They do an internship; they go into the parish and begin to work in many different ways. Some do it in a block of time — for three or four months; others spread it out through their whole time in the seminary. For example, there is the "teaching parish," where the person is involved in a parish for four years and really becomes part of it. The goals of those who are directing the field education — the supervised ministry — are: to get more participation from parishioners, to help students see how parish structures are changing, and to have them become more aware of the collaborative model of ministry.

All of these formation programs relate, of course, to the needs of the Church today. And that's the last thing I would like to talk about. The needs of the Church are multiple and manifold, as we all know. The ethnic groups mentioned by Archbishop Murphy in his contribution, the aging population, the young people: How can we relate to all of them? How can we develop the sociocultural perspective that is needed to understand the various situations from which people are coming? Many of them are not imbued with the faith in the ways that we were as children. We learned the catechism; we learned about our faith and the doctrines of the Church in a much more systematic way. Now, young people have different approaches. When they come to seminaries, they often are unaware of some of the basic things that we assume they would know. Yet, in a few years, they will be out of the seminary, dealing with well-educated Catholics — Catholics who are much better educated than they were twenty or thirty years ago.

The whole ethnic makeup of the immigrant population has changed. We must develop ways and means of helping the large number of Hispanic and Asian people who are in need of the services of the Church. This poses a challenge for the future.

Another change, which I think is a serious challenge for both seminaries and the Church at large, is the shift of the Catholic population to the South and the Southwest in the last fifteen to twenty years. The seminaries are primarily in the Northeast or the Midwest. This unbalanced distribution of seminaries is in need of some shifting and adjusting.

Goals and Directions

Planning for seminaries is another essential element in facing the future. I went through all the catalogs of the fifty or so schools, and only five have directors of planning listed. Planning has not been done in seminaries to any great extent, but I think that it must be from now on.

If planning does not take place, decisions are made without the necessary background and information. Planning is needed not only on a local institutional level but also on a national level, because without it, I think we will have poorer allocation of resources and lower-quality schools.

An evaluation of the ministerial effectiveness of those who become priests should also be considered for the future. Such an evaluation might look at the differences in the various seminary models. Does it really matter in what kind of a school or seminary a student was educated? Does it matter that it was one in which there were only seminarians? Is it better if the seminary was a mixed model? We don't know the answers to these questions, but I think they would be the source of some good research.

In considering my four main points, I think we are concerned with both survival and quality. It is not one or the other. It is really both.

The issues of mission and management include: what kind of school is best; the emerging role of boards; clarifying finances and building endowments; and distributing the charges for seminary education more equally.

The issues concerning personnel and students are: ongoing training for major administrators; design of administrative structures; training for second-level administrators; faculty development; student scholarship programs; ministry transition programs (continuing education for new ministers); and transitional programs (return to seminary for reflection periods).

Concerning programs, curriculum development is needed to address some of the issues from *A Shepherd's Care:* how to serve in parishes that are very different; collaborative ministry; matching the needs of the parishes with the kinds of services that can be rendered; dealing with conflict; and dealing with different groups of people.

And finally, for future goals and directions, operational and strategic planning is central. In addition, meeting regional needs (e.g., the population shift and the variety of people being served) and measuring ministerial effectiveness in the context of the Church today are important areas demanding our attention.

My final comment is one of hope. Doing this research during the past three years, I have been touched deeply by the quality of persons serving in the special task of preparing men for priesthood and others for Church ministry. The dedication, skill, and goodness of their work makes me believe that all things are possible for a spirit-filled future. And our cooperation and participation in that, I think, is very important. We may all be surprised by the direction in which the Spirit leads us, but let us pray for each other, that we will be open to the Spirit.

12.

U.S. Catholic Seminaries: Anticipating Their Future

Archbishop Thomas J. Murphy

I HAVE BEEN ASKED TO LOOK AT U.S. CATHOLIC SEMINARIES and to see if I am able to anticipate their future. My task is as enviable as that of a Wall Street analyst asked to tell the future of the stock market. In many ways, that analogy is far from irrelevant. Certain realities within both society and the Church have an inner strength and stamina, yet must face the future subject to forces that impact on them.

The question "What is a priest?" is of tremendous significance, because when we are able to articulate a theology of priesthood that is appropriated by the Christian community, then we will have a clearer idea of the direction of seminary education and formation today in its task of preparing ordained leaders for the Church of tomorrow. At the same time, we recognize the need to prepare qualified lay personnel, who are assuming an ever-growing role and responsibility in the Church, and we must ask questions regarding their ministerial formation and education. Such increased roles and responsibilities by laity within the Church are not self-directed, but they come from the challenge of Vatican II, post–Vatican II documents, a theology of baptism, and the real needs of the Christian community.

Archbishop Thomas J. Murphy is the Archbishop of Seattle and a former seminary rector.

If future years prove me correct in my beliefs about the future of U.S. Catholic seminaries, then I have helped to shape that future by being able to identify the tensions, forces, and vision that will create that future to which we must respond. If my vision is blurred, then my remarks will be part of that ever-increasing limbo of "what might have been if they had only listened to me." Allow me to outline what I hope to share with you. The future is unknown, yet we do know that so many dimensions of the future are determined by present realities. Consequently, I would like first to offer some insights on present realities within the Church as well as within seminary education and formation today. Second, I would like to reflect on forces operating within society and the Church today that are helping to shape not only seminary education and formation but the Church as well. In light of these realities and the forces that impact on them, one is able to see some possible future directions for seminaries in the United States as we conclude one millennium and begin another. Finally, I would like to offer some personal observations in the light of these realities, forces, and future possibilities.

Realities

It seems appropriate that as we anticipate the future of seminaries in the United States, we recall certain realities that are in place, which serve as agenda items that will help determine their future.

Organizationally, the Church is hierarchical. Though themes of collaboration, shared responsibility, response to local needs, and a host of other theological insights have influenced much of the life of the Church, it has to be recognized that legislation for the governance, purpose, mission, and ministry of a seminary cannot be isolated or independent of the expectations of the universal Church. Canon 242 states that "each nation should have a program for priestly formation which is to be determined by the conference of bishops." But it goes on to say that this program of priestly formation should be developed "in light of the norms issued by the supreme authority of the Church and which is also to be approved by the Holy See." Even when new circumstances require the program to be updated, approval of the Holy See is also a requirement.

Seminaries after Vatican II responded to the challenge of postconciliar expectations for the formation and education of its ordained ministers. There were innovative and intelligent responses to this challenge of meeting the signs of the times. Different forms and structures began to develop within seminary programs. Trying to utilize the resources of finances and personnel in the best way possible, many seminaries developed into centers for the formation and education not only of priests but also of other ministers. Seminaries began to use the gifts and talents of religious, deacons, and priests as faculty members. In doing so, seminaries believed they were faithful to the broad principles of seminary formation and education articulated in the "Program of Priestly Formation," which allowed for adaptation and response to local needs.

Yet the recent program of visitations to seminaries called for by the Holy See has raised a new consciousness of the norms for seminary formation and education found not only in the "Program of Priestly Formation" but also in the universal law and norms of the Church. In light of the visitation experience, significant issues have surfaced that need to be addressed by seminaries.

As institutions established for the formation and education of candidates for the priesthood, seminaries are only able to accept male students who are willing to make a lifetime celibate commitment as candidates for holy orders. According to many surveys and recent studies, this is a reality that has had a profound effect in the recruitment of candidates for priesthood, besides being an issue for some women who wish to have a more significant participation in the life, governance, and leadership within the Church.

Within seminary education and formation today, there is the growing realization that programs of preparation for candidates to the priesthood in religious communities are different from those for diocesan candidates. The last edition of the "Program of Priestly Formation," published in 1981, spoke of one program for both sets of candidates, in direct response to the request of the formation committee of the Conference of Major Superiors of Men. Within a very short time, however, it became obvious that a new dimension in seminary formation and education was evolving.

The research from various studies over the past five years indicate that increasingly the candidates for priesthood today are older, possess different educational backgrounds, and have different interests as far as ministry is concerned. This places new expectations on seminary programs.

For various reasons, there seems to be an ebb and flow of enrollment trends among individual theologates. The number of candidates for ordained ministry remains more or less the same, which means the dramatic increase in enrollment in one or more seminaries involves a decrease in others. Enrollment statistics in individual seminaries are a constant reminder of the good news/bad news adage. Ways must be found to stabilize enrollments in individual seminaries as well as to encourage the recruitment of qualified candidates.

Priests, especially those involved in diocesan and parish ministry, expect collaboration in ministry with others in service to people in the Church today. Though opportunities to prepare for such collaboration are present within the seminary program, this will remain an issue that seminaries will continue to address.

Finally, seminaries need to articulate a theology of priesthood that will be a basis for the educational/formational process in seminary programs as well as for future priestly ministry. Church statements, as well as ongoing references by Pope John Paul II, ask us to recognize the difference between the ministry of the ordained priest and the ministry that comes from the baptismal call.

These realities are but some of the forces and issues in place that need to be considered in any discussion of the future of Catholic seminaries in the United States. To plan for the future without taking these realities into consideration would be unrealistic.

Forces

Besides these factors that impact directly on seminary education and formation, there are also forces within the Church and society that will influence the seminary of today and tomorrow. Some of these forces follow.

The ongoing development and change in the lived experience of ministry in the Church today has been broadened to include an ever increasing number of nonordained persons in service to the Church. These ministers expect and want the professional training and expertise needed for their respective positions. Such training and expertise have become requirements within Church structures. The question continues to be asked where and how this training can best take place.

The reservoir of degreed, competent, and interested priests, who were once the exclusive component of seminary faculties in all areas of seminary formation and education, is not present to the same extent as it was a few decades ago. This places severe tensions on seminaries that want to offer quality programs in conformity with Church norms.

The escalating costs of seminary formation and education have become a significant factor in the life of the Church. The cost factor is not only a material one; the person costs, in terms of the time and resources needed to prepare qualified faculty members whose effectiveness is limited because of the relatively few students who are able to benefit from the faculty person.

We have witnessed a decline in the number of vocations for priesthood and an aging of the clergy presently serving the Church, in addition to the departure of priests from the active ministry. Publicity given to tensions in the Church and the inappropriate actions of clerics all combine to place new pressures and incredible expectations on seminaries.

At the heart of many of the issues impacting on seminary formation and education today is the broader issue of ecclesiology, which touches almost every area of Church life. It seems that people have different experiences, understandings, and expectations of the Church, which influence the program of preparation of candidates for ministry to serve that Church.

Forces within the world that impact on the future of seminaries in the United States can range from new forms of individualism to a new sexual morality, to the materialism that reduces the value of the spiritual and the transcendent.

A final force that is having a profound effect on the Church as well as on our country is the increased and growing presence of Hispanics as members of the Church. They ask us to respect and appreciate their language, culture, traditions, and values. A consciousness of the Hispanic presence also demands an awareness of the other growing minority communities within the Church—the blacks, native Americans, and Asians.

These factors within the Church and society do not exhaust the forces bearing on seminary formation and education today, but they give some idea of the issues that need to be addressed if seminaries are to fulfill their purpose and mission.

Future Possibilities

I believe it would be helpful to determine what will be asked of the ordained priest in the years ahead. If we know what is expected of him, then we will be able to provide a seminary experience that will meet this reality.

In the fall of 1987, the Bishops' Committee on Priestly Life and Ministry published a book titled *A Shepherd's Care: Reflections on the Changing Role of Pastor* (USCC Office of Publishing and Promotion Services). Though the document has as its primary focus the role of pastor and the changing roles, relationships, and environment that have occurred over the past twenty years in fulfilling that role, much in this book could apply to every priest in any ministry within the Church today.

Chapter 5 of *A Shepherd's Care* speaks of the future in terms of a challenge to continue. It describes trends that will continue to have significant impact on the role of the pastor, and it suggests challenges that need to be considered in the face of such realities. The three distinct or interrelated trends that will impact on the Church include the following: (1) the changing profile of the American parish; (2) the changing resources for parish staffing; and (3) the changes in parish status and leadership structures.

I believe it is worth considering what these trends suggest to seminary programs, in addition to the challenges they offer to pastors. In identifying such trends and challenges, we are offering seminaries an agenda for the future.

The first trend is the changing role of the American parish. Population shifts, ethnic changes, the growth of the older and younger populations, combined with what is described as a "spirit of selective compliance," together offer a unique challenge requiring evangelization and pastoral service.

How the parish will respond to the challenge of growth or decline will depend a lot on the leadership offered. There will be pain as parishes are consolidated in some areas, and struggle in others as the Church tries to meet growth and expansion. The parish will be asked to meet especially the needs of the ever-changing ethnic and cultural character of communities and respond to the even greater urgency to serve the needs of the growing senior-citizen community. Pastoral service will continue to be the model for parishes, but there will be a greater need for Catholic forms of evangelization and outreach, especially in service to the Hispanic community and in response to the growing problem of fundamentalism.

Are seminaries today recognizing this trend and preparing candidates to meet this challenge?

A second trend is the needed adjustment to the decline of the number of ordained priests available for parish service. The transfer of priests from administrative positions to pastoral assignments, the extended service of pastors beyond retirement age, the continued growth of the permanent diaconate, and the increased presence of professional and volunteer lay ministers will become realities in almost every local church in the United States.

Priests will have to face the adaption from an almost exclusively sacramental ministry where the priest is the indispensable and only minister. The priest will be challenged to exercise ingenuity in forging new relationships that will enhance his relation with deacons and lay ministers, especially women. Pastors must face the practical issues of certification processes, appropriate compensation systems, and job security for nonordained ministers. Pastors will be asked to help develop a spirituality of lay ministry and respond to the needs of lay and family life.

Are seminary programs today recognizing this second trend and responding to the challenge that it offers?

A third trend will be significant changes in parish status and leadership structures. Some parishes will close; others will become missions; some will be consolidated. The clustering of parishes will become a greater reality, bringing with it the challenge to maintain some distinct identity for the parish community despite the consequent reduction or sharing of pastoral services.

The many challenges that this trend suggests will include both the transformation of people's anger and frustration into energizing sources of new life and the support and development of people other than priests exercising pastoral supervision of a community.

Are seminary programs today recognizing this third trend and responding to the challenge that it offers?

In light of these trends, are seminary models called for by Church laws, norms, and guidelines able to prepare candidates to be the pastors or priests described in *A Shepherd's Care?* Are they able to prepare candidates to have the theological competence, spiritual formation, and ministerial skills to be such a pastor or priest in an effective way?

Seminaries in the United States since Vatican II have been, for the most part, very effective in meeting the signs of the times, in responding to the needs of the Church as lived and experienced by people within the Christian community. In many ways, seminaries have been faithful to the challenge of *Evangelii Nuntiandi* in preparing ordained ministers to proclaim the gospel in a way that meets the needs of place and culture, while remaining faithful to our tradition as a Roman Catholic faith community.

The recommendations, norms, and guidelines to be articulated by the Congregation for Catholic Education as a result of the total visitation experience will be proposed as the basis for seminary education and formation in the years ahead. Some guidelines have already been shared; more will be offered.

The question must be asked whether a dialogue might take place regarding such norms when, in the minds and experience of some, the purpose and goals of seminary education and formation of future ordained priests might best be achieved in another way. This becomes the key question that will help determine the future of Catholic seminaries in our country. In proposing this question, however, we must also be open to the response given.

The seminary is more than an educational institution or a place for the formation of candidates for priesthood, because of its unique collection of students, staff, and faculty and because of the influence that its sponsoring religious community or diocese has on it. In the reality of Church life and experience, the seminary often becomes the lightning rod for tensions, ideas, and trends and provides patterns for what is happening or will happen in the Christian community. Whether in future years that lightning rod can capture and harness the energy that comes from its search to fulfill its mission or whether it becomes a conduit for its own self-destruction will help to determine the future of seminaries in the United States.

In western Washington, we are blessed with countless examples of the beauty of God's creation. But the fog, clouds, and rain prevent many visitors to Seattle from being able to see Mt. Rainier, one of the best examples of that creation. Yet the mountain is there, with its unique beauty and its symbolic strength, as it stands etched against an endless sky. When days are clear — and there really are many such days in Seattle — Mt. Rainier is an incredible sight.

Seminaries in the United States are much like Mt. Rainier. They are often hidden from view by various forces and people who are unable to see the strength and vision they offer. Yet that strength is present as a powerful force and gift to the Church today in preparing candidates to be priests who serve the people of God in the Church of today and tomorrow.

To those responsible for seminary education and formation in the Church today and to those who help make this enterprise possible, thank you for all you share and do.

13.

People, Structures, and Values: Roles and Responsibilities on Promoting Priestly and Religious Vocations

Delores Curran

THE INVITATION TO ADDRESS THIS TOPIC WAS TIMELY FOR me, because I was already interviewing parents for a major Catholic magazine article on parental attitudes toward vocations. I interviewed 128 high-profile or committed, active Catholic parents—as opposed to passive, cultural Catholic parents—and one of the criteria I used was a rich faith life at home. In other words, my subjects performed family prayer, couple prayer, and rituals. These types of families produce vocations. These parents were people I met and worked with in various areas of the country, at theology institutes, family ministry conferences, marriage encounters, and engaged encounters. I asked them if they would like to see a son or daughter enter professional religious life. If yes, why? If no, why not? Well, my report is not very optimistic.

Initially, I was puzzled to find that while most parents would like a son or daughter to enter religious life, very few—aside from the Hispanic families—are actively encouraging them to do so.

The same was reported in a study by Dr. Dean Hoge of Catholic University: "A recent study of Catholic adoles-

Mrs. Delores Curran is a syndicated columnist and author who specializes on marriage and the family.

cents and young adults found that encouragement was the most important factor influencing whether or not they had ever considered a religious vocation for themselves." The same report later stated, however, that 58 percent of the parents did not think they should actively promote vocations for their own son or daughter. This does not imply that they were opposed to vocations, since 74 percent of the parents thought vocation talks for elementary-school children were a good idea.

Obviously, the question is: Why the dichotomy? If parents would like to see their children enter professional religious life, why aren't they encouraging them to do so? I posed this question to those I interviewed, and the responses revealed, not the selfishness we so often attribute to parents, but a parental concern for their children's future life fulfillment and satisfaction.

I heard five recurring reasons. The first reason is: "I do not want to pressure him; I just want him or her to be happy; I do not want to be responsible if my child makes the wrong choice."

In other words, parents are not really guiding their children into future life in any area today. In family ministries, we are seeing this with marriage. We are also seeing it in choices of college and education. Parents are abdicating responsibility in this area, and I found there are several reasons. Parents themselves felt pressured into a career or marriage that they did not find very satisfying. They feel uncertain about what careers are available and viable today. They are afraid their encouragement might be perceived as pressure and might backfire. It is a rule of parenting that adolescents reject something simply because parents encourage it.

The second reason is that many parents are not very happy in their own life's work, and they simply do not want to assume the burden of their children's future life. One parent said, "We do not want to assume that our children want the same roles in their futures as we did. We expect them to create their own reality."

It is a wonderful euphemism. "Create their own reality" really means "You are on your own for the future." And this leaves a giant void in adult guidance for young people today. Lack of adult counsel and guidance indicates a lack of responsibility and faith in the future on the part of parents — the very models that are most influential in children's lives.

My suggestion on dealing with this particular concern is that we build guidance for the future into our parenting education and family-ministry efforts in the Church. Our young people are not getting it elsewhere, and they need it. I envision the development of some kind of program or film series—which would be made available to parishes, schools, and family ministry programs—on the theme of helping your child make wise decisions about the future. Through this medium, parents would be made aware of their influence and expertise. It may also help parents as they guide their children toward the investigation of vocations, in the context of lifelong career and lifestyle choices, without pressuring them. I believe that one of the reasons parents are abdicating in this area is that they do not know how to do it without pressuring their children.

A second concern I heard is: "I do not want to encourage my children to go into a field that seems to be so unstable and unhappy today." Parents who do feel a sense of responsibility in encouraging their children to consider future careers do not witness a lot of observable joy and satisfaction in religious life today.

Every priest that leaves, every sister that is fired, every new story that deals with dissension between or among clergy, religious, laity, and Church leadership diminishes parents' courage to advocate religious life for their children. I do a lot of work with military families, and parents there feel the same reluctance as they see young military people and officers struggling with the present peace movement. These parents are not actively encouraging their own young sons and daughters to enter the military "until things settle down."

Parents do not want to encourage children into a life that is fraught with tension, unhappiness, and constant soul-searching.

"You do not push your child into a dying career," one father said to me when I asked about vocation counseling. I think that is harsh, but understandable in the light of today's open press and ecclesiastical structures. Whether this image is true or not, it is that perceived by many laity.

Many of the parents I interviewed noted the stigma attached to leaving, something not present in another career when a young person decides it is not for him or her. It is considered an embarrassment to the Church, to the family, and to the one who has to live with being a former priest or religious the rest of his or her life.

In our culture we may experience three or four careers in a lifetime. Many parents of potential vocations have, themselves, changed careers. They do not want to encourage their children to lock themselves into a choice—where unhappiness and stigma are the only way out—unless they are absolutely certain. But how many people are so sure at age twenty, especially when their parents are not at age forty? Many parents ask me rhetorically, "What if they make a mistake? Are they failures for life because they broke their sacred vows? I would rather see them go into lay ministry."

I suggest that we offset this stigma by honoring priests and sisters who leave, just as we do when they retire, or when people change careers. We thank them for their ten or twenty years of service. This would reduce the fear of making a lifetime mistake at a young age and having to protect the family honor by fleeing the diocese and denying oneself future service to the Church.

The third theme I heard repeated is that you do not have to be a priest or sister to work in the Church anymore. The explosion of lay ministries has had a dramatic impact on parents' attitude toward professional religious life. In many parishes, lay ministers are more visible than the ordained or the professed.

Many of the parents most likely to foster vocation are teaching in the parish school, serving as directors of religious education, youth ministers, family ministers, and adult educators. These committed and active people serve as models for youngsters who rationalize, "Why should I go into religious life, when I can do almost everything a priest or sister can do and have marriage as well?"

Two-thirds of the adult students in the Master Degree Program in Family and Adult Ministries at Denver's Regis College are lay. Many of them are couples studying theology and ecclesiology and preparing to enter some type of professional ministry. If their children are drawn to church work, they are unlikely to opt for the priesthood or convent—as they might have a generation ago—simply because their parents are doing this kind of work.

Two parishes in my archdiocese, Denver, are now being pastored by nonordained laity and religious, with visiting clergy coming in for Sunday liturgies. The message is clear in these parishes that one does not have to be a priest to be a pastor.

And finally, at a large youth-ministry gathering, I discovered that while the majority of youth ministers were committed and faith-filled laity and many young adults were interested in youth ministries, none was interested in entering the priesthood or professional religious life.

The fourth concern I heard is: "We do not support the Church's attitude toward women and are not encouraging our sons and daughters to be part of it." This is likely the most controversial of parents' concerns, but the parents I meet and work with are the most active in church ministries, as opposed to those who belong to the parish women's or men's societies. They are teaching or active in marriage encounter, family ministry, scripture groups, and prayer groups. They have a strong sense of equality. They do not have to achieve through their children. They know they can make it in the world but have chosen to work within the Church because of their faith commitment. Most of them have marriages where they model full personhood and a balance of power.

Our most active and committed parents today are not encouraging their daughters to enter religious life if it means lifelong second-class status, and they are not encouraging their sons to enter a structure that defends this inequality, because they know the pain these men feel whenever a statement comes out that diminishes women simply because they are women.

In earlier times, the Church was open to women because the world was closed to them. They served by building parish schools through bazaars and bake sales, by cleaning altars, and by producing priests and sisters to do the real church work. They became mother superiors or superior mothers.

In a world that is opening to women, the attitude of the Church seems anachronistic, and parents are not encouraging their gifted daughters and sensitive sons to be part of this attitude. Whether it is popular among churchmen or not, this feeling exists among our most active parents. If the mother is the most formative influence on a young person considering religious life, then we had better look at the kind of mothers our seminarians and novices have. I suggest in-depth research on this issue, probing questions such as: What are the attitudes of seminarians' and sisters' mothers toward women's equality? Toward women working outside the home? Toward laywomen active in professional church work? Toward women in management and professional positions? In short, what kind of mother is producing today's vocations? If most of our seminarians and novices are coming from a traditionalist family, with a mother at home functioning under traditional roles, then we must either bend our efforts at targeting these families—which are becoming fewer annually—or attempt to move the family back into traditional roles, or undertake a massive change in attitude toward women in our Church. I see these as our only three choices.

The fifth concern I heard is that parents sense the futility of encouraging children to religious life if the children do not have any personal contact with priests and sisters. This contact is becoming increasingly rare. "My kids do not know any priests or sisters" is a comment I heard over and over. Children can go through parish school and encounter perhaps only one or two sisters. Chances are good they might admire one of the lay teachers rather than a religious teacher—who was always a drawing card for vocations in the past.

Few parishes can utilize their overworked priests as youth ministers, and campus ministry is drawing fewer clergy. So both of these ministries are becoming increasingly lay fields. And if young people do not know and interact with someone in a career, they are less apt to consider it themselves.

To answer this concern, I would suggest a well-developed program designed primarily to bring together adolescent, priest, and religious. This could include weekend and summer internships at the rectory, convent, and seminary, or work on projects with priests and sisters. I do not suggest this structure for those who have already indicated an interest in a vocation, but for confirmands and high-school students who do not have any relationship with clergy or religious beyond Sunday Mass.

I work a lot at El Pomar Renewal Center in Colorado Springs, which hires young people—high-school students—to work in the kitchens and on the grounds. They interact not only with the Sisters of Charity, who run the center, but also with clergy who come in to conduct retreats or live there while they write books.

The sisters have drawn two potential vocations out of these students, who simply came to the center for part-time jobs. The young people worked around the sisters and knew them as people. Youth today do not experience what I call the Mother Teresa syndrome. They do not have the opportunity to recognize the wide variety of interesting, caring, and serving activities that are a part of religious life—visiting the ill, working with the grieving, and so forth. We have many Mother Teresas working in this country, but no one knows about them. To many young people, the priesthood and the sisterhood mean Sunday mornings, bulletins, meetings, and other activities that do not excite them very much.

All right. So this is very depressing. But then there is the important question I posed to the parents: Why would you like to have a son or daughter in professional religious life? Their responses represent a positive note, for they felt that religious life can be a satisfying, faith-based, caring profession in a world that is becoming increasingly secular and technological. Many of these parents are not happy in their own jobs, although they are successful in them. The high number of middle-aged adults who are turning to caring and helping careers testifies to this. I have a friend in Los Angeles who has a successful career with IBM, but he volunteers a great deal of his time to help others prepare for marriage. My friend said, "If I did not have that, I would go crazy, because my job is so boring!"

If I were to put my money to best use in attracting parents' support, it would be in this area. In advertising jargon, we call it the touchable nerve. The parents can identify with the situation, because they have experienced similar feelings in their own lives and careers. It will not offset the earlier-mentioned parental concerns—which must be addressed if we are going to get the support of our most committed parents—but it will give parents support in encouraging vocations as alternative careers to those in computers and plastics. I would begin my media campaign by publicizing the witness and testimony of fulfilled and happy adults in the priesthood and religious life today.

Sister Helen Flaherty, a leader among U.S. religious women, pointed out to me that a papal study of religious life today reveals a new maturity and depth of spirituality and satisfaction among women religious, compared to twenty years ago. True, 20,000 sisters may have left, but 130,000 have stayed.

Let us use the media to tell their story, to show their work, and to publicize their personal fulfillment. This will offset the image that the priesthood and sisterhood are filled with tension, and will give parents models of faith-filled and happy religious to present to their children when guiding them toward the future.

14.

How The Notion of a Calling Manifests Itself in the World of Business: One Viewpoint

Thomas S. Johnson

ALL OF US HAVE HEARD OUR PARISH PRIESTS AND OTHER religious leaders talk about the different vocations followed by members of our community: the vocations of the lay person, the vocations of marriage, parenthood, and others. But I sometimes have wondered whether most of us who are not following formally a religious vocation really believe that we are anything other than second best in having chosen a lay vocation. We all give a lot of lip service to our responsibilities in our professional lives and in our families, but do we secretly harbor a sense of guilt or inferiority because our vocations are somehow less seriously committed to serving God?

We can contrast our daily existence in many ways with that of priests and other religious figures. As we mature in life, however, and particularly if we have the opportunity to become familiar with individuals who have followed the religious vocation, isn't it true that we come to see they are people who have lives much like ours? The parish priest celebrates mass and tends to other sacramental duties in ways that we can never share, but he also administers an organization that requires resource allocations, supervision of labor, and many other ele-

Thomas S. Johnson, a former Chairman of Manufacturer's Hanover Bank and the Chemical Bank, has served as Chairman of the Board of Union Theological Seminary and as an advisor to the Woodstock Center for Theology.

also administers an organization that requires resource allocations, supervision of labor, and many other elements of the businesses where we work. I suspect that if you measure the number of hours that religious people devote to uniquely religious activities, as opposed to administrative or teaching or health-care pursuits, you might find that there are relatively few differences in a twenty-four day between how they spend their time and how we laypeople spend ours.

So the secular occupies all of us, whether a business man who is religious, a priest whose field is economics or physics, or a sister who administers a school or a hospital. So, in greater or lesser degrees, we all probably need to answer similar questions about the meaning and the goodness of what we do. For we all have to understand how all the varied activities that fill a day in our lives can be made to fit together into a pattern consistent with God's plan for us. It is somewhat comforting that I have been only asked to present "one viewpoint," for that certainly excuses me from having to prove my claims. But I hope I will provoke greater understanding and clarity on how to make our secular lives a part of our journey through life according to God's plan.

The Macroview

I am starting off with some basic premises in my reflection on business and professional life as an opportunity for a morally good existence. First, I think most would agree that the system of democratic capitalism in which we pursue our professions is demonstrably good. It has created, for a large part of the world's population, great prosperity, compared with earlier days. This has given people the opportunity above all to enjoy the dignity of self-sufficiency. It has changed societies in profound ways, perhaps most dramatically by producing a degree of social mobility in Western society previously unknown anywhere in the world and still not experienced in many other societies. This system is the source of much of the pride we have in our society. It is the engine that has created prosperity, but above that, the freedom that is sought after by untold millions of refugees from Asia and from Latin countries, and recently, in Western Europe, by tremendous numbers of people from Eastern Europe.

Second, the institutions of this system can, therefore, be regarded as inherently (or at least potentially) good, and their efficient functioning is good. From observation of individual companies and industries and, indeed, countries, I have concluded that striving to make the institutions of democratic capitalism work well is a worthwhile pursuit. This includes not only the companies and firms that pursue profit and compete with each other for success, but also the structure of rules governing them, as well as the development of the economic infrastructure that only government can provide. Thus, the overall system includes education, transportation facilities, police protection, and the like. It is the interplay, after all, among all of these elements that makes our system work. We are barraged by the word "interdependence." But consider how we in business rely on education to provide the sound foundation for our employees, and how a country is at peace internally and has a semblance of tranquility when it possesses adequate police protection and a reasonable consensus within its population on what it should be doing. The functioning of this system is at the same time a marvel and something not to be taken for granted.

Third, therefore, for the sake of the individual human being, it is demonstrably good to apply one's talents to the success and improvement of the institutions of this great system. Striving for your firm to succeed or win over the competition and endeavoring to get ahead by competing with others for that next promotion, if done the right way, will lead to greater personal development. This greater accounting, therefore, for the talents that we have been given, can be regarded as good, even though it can have heavy costs at times.

But these premises, or what I might call the macroview, are really not enough to convince us of the moral quality of our lives. If we really held the view that single-minded pursuit of efficiency is a sufficient criterion for moral goodness, we would not need to complicate our journey by questioning whether there is not more to the moral life than just that. There are those, of course, who come close to arguing that the single-minded pursuit of profit is enough. They, mistakenly in my view, frequently argue that the invisible hand mentioned by Adam Smith makes everything come out for the good and we do not, therefore, need to worry very much about the complicating factors of competing claims on resources, the impact of these institutions on human lives, or the question whether these institutions have any responsibilities other than to make a profit. I think a proper and complete reading of Adam Smith would probably lead us to say that he never intended for his thoughts to be regarded as offering a comprehensive prescription for how all our social institutions should work. He only meant to demonstrate how the pursuit of gain and efficiency works to create greater wealth than the other systems of organization of work conceived up to that time. The macroview is clearly not sufficient for a number of reasons.

First, not all consequences of this great system of creating economic value are benign. While much good is obviously created, we cannot look around us without justifiably questioning the costs of this system on our environment, without observing the inhumanity of some excesses of the system, without recognizing that cheating and lying occur within, and sometimes in the name of, the system. We need, therefore, to question not only how the system operates, but how our personal work within the institutions of our capitalist system can be considered to be moral.

Second, the intensity of the race for success frequently seems to blind us to the other aspects of what I would characterize as a truly civilized society. If we achieve striking material success and create wealth beyond the dreams of earlier generations, as indeed we have over the last two centuries, most of the human beings within our society benefit. But if we cannot somehow elevate those who are the most deprived, if the way we hone the economic engine fails to be cognizant of the legitimate claims on its product by the least among us, we have to question whether the system is as morally good as it can be.

Third, we all know that the heavy personal commitments of time and energy demanded by our involvement in professions or in business lead to conflicts — and that these conflicts can be quite intense and extensive. We frequently complain how the time demands of business conflict with our responsibilities to our families and with our own personal development, such as our need for leisure and for reflection. Moreover, the work is often so intense and demands such total immersion that we sometimes find it difficult to see a direct connection between what we do and the good God wants us to do. Often we are distracted from considering the negative consequences our actions may have on human beings.

As exciting as our work can frequently be, I'm sure all of us have reflected from time to time that it can be such an all-consuming experience, lacking in diversity, that over time it becomes a confining and narrow existence, when it really should be a broadening and enriching one.

Fourth, and perhaps this is the most difficult question of all, don't we need to reflect on the perverse effects of competition, and not just the positive and enriching results that occur as the fittest survive and rise? What about the individuals who do not get the next promotion, the companies that fail, and the employees who lose their jobs? Is it sufficient for us merely to be comfortable with the demonstrably favorable wealth-effect that occurs cumulatively from competition without at the same time wondering about the costs imposed by this very same wonderful machine on the individual?

Making Our Lives in Business More Moral

I'm sure there are other questions that can be raised about our work and business. But these are sufficient to convince me that there is a moral dimension to our work beyond the fact that the overall system works to create wealth and opportunity for a great many people. How can our lives and business be made moral, or more moral, or as morally good as possible? If contributing to the overall operation of such a beneficial system can be regarded as good, then how much better it can be if we pay specific attention to the moral challenges and opportunities it presents. Let me just suggest three perspectives according to which our lives and business have very significant moral dimensions.

First, if making the enterprise successful is inherently good, it is even better, in addition to achieving that success, to accomplish as many desirable objectives as possible beyond efficiency and profitability and to minimize potential negative consequences of our business activities. Examples of obvious responsibilities, but ones which can be enhanced if we put our minds and consciences to work, include protecting employee welfare, honestly serving customers, and making contributions to the community in which the business exists. These endeavors serve the long-term self-interest of the business. They are even more positive from a moral perspective when they use the influence and resources of the business beyond self-interest to enhance the general good. Conversely, morally conscious executives can make special efforts to avoid business policies and operations that are harmful or potentially dangerous to employees, to abstain from providing misleading product information, and to be conscious always of the impact of the business on the social and physical environment.

The role of business in preserving and protecting our environment for future generations is an evident responsibility. But the real challenge is to represent the interests of the business vis-a-vis community interests in a non-single-minded way. Can we challenge ourselves to think not just of how to defend ourselves from unreasonable demands on the business? We know more about our technologies and our plans for future growth and development than anyone else possibly can. Will we go beyond our defensiveness and affirm that it is highly desirable, from a moral perspective, for us business leaders to consider environmental concerns a special moral responsibility of ours, not just on behalf of the business but on behalf of our fellow human beings? I like the word "stewardship" with an expanded definition beyond the very strict traditional sense of managing shareholder resources. It is obvious to all of us now that stewardship should be defined in ways that include the preservation of our planet, the advocacy of conditions assuring a more bearable life for less fortunate people, and setting the right kind of example in the way we do business.

A second perspective is that our involvement in business and professional life brings opportunities for leadership and influence that can be a genuine calling or vocation. Using the personal influence that we have can be a force for positive moral good. Sometimes I am shocked at the amount of attention given to what I say, and in fact I have had to learn over the years to be careful about a somewhat acerbic and cynical manner that is part of my nature. The real influence we can exert as individuals because of others' respect for our leadership positions cannot be overstated. The little extra attention that we can give to using this influence in positive moral ways can, I think, be regarded as truly part of our spiritual and moral development. Setting the right kind of example and letting others know of the genuine unity we affirm between our business or professional responsibilities and our personal and moral life can be a powerful force for good. We frequently hear the sermon about not leaving our religion to Sunday morning in church, but I wonder how much more we could do with our influence if we reminded ourselves from time to time how carefully and closely people watch what we do. Think of the positive example we could set if we found ways to let people know that we regard doing the right things in our business existence as an inherent part of a complete personal moral life.

We can also make our roles in business a positive moral force by choosing a style of leadership that brings out and recognizes the best in others. We are taught that we are not put here to be alone, that we are meant to live in communities, and that we are to use the talents God has given us to the fullest extent. But we need help to do this. Every one of us can remember those who have helped us to develop, whether teachers, business mentors, or colleagues. We should remind ourselves that, particularly when we get to positions of leadership and influence in business, we have immense opportunities to help others maximize their own development. If we can also assist them to recognize the wholeness of their lives, including the moral aspects of their jobs and business, we can regard this as a real calling and a real answering of God's demands on us.

Perhaps most important, our positions of leadership provide us opportunities to minister to those around us. I use the term "minister" because it evokes the religious vocation. The amount of time we spend at work is, for most of us, way over half of our waking hours throughout our entire working life. The personal relationships that develop are such that we have many, many opportunities either to ignore or to show concern for the problems other people are facing. What a marvelous opportunity this is, truly God-given, for us to share in the work of his priests. If we can view our management roles not just as controlling and administering, but also as caring and providing moral leadership, are we not then conducting our lives like the good shepherd of the Gospels? Good managers are often described in terms that boil down to ministering to others. A good husband or wife helps his or her partner to come down from the intensity of the day's work, to regain a sense of self-esteem after the sometimes unpleasant aspects of work, and to expand one's value horizons beyond work to family, leisure, culture, and self-development. Can there not be an analogous aspect in our working day? After all, each of us has problems and suffers from confusion and pressure. Is it too much to ask that we minister to each other during the hours we spend together at work, by showing understanding and compassion, by offering advice and support, and by establishing an atmosphere that explicitly honors the whole person? Do we have to go home to become human and to enjoy support in our personal struggles, or is there not a higher calling for those of us who have leadership positions in business to see that the work day is not an interruption of moral responsibility but an opportunity to help our fellow human beings in their journey?

And this brings me to the third perspective on how our lives in business can be moral, that of our own journeys on this earth. If our accomplishments in business and professional life are good not only in and of themselves but also because our conduct conforms to God's plan for us, we can then consider work, not as separate from our spiritual life, but as a major part of how we conform to God's will. If we can elevate our goals above the merely mundane and pragmatic, by keeping our eye on how best to use the opportunities we have to help our fellow human beings, could not work then take on the aspect of what theologians call charity, that is, a love for others seen both in their need and in their imaging of God himself? For example, our interest in community or education can go well beyond the pragmatic need to secure and protect resources we need for the business.

These interests, if they arise out of a true sense of responsibility toward the less fortunate and toward future generations, truly constitute a spiritual vocation.

One of the greatest burdens of business leadership is, of course, the competition for time among our job, family, personal development, leisure, and spiritual life. If we can look on these pressures, not as negative or bothersome, but as opportunities to make choices for the good, they become part of salvation.

The ways we use the material rewards that come from business success are, of course, also important. The decisions we make about conserving wealth or using it to alleviate suffering of fellow human beings or to prepare for a better world in the future are other ways in which our leadership positions in business are opportunities for personal development along the lines God has in mind for us. If we can avoid the ever-present personal pitfalls, if we can avoid a selfish attitude, if we can win the battle over pride by reminding ourselves constantly that our talents come from God, if we can fight the temptation to imperiousness and a patronizing style, if we can fight intolerance and defensiveness, if we can shun isolation and exclusiveness—in short, if we can act for the love of our fellow human beings more than for the love of ourselves — we will be working for the love of God and our jobs will become part of our own salvation.

We all know that business is not all there is to life, and have expressed it in different ways, but we also cannot deny that business is a part of our moral life. Nothing that we spend so much time and energy on can be separated from our journey as human beings seeking to serve our creator. If we can reconcile and harmonize our business and professional lives with our own personal development and our other responsibilities to family and community, then business becomes a real calling and an opportunity to serve God.

So the task of business leadership really isn't separate from our moral and spiritual lives and perhaps is not

166 \ *Thomas S. Johnson*

so inferior a calling. Just different and complementary means to a common end. Each of us is called on to struggle through to the moral life and salvation. I hope that you will agree, on the basis of these simple perspectives, that our business and professional lives bring many wonderful opportunities to serve our fellow human beings in a moral way. We business leaders will continue to question our lay vocations, and whether they really measure up, but at least for me, that uneasy feeling helps me to focus on accepting moral responsibility in what I do, and to seek opportunities to make moral convictions count. By striving always to understand how our decisions and actions can be made more to reflect God's teachings, business can help us in our own path to the good life.

Youth Ministry and Catholic Schools

15.

Is Our Church Losing the Next Generation of Catholics?

John M. Roberto

I WOULD LIKE TO SHARE SEVERAL PERSPECTIVES ON YOUNG people, particularly adolescents. I will offer ingredients for effective ministry with youth that I see working nationally, and finally present five challenges that leaders in ministry with youth are currently addressing.

My focus will be on the adolescent years. Early adolescence runs from 10 to 14/15 years of age, and older adolescence from 14/15 to 18/19.

The question "Is our church losing the next generation of Catholics?" is the right one because the problem is not with young people, be they adolescents or young adults; it is a problem or concern for the entire church community. For the past fifteen years Catholic youth ministry, that is, ministry with adolescents, has been addressing this question. So today we stand in a very different place than in the mid-1970s, when there was a lot of disarray in the church's approach to young people.

Nationally, over the past two decades, the growth of parish-based youth ministry, of youth ministry training programs for leaders, of Faith, Service and Values resource materials for leaders and youth, and of program

---

John M. Roberto is Director of the Center for Youth Ministry Development in Naugatuck, Connecticut.

development for youth has provided an excellent foundation of experience. I would like to elaborate on that foundation today.

The Perspectives

Let me start with several important perspectives on adolescence arising out of research and pastoral experience.

Perhaps the most important perspective as we approach the question today is to view adolescents and young adults as resources and causes for hope rather than as problems or concerns. This starting point is extremely important. If young people are problems to be solved, we will approach them in a problem-solving mode. But if we view them as resources, as signs of hope and energy and idealism, as an asset to the church community, our approach will be very different.

Second, we need to view youth holistically. In the past we only considered their individual faith growth. Viewing them holistically rather than just as individuals broadens our outlook. We look at their total growth, not just up to eighteen years of age but right through the entire life cycle, and we see them as participating members of families in the family life cycle. We also regard them as integral members of our faith communities, as part of the local community to which they belong. This broader view thus includes both psychological and social perspectives.

Third, we also need to view faith holistically. Faith is more than just the act of believing, in which we come to understand, internalize, and articulate the Catholic Christian faith. It entails the development of a trusting relationship with God in Jesus Christ and with God's people. Our faith also has consequences for the way we live, as individuals, as members of communities, and as citizens of our world.

We also have to approach faith from a developmental perspective, as growing, evolving, and expanding over a lifetime. And we need to ask what is the appropriate intervention to make in the lives of adolescents and young adults.

Using a developmental perspective, I would like to suggest five styles of faith that have relevance in adolescence and young adulthood. There is great diversity of styles within any age group. Many adolescents, especially younger adolescents, still derive their faith primarily from parents and family, with the parents serving as role models for faith and values. Many other adolescents ground their faith in the life of the faith community. This is a conventional faith. Through participation in the life of the community, they learn the ways, beliefs and practices of the community, an important aspect of faith growth for many adolescents who seek belonging and active engagement.

Still others, especially during older-adolescent and young-adult years, begin to take a critical look at the faith they have been socialized into, the faith that has been handed down to them. We commonly call it "losing your faith." Youth do not really lose their faith; rather, their faith changes and evolves. They may shun external dependence on the community, and so the efforts of teachers, youth ministers, and parents may seem to have been in vain. But in a sense, one does not grow into a searching style of faith and reflect on the faith that one has been given unless one has a grounding in the faith of the community.

Young people, especially in the older-adolescent and young-adult years, often exhibit this critical reflection. It is a restructuring of faith, helping them to internalize and then make the Catholic faith their own. We see questioning, reflection, and the process of "taking responsibility for my own life," in terms not just of faith but also of lifestyle, identity, commitments, convictions.

Still others, again especially older adolescents and young adults, view their faith primarily as a personal belief and relationship in Jesus Christ and his message. They have found in Jesus Christ a meaning for their own lives, a relationship that permeates and guides their lives. Though it is more common in young adults and adults, some adolescents have moved through searching faith, developed a personal-relational faith, and made a firm commitment to a personally held faith. We normally call this adult faith — the faith of convictions, the faith that is internalized and owned.

It is essential for those in ministry with youth or young adults to recognize the pattern of faith growth and respond appropriately, to know what to expect, to know how to foster and nurture faith, and to realize that the ongoing process of faith does not mean that faith is being lost, but that faith is evolving and expanding.

In summary, the perspectives I bring to adolescents and their faith development are: to see them as resource and hope; to regard them holistically, not just as individuals but in the broader context in which they grow and develop; to view faith holistically; and to look at faith growth in its patterns of development—changing, growing, and evolving.

The Ingredients

Now to the second part of my presentation: What do we see is working in youth ministry? When we pose the question "Is our church losing the next generation?" we often do not see the signs of hope. In this connection, as I get halfway through the ingredients for effective ministry, you may ask yourself, "Does any parish like this really exist? Does any campus ministry like this really exist?" The answer is yes. These are the elements around which people are actually building their ministry.

First, I find that leaders are working for three goals for their ministry in parishes and on campuses: 1) to promote the personal and spiritual growth of youth; 2) to promote responsible, active participation of youth in the life, mission, and work of the faith community; 3) to empower youth by promoting discipleship in Jesus Christ, which inspires people to go out and transform this world, in particular by living and working for justice, peace, and human dignity. The activities and programs of ministry with youth are organized around these goals.

The second hallmark or ingredient of effective ministry with youth is that it is comprehensive. Many of us grew up in our adolescent years participating in youth programs or youth groups like CYO. But ministry with youth is not a question of a particular program or group or organization. Rather, it is a broad ministry, comprising in a sense all the parish's ministries focused on the particular life tasks and needs of youth and young adults. Through the ministries of evangelization, catechesis, community life, prayer and worship, justice and service, pastoral care, leadership development, and advocacy, the church responds to young people, thus providing a broad context for ministry and belonging. This relational and community-based ministry affords opportunities for relationships with adult role models and with other peers in faith sharing and faith growth.

A third hallmark of an effective ministry with youth and young adults is leadership development and ministerial involvement — actively helping young people to assume leadership roles in the faith community and to minister with each other. Youth will need specific training to take on these responsibilities.

A fourth hallmark is variety. Ministry with youth does not operate from one set program model. Perhaps we do not recognize the signs of effective ministry easily because there is no one program model that works in all places at all times. In fact, with the nineteen thousand or so parishes across the country, there should be nineteen thousand different models of ministry organized around the needs of their youth and the communities of which the youth are a part. What integrates these youth ministries are not the great variety of programs, activities, schedules, and formats, but rather the concept, goals, and philosophy with which they operate.

In years past, when the needs of young people and the society we lived in were relatively stable, a program-centered focus, rather uniform across the country, could be maintained. That is not true today. What is unifying leaders today is a common set of goals, philosophy, and approach.

Another hallmark of effective ministry is a family perspective. Ministry with youth views the family as a most important context for the promotion of faith growth, and this perspective is built into all programming. The more that ministry with youth supports and encourages the role of families, the more that families are involved with youth ministry and youth ministry is involved with families, the stronger will be the faith of young people.

Promoting multicultural awareness is an increasingly important ingredient of an effective ministry with youth as they come to live in an increasingly multicultural world. Ministry programs will need to develop the skills, knowledge, and understanding necessary to live our faith in a diverse church.

My last ingredient is cultural awareness. Ministry with youth raises the consciousness of young people to the impact of youth and popular culture and the media upon their own faith and identity. Culture is a faith- and value-formation system. We attempt to get youth to reflect critically on that system, to compare the Gospel to cultural values, and to critique those values in light of the Gospel.

All these ingredients together form a multifaceted approach to faith growth and ministry that seeks to create both a network of families and a vibrant community of young people within the parish community. To be effective and successful in working with young people, we need to combine a common philosophy, comprehensiveness, a relationship with a community, and a wide set of programs and activities that involve young people more deeply in the church, more deeply with each other, and more deeply with their families.

The Challenges

But despite all these positive elements, leaders face today a set of challenges. I would like to pinpoint five of them.

The first challenge, certainly one of the most important for me, is the changing expression of Catholic identity. The Catholic identity that so many of us were socialized into and that became integral to our own lives is developing new expressions in the young generation. Let me identify four points about Catholic identity and then elaborate: 1) At the core of Catholic identity is the life, death, and resurrection of Jesus Christ. Catholic identity is Gospel identity. 2) The life, death, and resurrection of Jesus is mediated through expressions such as doctrine, liturgy, sacraments, ethics, and organizational developments. Over time the life, death, and resurrection of Jesus Christ are mediated in a variety of ways. Sometimes these expressions get so closely identified with Catholic identity that we forget they are not the only ways to express it and have an historical origin. 3) The ability of our well-loved historical expressions of Catholic identity to continue to mediate our relation with God in Jesus is being questioned by vast numbers of youth and young adults today. It is not something new in the history of the church; it happens quite regularly. 4) As we look at expressions of Catholic identity in youth today, we will find new and revitalized, as well as many historical and traditional, expressions that mediate the reality of the life, death, and resurrection of Jesus Christ for them. While

the expressions often look and feel different, I contend
that they seek to mediate the core of our faith. The expressions may change, but the reality that they try to mediate and articulate does not. At the core is still Jesus
Christ.

Let me illustrate these points. As young people explore the Scriptures today, they often find other images of
God besides the traditional one of God as father. These
"new" images may mediate God much more as mother, as
friend, as lover, as liberator than as father or king. And
these images are in our tradition. The Hebrew Scriptures
are filled with dozens of images, but youth are discovering
them in new ways. For the many young people who grow
up without a father image at home find in the Scriptures
other images of God that can nourish their faith growth.
Also, the devotion of youth, with all their energy and vitality, to serving those in need and to acting for justice is
a distinctive emphasis today, but it is certainly part of the
tradition of the Catholic Church. Different expressions of
Catholic identity — whether it be music, prayer styles,
lifestyle, or images of God — are part of the changing
scene, part of the challenges that help young people discover new expressions and revitalize older ones that give
form to their Catholic faith. One of the primary challenges
leaders working with youth and young adults face is to
help youth give birth to new expressions of Catholic identity and new life to traditional expressions, all the while
maintaining continuity with the tradition. There are forces
on both sides of the question who want to emphasize one
task over and against the other. In fact, they are one task
done in two different ways: to give birth and to maintain
continuity.

The second challenge that I think leaders ministering
to youth and young adults face is to provide youth with a
spiritually challenging vision. I call this the challenge of
discipleship. Young people in our society are looking for a
worthy venture to which they can commit their lives. If
the church does not offer that, they will find it somewhere

else. Most do not leave the Catholic Church for another church; they leave it for another meaning system. One has to give meaning to one's life; one has to invest one's life in something, even if it is a consumeristic society. Can we make faith in Jesus Christ and discipleship a spiritually challenging vision? Again, it is a question of how we give that two-thousand-year-old message new life and new vibrancy to respond to the life concerns of youth and young adults in our communities. It is a task that every generation has faced, one from which Jesus did not hide. He made the good news appropriate to the life concerns of the people in his day by speaking in images, symbols, and stories that directly related to the world of his audience. If we do not provide a spiritually challenging vision—not comforting but demanding—youth will look elsewhere to invest their considerable time, energy, and idealism.

Third, we have to be communities worthy of allegiance. This is broader than a youth issue. We have to be communities worthy of the allegiance or loyalty of youth so that they are willing to invest in these communities and become active participants. We risk marginalizing youth to the peripheries of our communities by not giving them active roles in the life of the community—active roles in liturgy, in leadership, in service, in the very life of the community. The more actively they participate in the community during the youth years, the more likely they will be religious and loyal to their church as adults. We need to be worthy of their fidelity by calling forth their allegiance with a sense of challenge and urgency and by providing concrete ways for them to try out what their faith means. In, for example, service, action for justice, leadership, and peer ministry, young people have an opportunity to see what their faith feels like, what it looks like. The more youth are marginalized from the adult world and from our communities, the less opportunity they have to experiment with their faith and to discuss that faith with an adult role model.

The fourth challenge is more of an "in-house" concern, one that I face as I go around the country teaching youth ministry and helping leaders organize youth ministry programming. Simply stated, the issue is that so much of our youth effort in the United States is being taken up with confirmation, not with organizing and conducting comprehensive ministries. In addition, despite all of the time and effort we are putting into high-school confirmation, we face the terrible paradox of fully initiating young people who then leave our communities and no longer actively practice their faith, sometimes only a week or two after they are confirmed. This is a structural problem, for confirmation is viewed as graduation, as if from high school, not only by the young. Our efforts are not producing the intended result, so we better analyze the causes and take a different approach. In my judgement, we need to broaden our emphasis away from just preparation for the sacrament of confirmation to a broader, comprehensive youth ministry and situate confirmation within this broader framework. Presently we are not empowering our youth to live their faith or guiding them on a trajectory toward adult faith.

Fifth and finally, what I have been suggesting throughout this presentation is the need for a total systems approach to faith growth and faith transmission. In past decades, the Catholic school system provided this systems approach, but this structure no longer exists for the vast majority of adolescents across the United States today. We have not replaced it with a new system; instead, we have tried to replace it with one hour a week of religious-education classes or youth group meetings. And we have found that wanting. The system of socialization, faith growth, and faith transmission that has served us well for many decades cannot be supplanted by a one-hour- or two-hour-a-week program. It has to be replaced with a corresponding systems approach that involves the family and the parish community, as well as comprehensive youth programming. Otherwise, we will never respond adequately to young people's growth in faith. We cannot go back to our old system. But if we tackle the task of creating a new system that includes family ministry, comprehensive youth programming, and the involvement of youth as integral members in the total life of the faith community, then we will find a way to serve young people into the next century. In this way they will receive a great resource that will empower them to experience continued faith growth throughout their lives.

16.

Why the Catholic Inner City School Is Worth Saving

John E. Coons

WHY SHOULD WE SAVE THE CATHOLIC SCHOOL? FOR TWO general reasons. One is that it would be good for the civil order, and the other is that it should be good for the Church and for religion.

Now, why would saving the inner-city Catholic schools be good for the civil order? For two reasons, I think: because parental control is absolutely essential to the reform of education, and because Catholic schools are essential to any such reform.

The first proposition — that choice is good for education — is the easiest for me to explain and consists of several propositions.

We have contrived for ourselves in America a market-oriented society in almost every way, but obviously we have done something very different in the educational economy.

We call it a system of public education, but indeed it is quite the opposite. If you are able to afford to live in a nice suburban neighborhood, you probably have a nice public school, a nice government school. And if you'd like to live instead in a fancy apartment somewhere in San Francisco, you probably go to a private school. You and I

Dr. John E. Coons is Professor of Law at the University of California Berkeley and an expert on constitutional law and American education.

where they are told to go, and study what they are told to study. A system of lobbying determines the content of instruction, and parents have very little say about it or about who the strangers are that are going to teach their children.

This is a poor way to run education. In the first place, it's definitely not public in the sense that we use the word "public" for most of our institutions, our governmental institutions.

The schools of Piedmont or, say, Palo Alto, California, or even my own neighborhood, are not open to everybody. They're open to people who can afford to buy a house there. In no sense do we have public education, except possibly in the private sector, where, so long as you can afford to pay the tuition, most of the schools are quite willing to take whoever comes along. Catholic schools are much more public in any meaningful sense than the system of government schools that have coopted that particular label.

So in the public-school system we have very bad education, as you would expect from this monopolistic kind of enterprise. People have very little incentive to be good teachers or administrators. They know that they will have customers tomorrow, irrespective of how well or how poorly they do their job, and that those customers will pay their way through the forms of financing that the government provides.

The teachers and administrators are not going to improve even if there's a system of choice in the public sector created through President Bush's initiative or otherwise, because in the end nobody's going to be fired. No blood will be shed in the public sector: nobody is going to lose a job because a child moves from some bad school to a good school in East Harlem.

Instead, a teacher will merely move from a school that fails to another school, maybe to the very school that the child transferred to because he didn't like that teacher. So he'll meet the same teacher at the other end, all will remain pretty much the same, and the system as a whole will not improve. Some people will get a better deal, people who happen to have more sophistication, perhaps middle-class people who have a chance at finding out more of what the schools are about.

How can we fix this system? It seems to me the simplest solution — even if it gets more complicated in practice — is one modeled on the GI Bill.

Children from kindergarten through the twelfth grade would receive from the state of California (or your state) a scholarship worth perhaps $4,000, or in any case something substantial for capital investment in private education.

This kind of system would reduce the expenditures in education and enhance cost efficiency. And that's the first thing, isn't it — that education so function that if you spend more, you get more. With a system of choice, we could reduce educational expense and at the same time educate as well as, or even much better than, we do today. Catholic schools, for example, spend about half as much as the public system, that is, roughly $2,500 as compared to $5,000 in the public sector.

Quality, then, can be had with efficiency. It's simply an application of market principles. But I think we would get more important benefits for our society out of this system. We have been plagued with class division. I've already described how it works in our educational system: the rich go to school together and the poor go to school together; minorities go to school together and whites go to school together.

We have tried to change this pattern by force through the judicial process, but it would be wonderful, I think, if we could begin to do that in another way.

Let me tell you a short story. In Kansas City the school district has been found guilty of de jure segregation because, of the 33,000 children in the district, 25 percent are white. Not much you can do, is there, to achieve desegregation in Kansas City. It's even worse when you discover that the suburban government schools will not take the black children from the inner city because these districts were found innocent. They say, "Well, we don't have to take these children; we're innocent." So there's no place for the children to go.

Several black children, however, filed suit in the federal district court in Kansas City, asking to attend private schools at one-third the cost of the Kansas City schools. Surprisingly, fifty private schools volunteered 4,100 racially integrated places for inner-city children.

The point is not whether we will win that suit but that these schools — mostly Catholic, some Lutheran, some Episcopal, some nonsectarian — demonstrated that they are not the problem, they're the solution for children in the inner cities who desperately want to go there, but cannot afford to do so. And of course the schools cannot afford to take them because they're already subsidizing too many other kids just like them.

Imagine a scholarship system like that operating in Detroit, Chicago, or the District of Columbia. Choice would provide less class discrimination, which can't get any worse, and an amelioration of one of our most serious social problems, racial division, in a form that can at last be stable and is by choice.

And for teachers, choice would, interestingly enough, probably raise salaries, even in the public schools if they are included. The public sector now spends only forty cents of each education dollar on the classroom teacher. In the private sector, on the other hand, seventy-five or eighty cents of each dollar is spent on the teacher, precisely because the customer wants the money to go into teaching. That is the way all education would go in a system in which there was competition and choice, in which students could leave a school and go to another.

The teacher would benefit not only economically but also professionally, because at last the teacher would be dealing with parents in a relationship of equality and dignity, instead of superiority, domination, and social distance from the family.

A system of choice would also begin a true family policy in the United States. Except perhaps among the wealthy, a child's experience with school is very disruptive for most families in the United States. The parent, who for the first five years has stood at the center of the child's life as the authoritative advocate, the leader, the child's defender, is stripped of dominion over education. The child is sent off, irrespective of the parent's wishes, to a school operated by strangers who will administer and control the education.

This experience, it seems to me, is destructive to the child's image of the parent. For the most unfriendly thing we can do to the American family is to show the child that the parent is impotent to protect the child in this very important aspect of the child's life.

From the parent's point of view, it is as equally debilitating and frustrating. Put in social terms, there's no better way to build division and dissention among our citizens, it seems to me, than to tell people that we don't value their opinion simply because they haven't enough cash to pay the tuition to go to a school of their own choice, and that we won't give them the cash, even though it would be easy enough to contrive a system for doing so.

That way, it seems to me, lie hostility, resentment, and the kind of apathy observed in the public schools, in which the public-school leaders blame the parents, whom they have disenfranchised, for their part in the student's failure.

But through a system of scholarships, we can have quality, social and racial integration, good teaching, and a good life for teachers. We can have a policy that respects the family of the lower-income classes. And I believe that it is our duty to contrive a way to establish such a policy.

I believe that a choice system will benefit not only the social order in the city of man but also the Church itself;

not so much because the inner-city schools, our Catholic schools, are designed to proselytize, although that seems to me a perfectly legitimate and wholesome function for our schools. Rather, it is a very natural thing for Catholic institutions to be doing as part of our normal relationship to the civil order. We should provide good education to those who want to come and get it by choice, by free association with our institutions, public and private.

It would improve our picture of ourselves, who we are as Catholics. At the same time, we must avoid going broke, destroying our institutions financially, and losing our independence. So the terms on which government involvement comes are important to examine.

Can a system of scholarships become reality? There are encouraging signs that it can.

In Milwaukee the black community celebrated when Governor Thompson and Polly Williams managed to get a bill through the Wisconsin legislature providing scholarships so that 1,000 black children in the inner city could go to private schools on the outskirts of the city.

This was a great breakthrough because nothing comparable had ever happened in American political experience. Maybe the best part of it is that Polly Williams is black and the people who finally pushed the ball over the line in Madison, the state capital, were black families whom she organized. They succeeded in pressuring the reluctant senators on the education committee to do what they should have done long ago.

How far is this going to go? Nobody knows. But in the neighboring state of Michigan, a wonderful young medical doctor is putting together a coalition that shows very good promise of getting an initiative on the Michigan ballot.

Michigan and Missouri, plus six states in the West, now have the initiative process. In this political scenario, the people can put on their state ballot a constitutional change by getting signatures on the street. The proposition then goes to the entire electorate. In California, we have had our famous propositions 13, 98, and 103, and soon we'll be voting on several others.

Proponents can even change state constitutions, the primary barrier to choice in education, but they face many other challenges, of course, in the political order. As you consider the possibility of political change, you must ask, for example, how big a bite to take at the beginning. Should you use the initiative process? How can you use litigation skillfully, artfully? With whom do you make alliances?

It seems that a majority of persons would like to see a change in this direction, as all of the polls on this issue show strong support for change. The most interested groups are minorities in the inner city, but they are very difficult to organize. Families are very difficult to organize. I cannot predict the final outcome, but a lot of attempts at change will be made.

Over the last fifteen years something has been learned about the politics of school reform. I think we've learned that choice should never suggest antipathy to the public schools, the government schools. Why? Because the basic proposition is parental choice, not an opposition to anything. The goal is to provide families with autonomy to choose the kinds of education that they want and not have to accept what somebody else thrusts upon them. And many will want public schools. (You have to swallow hard, because lots of families are going to make decisions that you don't like if this kind of system should ever come to be.) And so it is not anti–public school, it is not pro–private school. It is not even pro-religion, because a lot of families will not want a religious education.

In the end, though, this is all closely connected to the idea of the inner-city Catholic school. The connection is odd, but it is real. We belong to a Church with not only a big *C* but also a small *c*, a Church that historically has taken a long view on its role in the good society. And here's a role I think it could play to the benefit of all.

17.

Catholic Education and Its Impact on the Value System of Low Income Students

Peter L. Benson

I WANT TO SHARE WITH YOU WHAT WE KNOW NATIONALLY about two great passions in my life. One is Catholic schools and the other is values, particularly the values of adolescents. My primary thesis is that this nation needs Catholic schools more than ever. And implied in that thesis is the fact that not only does the Catholic Church need Catholic schools, but the nation needs Catholic schools.

Catholic schools are an important resource to the nation as a whole. Without Catholic schools, the problems we face as a nation would be greatly compounded. But in raising future generations of parents, workers, and voters, we are experiencing two significant problems. One is academic, and the other has to do with character.

On academic grounds, we are a nation at risk. I hardly need to document this. If you read the papers, you are always seeing stories about how the United States ranks toward the bottom of industrialized nations in academic test scores in almost all fields. We also lead the industrialized world in the dropout rate for high school

---

Dr. Peter L. Benson is President of the Search Institute of Minneapolis and has directed numerous national studies on private education, youth, and American religions.

students. It's a real blemish on our reputation internationally.

But that's only half the problem in raising young people today. As serious, as compelling, is the problem of values. At Search Institute we monitor the well-being of young people in this country, not only in the Catholic world but more generally, in the public-school world. Right now, in 1990, we are surveying all public-school students in 150 cities from coast to coast — probably the largest effort ever to look at the state of health among young people in this country. And I want to say a word about that, because it helps capture this second problem of a nation at risk in terms of character, or values.

In these national surveys — it's going to grow to 300 cities by the end of the year — we are trying to document the percentage of kids who are at risk, that is, who are developing some kind of behavior pattern or emotional scar that could jeopardize adult happiness or productivity. The signs in adolescence might be: frequent alcohol use — say six or more times per month by a ninth grader or tenth grader; fairly frequent use of an illicit drug such as marijuana or cocaine six or more times in the last year; sexual activity; constant depression or suicidal thoughts; bulimia; or antisocial activity like vandalism or theft.

The first chart shows the percentage of young people in U.S. public schools who have already developed at least one of these at-risk indicators.

At-risk Indicators									
	6	7	8	9	Grade (%) 10	11	12	Grade (%) M	F
Those with 1 or more indicators	45	55	62	68	75	81	85	70	68
Those with 3 or more indicators	15	19	28	34	44	53	58	39	36
Those with 5 or more indicators	5	8	14	17	24	30	37	21	19

The percentage of young people in the 150 cities who already have one of these at-risk indicators grows to 50 percent in the sixth grade and 85 percent in the twelfth grade. And the results reveal a new "gender equality" that is disturbing. These figures signal that we have problems nationally in fostering the character of young people.

And so our problems are not only academic; they are equally or primarily about raising young people to bring into their own personalities a responsible set of values — values that lead young people to make wise decisions. Internationally, we lead the industrialized world not only in dropout rates but also in teenage-pregnancy rates. In the industrialized world, we lead in alcohol abuse and illicit-drug abuse by teenagers, and we have the fastest rising suicide rate among teenagers and the highest divorce rate, twice as high as Sweden, the country in second place. At the same time, we are the most churched country in the industrialized world, an interesting juxtaposition to the condition of our young people.

This national picture of academic problems on the one hand and value crises on the other knows no racial or income boundaries. But both are more pronounced among those who are in poverty in this country. And a final indicator on which we lead the industrialized world is the percentage of children and adolescents we raise in poverty. Nearly 25 percent of all people under the age of eighteen live in families with incomes under $10,000. And we have yet to find a way to prevent poverty or to help young people who grow up in poverty to break out of that cycle.

In our work at Search Institute, we seek to find solutions to the national problems of academic failure, value dysfunction, and poverty. And out of all the resources that we look at nationally, out of those resources which can serve us as a nation, none, I would argue, is more powerful than the Catholic schools in academics, in values, in serving the poor. It is both ironic and tragic that the closing of Catholic schools happens precisely at the time we need Catholic schools the most.

Now that's the big, national picture: raising quality young people who will serve our nation as adults. But if you take the more particularistic view of concern about the Catholic Church, the case is equally strong: for the future health and vitality of the Catholic Church in this country, we need strong Catholic schools. And so it is very clear to me, on both national grounds and on Catholic grounds, that Catholic schools matter, and matter a great deal.

Now all of this serves as preamble to the data I wish to share about the role of Catholic schools in the academic and value development of young people, with particular emphasis on low-income students.

This data will help build a strong case for Catholic schools and provide additional incentive to people to continue the troublesome battle of preserving this important national and Catholic asset.

First, I want to say a word about the national stereotype about the nature of Catholic students. People outside Catholicism often say that private schools serve a wealthy, privileged clientele. That may be true about elite private schools in this country, but it is not true about Catholic schools. When you compare information on Catholic students (the only data we have is from 1983) to 1982 census data on United States families in the second chart, you see something quite different from the stereotype. It is true that, though 11 percent of U.S. families were under $10,000 in income, only 6 percent of students in Catholic schools were at that level. But at the very top level, over $50,000 income in 1982 dollars, Catholic schools have a lower percentage than what is the case nationally. If we look at the total percentage of students from families with income under $20,000, we see that the Catholic school plays a significant role in serving young people from families whose background does not include economic privilege.

The Income Stereotype		
	Total, U.S. Population (1982)	Catholic High School Students (1983)
Under $10,000	11%	6%
$10,000 - $19,999	20	22
$20,000 - $50,000	55	61
Over $50,000	14	11

I would also like to share a few comments about the demographics of Catholic schools. Those serving fairly large percentages of young people in low-income families — under $10,000 in the third chart — tend to be not the private schools, but the diocesan or parochial. That comes not as a surprise. But it is striking that 43 percent of the Catholic high schools serving significant percentages of low-income students have under 300 students. The fact

Demography of Low-Income Schools		
	Low-Income Schools	*Other Schools*
Diocesan	43%	39%
Parochial	21	12
Inter-parochial	8	6
Private	28	43
Under 300 students	43	28
300 - 500	25	23
501 - 750	12	20
751 - 1000	10	16
1000 +	10	14
Communities under 10,000	15	7
10,000 - 99,000	21	33
100,000 - 249,999	10	12
250,000 +	54	49

that smaller schools have a harder time surviving speaks to the fragility of those schools serving low-income students. The bottom of the chart shows how low-income-serving Catholic high schools are distributed by community size. Though 54 percent are in central cities, 15 percent are in small towns of under 10,000 people. So we serve not only the low-income urban poor but also a very significant proportion of young people in small towns, presumably from agricultural or other small-town backgrounds.

Interestingly, those Catholic schools serving low-income students do so at a much lower per-pupil cost. For example, several years ago the average amount of money spent per pupil in low-income-serving high schools was $1,000 less than in other Catholic schools. Part of the reason is that schools serving low-income students are much less likely to raise money from fund-raising sources or from investment-return sources.

The fourth chart compares Catholic high schools serving mostly low-income youth in central cities and in

Central City Low-Income Schools		
	Types of Low-Income Schools	
	Central City	*Non-Urban*
Percent single parent families	30	13
Percent income under $10,000	31	14
Percent income under $20,000	75	56
Average enrollment size	610	290
Per pupil expenditures (1983)	$1866	$2809
Teacher/student ratio	1:20	1:15
Administrator/student ratio	1:167	1:109
Subsidy income (per student average)	$168	$712
Fundraising income (per student average)	$116	$199
Investment interest (per student average)	$ 22	$ 49

non-urban centers. Low-income schools in large urban centers are particularly fragile from an economic point of view. The per-pupil expenditure in central city schools was $1,866 dollars in 1983, compared to about $1,000 more in the non-urban schools. The chart also reveals a vast disparity between central city schools and other schools in sources of income — subsidy income, investment income, and fund-raising income.

Another point is the impressive impact of Catholic schools on low-income students. High School and Beyond, a national, federally funded research project that tracks tens of thousands of young people from their sophomore year through their college years, is our primary source of information about the impact of Catholic schools. And every time High School and Beyond is analyzed, almost always something positive and favorable is said about Catholic schools, particularly about low-income students in Catholic schools.

We know now that there is a Catholic-school effect. After we have controlled for family background differences, income differences, and other differences, Catholic schools make an additional difference, over and above public schools, in what students learn academically. But what is particularly exciting is that this special Catholic-school impact is dramatically greater for those students who are poor. And the academic gain by poor students is very dramatic in Catholic schools, compared to those in public schools.

Why do Catholic schools perform better overall than public schools? It may have to do with teacher motivation, school climate, and academic rigor, but what would lead Catholic schools to have an extremely positive impact on youth who are poor?

First, Catholic schools prevent student dropout much better than public schools, and particularly with low-income youth. A second factor is the success of Catholic schools in sending young people to college. The fifth chart shows that the rates of the disproportionately poor black

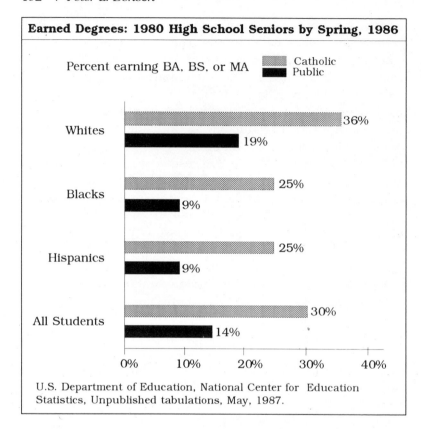

Earned Degrees: 1980 High School Seniors by Spring, 1986

Percent earning BA, BS, or MA   Catholic / Public

Whites — 36% / 19%
Blacks — 25% / 9%
Hispanics — 25% / 9%
All Students — 30% / 14%

U.S. Department of Education, National Center for Education Statistics, Unpublished tabulations, May, 1987.

and Hispanic youth who go on to complete college are so much greater for Catholic schools than for public schools. Of all black graduates in 1980 from Catholic schools, 25 percent had received degrees—a B.A., a B.S. or an M.A.— by 1986, compared to 9 percent from public schools, and the same ratio holds among Hispanics.

Public schools seem to place most of their poor students in general vocational tracks. Catholic schools still put most of their low-income students in an academic, college preparatory track. Even though the students may resist, saying, "I can't," the Catholic school says, "You can."

The sixth chart shows that in the Catholic school 55 percent of minority youth are in an academic track, com-

Academic Program and Homework, by Minority Status					
	Minority			*White*	
	Public	*Catholic*	**Catholic Advantage**	*Public*	*Catholic*	**Catholic Advantage**
Academic Track	29%	55%	**26%**	54%	72%	**18%**
Hours of Homework per week	3.76	5.01	**1.25**	4.72	5.62	**.90**

pared to 29 percent for public schools, a Catholic school advantage of 26 percent. And among white youth, the difference is 72 percent versus 54 percent. The bottom row shows that both minority students and white students do more hours of homework per week in the Catholic schools. In both of those items — the academic track and the amount of homework — the impact of Catholic schooling is more pronounced for minority youth than it is for Caucasian youth. In addition, the average low-income student in a Catholic school takes more math, more science, more English than the average public school student, regardless of income. That is a significant academic achievement by Catholic schools.

One of the most appealing things about Catholic schools is the equity in allocation of educational resources regardless of income level, as demonstrated by the seventh chart.

The center column lists the many resources to which low-income students in Catholic schools have equal or greater access than students of other income levels. The column on the far right lists resources to which low-income students have less access than other students. Now, if we did a chart like this for the public-school world, the size of these columns would be reversed. That is, there would be a considerable inequity in the distribution of resources, most of them shifted to the far right column, which represents less access for low-income students. In

Access to Educational Resources		
Educational Resources	Resources to which low-income students have equal or greater access	Resources to which low-income students have less access than others
Graduation requirements	English, Fine Arts Foreign language History/Social sciences Mathematics Religion/Science	
Curriculum	3rd & 4th yr. foreign languages Calculus, 2nd yr. algebra, Music	Chemistry courses Physics courses Geometry
Co-curricular activities	Drama, Music, Art Journalism Gymnastics Football Basketball	Tennis Swimming Soccer Golf Varsity debate
School climate	Academic emphasis Sense of community Religious emphasis Lack of discipline problems Morale	
Teachers	Teachers with more than five years experience Minority teachers Teachers with advanced degrees Quality of teachers	
Physical resources	Vocational labs Libraries & no. of volumes in library Remedial labs Audio-visual and media resources Biology, chemistry labs	Athletic facilities Physics labs
Financial resources	Per pupil expenditures	
Program tracks		Academic track

the Catholic school world, low-income students have access the same as, or better than, students of more substantial economic divisions. And I think that is a wonderful story — essentially an untold story within the whole schooling community in this country — attesting, I think, to the long-term commitment of Catholics to the education of poor students. Low-income students' access to resources and academic tracking help explain how Catholic schools serve low-income students very well.

Still, the academic accomplishments speak only to part of the Catholic school mission. For I believe that the commitment to heart and soul, in addition to mind, more fully describes the purpose of Catholic schools. Good academic achievement alone would make a very strong case for Catholic schools. But the commitment as well to faith and to values gives Catholic schools their unique mission. Catholic schools, then, that not only promote academic learning but also spark a passion for justice and a commitment to the Church — those are the kind of schools we want to continue.

Now the question becomes: What do we know about the impact of Catholic schools upon the value and faith formation of young people? We know so much about academic development; its stories are terribly positive, its research and literature, although unfortunately tilted almost exclusively to high-school students, is deep and rich. Our knowledge about values and faith is more limited, and the subject has not received the same scrutiny as academic outcomes have. There are several important exceptions. One is the work of Andrew Greeley, who for twenty years, until he started writing novels, documented nicely, through the retrospective accounts of adults, the long-term impact of Catholic schooling. John Convey has also done some significant research on the impact of Catholic schools on faith and church.

Still, we know little about the impact of Catholic schools on values. But we must understand that impact and keep that impact strong if we are finally going to jus-

tify the long-term help necessary to continue Catholic
schools. Two new research projects, however, are now beginning to round out our understanding.

The first one is bittersweet. It tells us that while the
Catholic high school passes on values as well to low-income students as to other students, overall there is a
backsliding, or an apparent backsliding, between the
ninth and the twelfth grade among young people who attend Catholic school. The eighth chart is a snapshot of
ninth graders and twelfth graders at the same point in
time, from one of our studies a few years ago. We can see
that the faith commitment of both low-income and other
students falls backwards — as is indicated in the paren-
theses — one point. So the backsliding by low-income
students is about the same as by all students.

Now adolescents are notorious, in any denomination or in any walk of life, for backsliding between the
ninth and the twelfth grades. Maybe we should celebrate how little backsliding there is. But church com-

Income and Values						
	Low-Income			Other		
	9th	12th		9th	12th	
Faith commitment	50.7	49.7	(-1.0)	50.5	49.5	(-1.0)
Church commitment	51.2	48.7	(-2.5)	51.3	48.9	(-2.4)
Social compassion	50.1	49.8	(-.3)	49.8	50.6	(+.8)
Responsible behavior	50.1	50.3	(+.2)	50.3	49.8	(-.5)
Global awareness	46.9	50.1	(+3.2)	50.9	52.9	(+2.0)

mitment and social compassion, the development of concern for other people, also decline among low-income students. We know from our and others' public-school research that between the ninth and the twelfth grade adolescents become more individualistic, not more communal, in their value sense. So this suggests that low-income students gain as much or fall backwards as little as

students of other economic conditions. The bittersweet
message, then, is that for low-income students the gain is
the same, but overall the gain is not what we would hope
it would be.

We have released with the National Catholic Education Association (NCEA) a newer study, called "The Heart
of the Matter," about the values of Catholic students in
Catholic schools and in public schools. If we think about
the impacts of the Catholic school and of the public
school on Catholic students, we'd better hope that the
value formation is stronger in Catholic schools than it is
for Catholics in public schools. When estimating value impact, right now we have to depend on national, federally
funded research efforts that don't have at heart a concern
about Catholic schools and values. They ask a rather
measly set of questions about values, because the federal
government is primarily interested in academic achievement.

But one interesting study, called "Monitoring the
Future," is done annually at the University of Michigan.
It is the federal government's way of taking a look at
the values and behaviors of exiting high-school seniors
in this country. Fortunately, every year since 1976, part
of the national sample has included Catholic schools.
And so, in collaboration with Michael Guerra at NCEA,
and with help from Dick Reuscher and the St. Marys
Catholic Foundation, we at Search Institute looked at
Catholic youth in Catholic schools versus Catholic
youth in public schools on a whole range of value issues, measuring them as best we could from this national study.

In our examination of this national study of values,
the question becomes: Can we isolate any impact special
to Catholic schools over and above what happens to
Catholic students in public schools? The ninth chart does
not contain the list of values that you might develop if
you had started with the question of the impact of Catholic schools on values. You see nothing here about sexual-

ity, nothing about ethical decision-making. There are a number of moral issues not included, and the church and faith measures are fairly weak. But it is interesting that this federally funded study includes some items about the importance of religion and about the importance of church.

We compared twelfth graders in public school and twelfth graders in Catholic school, statistically controlling for a number of family background differences between those two "pots" of students. And our findings in this fairly limited study are very affirming about Catholic-school impact. On this list are eleven school effects — eleven areas in which we can attribute the difference to schooling. And in ten of these eleven, the impact favors

The Outcome Variables	
Social Value	Militarism Pro-Marriage Racial Acceptance Equal Opportunity Materialism
Educational Values	College Plans Liking for School Cutting School
Pro-Social Orientation	Community Involvement Support Social Justice Helping Profession Concern for Others Contribute Money
At-Risk Behaviors	Anti-Social Cigarette Use Alcohol Use Binge Drinking Marijuana Use Cocaine Use Illicit Drug Use
Self	Self-Esteem Pessimism Loneliness
Religion	Church Attendance Importance of Religion

the Catholic school. These ten impacts occur largely in three areas.

First of all, in social values, we find that Catholic-school attendance reduces militarism, in concert with recent Church teachings, and promotes a pro-marriage attitude among Catholic students over and above what public-school attendance accomplishes.

In educational values, Catholic-school attendance promotes planning for college and reduces the cutting of classes during high school. The one index out of the eleven that favors public school is the liking for school. When students are twelfth graders, Catholics in Catholic schools are less likely to say they like school than Catholic students in public school. Why is that? I think that's related to the rigor of the curriculum, the homework emphasis, the premium on discipline — all of which come into conflict with adolescent needs for freedom and self-governance. It's thus a temporary phenomenon that will evaporate, I believe, as these students move out of twelfth grade into the college years.

A third set, pro-social orientation, shows a strong Catholic-school effect, promoting greater community involvement for young people, a greater concern for other people, an increase in contributions of money to charity, and a deeper commitment to developing a career later in life that makes a difference for people and for society.

And finally, several of the impacts are in the religion area. We find that attending a Catholic school promotes the importance of religion in young peoples' lives and fosters a positive attitude toward the institutionalized Church.

So except for that one case of liking for school, all the value impacts that we can attribute to Catholic schools or to public schools favor the Catholic schools.

In the tenth chart, I try to summarize what we know about the effects of attending a Catholic high school. After controlling for family background differences, we have

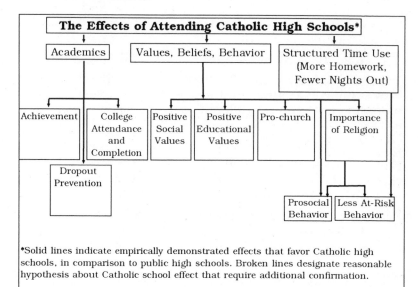

The Effects of Attending Catholic High Schools*

Academics → Achievement, College Attendance and Completion, Dropout Prevention

Values, Beliefs, Behavior → Positive Social Values, Positive Educational Values, Pro-church, Importance of Religion

Structured Time Use (More Homework, Fewer Nights Out) → Prosocial Behavior, Less At-Risk Behavior

*Solid lines indicate empirically demonstrated effects that favor Catholic high schools, in comparison to public high schools. Broken lines designate reasonable hypothesis about Catholic school effect that require additional confirmation.

found that Catholic schools have some clear academic effects over and above those of public schools — not only for upper-income and middle-income students, but very significantly for low-income students — in fostering academic achievement, in promoting college attendance and completion, and in preventing dropouts. Those are wonderful outcomes. But now, on the basis of this new study, we can add to this academic success an impact in the realm of values, beliefs, and behaviors. For the Catholic school also promotes positive social values, positive educational values, a pro-church orientation, an increase in the importance of religion, and an increase in pro-social behavior.

The right side of the chart has some dotted lines representing issues that need further substantiation but that make theoretical sense. We know that Catholic high schools structure the time use of adolescents better than public schools — both in terms of more homework and fewer nights out. These in turn perhaps may reduce the at-risk behaviors mentioned in the ninth chart.

Our knowledge, then, about the value-impact of Catholic schools includes the following: First, in Catholic high schools, low-income students gain as much as other students in faith development, pro-church orientation, and social values. Second, Catholic students in Catholic schools gain more than Catholics in public schools, and this holds for all income levels — low, median, and high. And so this research — along with that of Greeley and John Convey — helps to form a detailed picture of the impact of Catholic schools on all students, and particularly on low-income students.

One of the problems is that we do not understand the impact of Catholic schools on values nearly as completely as their impact on academics. And to understand Catholic schools fully, we need to do more research. I would suggest that there are a few things that we still do not know.

Because we have never done a good longitudinal study on adolescents, I would argue that nobody knows much about value formation for any adolescents in America, whether in the schools or in any other domain. So we don't know a whole lot about: how faith and values form between the sixth and the twelfth grades; what the key transition points are in that change; how all of that growth or backsliding in faith and church and values is related to gender, race, or income; what in school, family, and parish really matters for preventing backsliding and promoting positive steps in faith and values; and when in the sixth-to-twelfth-grade period young people need certain things the most in order to maximize positive faith and values development. And we don't know, finally, what ultimately is the biggest question: What adolescent experiences encourage the developing of bonds to church and faith at thirty or forty years of age? If we knew that now, we might restructure the way we do things in parish, family, and school life.

This is the perfect time, if there ever was one, to launch finally a longitudinal study that starts with sixth graders — I'd say 4,000 of them — and follows them every year. Some of those students will go to Catholic school and some to public school. We need to begin following them through the twelfth grade to pinpoint when change occurs in values, faith, and church and what features of family, church, and school make the most difference. If we had that kind of data, we could continue to look at those young people — when they are twenty, thirty, forty, and fifty years of age — to see what in the developmental experiences of growing up most led to positive relationships to the Church and the faith.

I believe that values in the 1990s will become a very important selling point for schools. We are now starting a decade in which values are being rediscovered by the American public — by corporations, by government, by public schools. Public schools are not afraid of the word "values" right now, as they have been for twenty years. Everybody is beginning to understand that part of our national dilemma concerns values. So the school or school system that can advertise strength in both academics and values will be extremely attractive to parents, foundations who might fund schools, and employers who are worried about the next generation of workers.

Relying on multiple studies in the academic area and slowly emerging research in values and beliefs, we are able to maintain that Catholic schools are a terribly important resource to Catholics and to the nation as a whole in promoting both character and learning. They form the twin purpose of Catholic schools, if you will, and the evidence to date is that Catholic schools are doing extremely well in these areas, though we don't know as much as we need to in the realm of values.

Evangelization

18.

Evangelization and the African-American: Is the Church Listening?

Bishop John H. Ricard, SSJ

I'D LIKE TO SHARE PART OF A LETTER THAT I RECEIVED A FEW years ago from an African-American student who had attended a Catholic college, which I will call St. Ambrose.

Dear Bishop Ricard: I would like to tell you a little bit about myself and about my experience at Saint Ambrose College. Saint Ambrose is a good college which gave me an excellent opportunity to learn and to sharpen my skills. I probably would not have had that opportunity had I not gone there, but my college years at Saint Ambrose were not easy ones. You see, Saint Ambrose is an all-male, all-white Catholic college. I was one of five black students there and it was very difficult for me at times to feel at home at Saint Ambrose. There was no question in my mind that there was a subtle racism on the part of the student body and faculty which the blacks students and I felt.

I experienced this many times when the priests and brothers would spend more time with the white students and when they seemed to be getting all the atten-

---

Bishop John H. Ricard, SSJ is Vicar General of the Archdiocese of Baltimore and Chairman of the Domestic Policy Committee of the United States Catholic Conference.

tion. It was also difficult for me to relate socially to the students at the college. Oftentimes I found myself completely lost, not knowing how to respond when they weren't very friendly.

There were occasions when we would get together and I would fake songs that the other students were singing just to show that I was part of the group.

I had to struggle to get through math and English, especially when I had little or no help, but I was able to make good grades.

But when graduation day came around, I held my head up high because I was so proud of myself. I knew as I marched down the aisle that I had accomplished more than any other student there because I had made it against odds which the other students did not face.

Don't get me wrong; Saint Ambrose is an excellent school. It just has to clean up its act.

Most African-Americans who are Catholic could have written this letter. It sums up the experience of African-Americans with the institution of the Church. It's an experience more often than not characterized by indifference, hostile reactions, and gestures, attitudes, and platitudes that spell rejection and exclusion.

But the most important part of the young man's story is at the end, for it tells the whole story: that this young man at Saint Ambrose College, like African-American Catholics generally, recognized this reality for what it was and was able to work through it. And when he graduated, he held his head high because he felt he had accomplished more than any other student there. In the same way, many African-Americans feel an intense loyalty to the Church, an intense attachment and bonding to the Church, and a sense of keen ownership because they had to struggle to be part of it. They had to struggle to feel that the Church was theirs and they were the Church.

Most African-American Catholics do not take their faith for granted. They don't assume it's going to be there. They love the Church intensely, and they want to see the Church more a part of them and themselves more a part of it.

The History

In the same way, the African-American presence has been puzzling, problematic, and perplexing for the Church in the United States from the beginning.

Catholic slave owners saw no contradiction between their Catholic faith and the ownership of slaves. In fact, not only lay Catholics were slave owners and participants in the slave trade; religious communities and Catholic institutions, like their secular counterparts, utilized the slave system to their own advantage as well.

But nowhere, in my observation, is this attitude of the Church more dramatically demonstrated than in the period immediately following the Civil War. I surface this example because I feel it offers a powerful lesson to us today and affords us another opportunity to re-examine the level of commitment towards the full inclusion of African-Americans in the Church and towards our outreach to evangelize the African-American.

In 1866, an opportunity for direct outreach to African-Americans presented itself to the Catholic Church in the United States, and in particular to the Catholic bishops who were assembled for the Second Plenary Council of Baltimore. On that occasion they were challenged with an urgent plea by the Holy See to take formal and direct action to respond to the needs of the newly emancipated African slaves in the South.

In a letter of genuine concern, one archbishop wrote: "It is the most urgent duty of all of us to discuss the future status of the negro. Four million of these unfortunates are thrown on our charity and they silently, but eloquently, appeal to us for help. It is a golden opportunity for reaping a harvest of souls which, neglected, may not return."

Of the four million blacks in the South at the end of the Civil War, some 150,000 were Catholics.

The bishops, during that plenary session, engaged in sometimes bitter debate over the request of the Holy See for some form of direct action. The Holy See had proposed to the bishops the establishment of a national director, who would have the status of a bishop and the responsibility of coordinating all activities for evangelization and outreach.

With a few exceptions, there was little support for this proposal. The northern bishops considered that it was not their problem. The southern bishops did not want to share their authority with a national director or, even worse, an ordinary for black Catholics and black evangelization if it would hurt their fund raising and their churches in general. So they decided to appoint no national director and to allow each bishop to do what he considered opportune for his own diocese.

In the end, however, little was done. The same golden opportunity was seized by numerous Protestant denominations, who began to go into the South and establish missions, orphanages, centers of outreach, schools, and colleges. And as a result of this activity of the Protestant Church in America and the inactivity of Catholics, the vast majority of African-Americans today are Protestant. Today there are two million blacks who are Catholic and roughly twenty-five million who are baptized Protestants.

But there is another side to this story. Of the two million African-American Catholics, almost half have entered the Church in the past three decades. In fact, most observers would see this period, the '60s, '70s, and '80s, as a time in the history of our church that offered another golden opportunity for reaping a harvest of souls. This period really began in the late '60s, when two important events shook the foundation of both Church and society: the Second Vatican Council and the civil rights movement.

Catholic leaders in the black community made a deliberate decision that if the Church was not only to survive in the African-American community but to expand and flourish, the Catholic parish had to respond to the exigencies of African-American culture emerging in many dramatic forms in the '60s and '70s. They also determined that the parishes had to meet the needs of neighborhoods where they were located and where social disintegration, violence, poverty, and many other social ills were clearly in evidence.

As a result of this decision, parishes began a variety of efforts towards social development and community change. Internally, the parish moved forward with the incorporation of gospel-style music and many other forms of African-American culture into sacred worship, and with a conscious effort to promote black leaders.

And so the Church in the African-American community not only survived the turmoil of the '60s and '70s, but thrived and expanded. And today, more than ever before, there are clear indications that the Church is on the move in the African-American community. For if the '60s, '70s, and '80s were a period of rapid and significant expansion for the Church in the African-American community, the '90s must be seen as a time of internal development — in strengthening African-American parishes, maintaining schools in African-American communities, developing catechetics that would reflect African-American experience, and increasing vocations to priesthood and religious life.

The bishops of the United States have seized this opportunity by endorsing the pastoral plan for black Catholics, which was established by black Catholics, by establishing a secretariat for black Catholics at the National Conference of Catholic Bishops to carry out the pastoral plan, and by enthusiastically sending their priests to be trained and to participate in the development of that plan.

The Challenges

Yet, as optimistic as all this may sound, many problems and challenges still lie ahead both for the Church and for the African-American community. I would like to point out those challenges to which the Church must respond if it is not to lose another golden opportunity.

I want to make two observations at the start. First, integration as we might desire it, or envision it, does not exist in American society today. And because the Church reflects the society of which it is a part, integration does not exist in our church either. Very rarely do blacks and whites live together, work together, or worship together.

Martin Luther King observed that the time between ten and eleven o'clock on Sunday morning, when most Americans are in church, is the most segregated hour. The overwhelming majority of African-Americans today live in a separate and distinct world that has little or no contact with the white world.

The August 1989 edition of *Demography* magazine coined the phrase "hyper-segregation" to indicate that in most large American cities African-Americans work, send their children to school, and live in circumstances that rarely bring them into contact with whites. The article stated that housing patterns, job conditions, schools, and institutions, including the parish church, are so designed that a black child could be born, baptized, attend school, go to church, and get a job, and yet rarely come into meaningful or significant contact with whites.

Unquestionably, our two societies, one black and the other white, are further apart today than they ever were. And we all know that living apart from each other can have its negative consequences. Misconceptions, distortions, and stereotypes arise and breed in segregated and isolated conditions, and inevitably, when the two societies do come into contact with each other, open hostility and conflict often ensue.

210 \ *Bishop John H. Ricard, SSJ*

My second observation concerns the stance of U.S. attorney general Edwin Meese before leaving office that racial bigotry and prejudice had virtually vanished from the United States and that self-serving blacks were keeping alive notions that discrimination still exists. I'm positive that any thinking American would agree that the events of the recent past tell us otherwise.

The murder by young white men of a young black man who happened to stray into the all-white neighborhood of Bensonhurst, Long Island, to check out a used car; the bloody clash and riotous behavior between college students who were black and policemen who were white in Virginia Beach over a recent Labor Day weekend; and the convenient exploitation of whites' fears of blacks by Charles Stuart in Boston to cover up the murder of his pregnant wife, together with a subsequent vigilante scourge of black neighborhoods by the police, the press, and the politicians — all these events happen in a context. And the context that we see developing in America today is an increase in overt racially motivated hostility towards black people.

I think we would all be kidding ourselves if we denied that there is an ominous resurgence of racism in American society today, the likes of which bodes serious consequences for us as a nation and as a church.

This racism, if we examine it carefully, is now being felt at several levels. On one level, hatred is becoming quite hip. In some isolated spots of pop culture, racial prejudice has slithered back into view.

Andrew "Dice" Clay, a popular comedian, performed to packed audiences on a nationwide tour a few years ago. He regularly mixes dirty jokes with vicarious putdowns of black people. On the *Tonight Show*, Johnny Carson, as the loco character Floyd Turbow, reminisced about baseball the way it was meant to be played: "on real grass with no designated hitter and all white guys." The studio audience gasped, then laughed nervously. The heavy-metal group Guns and Roses savors the word "niggers." In one verse, among many others in their songs, they shout out, "Niggers, get out of my way, don't need to buy any of your gold chains today."

But the developments within the African-American community today, especially among African-American males, are perhaps of far greater importance and consequence. African-American males make up 2 percent of the college population of American students today but 48 percent of the prison population.

The real income for African-American males dropped in 1988 and continues to do so. Real income for black males is 57 percent of that for white males, and African-American women command higher incomes than African-American males. It is no wonder that households headed by African-American females rose to 58 percent in 1988.

The leading cause of death in the African-American community, especially among young males, is murder by another African-American male. Rates of cancer, heart disease, and hypertension are significantly higher among African-Americans than whites, and concomitantly the life expectancy of African-Americans is significantly lower than that of whites.

African-American children suffer even sadder circumstances. One in two black children lives in poverty, and as they reach the high-school level, 47 out of 100 will drop out of school before receiving a diploma. And although blacks make up only 12 percent of the population, more than half of the babies born with AIDS are African-American.

These sobering facts indicate the enormity of the tasks lying ahead and highlight the need for men and women of vision in our church and society to respond to these challenges.

Clearly, the nation has abandoned its commitment to civil rights and has lost the collective will to incorporate African-Americans and other minorities into the mainstream of American life. And we are witnessing a void of leadership at the highest level of government, education, and other important institutions in American society.

But it is also obvious that the Church enjoys a unique opportunity in history to be a moral and positive force for social change and community development among our African-American people.

If you're brave enough to drive or walk through the sweltering core of any of our inner cities or some isolated spots in rural America, you will find that the single institution left behind after all others have fled in fear is the parish church and, usually, the parish school. Despite the apparently insurmountable odds, these faithful remnants have not only remained but have flourished in the African-American community.

The Old Testament referred to God's people as a remnant. In the New Testament, Jesus adopted a new metaphor to describe God's people. He named his faithful followers "the leaven."

In many ways, the segment of our church that best expresses the concept of the leaven is the African-American parish where the people not only survive and preserve what is good but increase, multiply, and change the world about them.

I'd like to point out several very important areas that the Church must address if it is to extend itself to the African-American community in a meaningful way.

The Church must, first of all, devote a great deal of its resources and time to the development of lay leaders in the African-American community. For fewer than three hundred African-American priests serve in the American Church today.

Emory University and the United Methodist Church have offered a summer course for laypeople on the establishment of parish congregations because these institutions are convinced that the indigenous lay leader is far more effective than a white clergyman or religious leader in attracting ethnic minorities to their church congregations. I think the same principle would hold in our Catholic tradition. We must utilize indigenous lay leaders if the Church is to further extend itself in a substantial way in the community.

I also feel that the Church must begin to retool and retrain the clergy who staff African-American parishes. Almost 80 percent of these priests are white. And the need for continued training and development of the skills so necessary to keep these parishes going is evident. There is no question that the rate of burnout and turnover in African-American parishes is significant. In the stressful conditions that are part of everyday African-American life, even the strong seem to need help coping.

A third area of very important concern for us is the continued development of the African-American family. If we as a Church believe that the backbone of society is the family, we have to admit that the African-American community faces serious problems.

We need to look at programs that develop parenting skills and that help single parents cope better with the many stressful conditions that they face daily. The premise is that people who are attached to a formal religious structure seem to do better socially and are better able to handle stressful conditions. And certainly, the African-American family that is attached to the Church seems to fare better regardless of its economic or social condition.

19.

The Pastoral Challenges of the New Immigration

Silvano Tomasi, CS

IMMIGRATION PERSISTS AS AN EXPRESSION OF THE INNATE search for betterment and of the aspiration to go beyond, but also as tragic evidence of the growing abyss between the rich and the poor of the world. This ambivalent social phenomenon has the double face of creativity and injustice. The United States debate over the implications of continuing and pervasive migration focuses on many enduring themes, such as how immigrants affect the social, cultural, and political values of society in general, the job and income opportunities of native populations in particular, and the sending countries' balance of payments.

In the public-policy debate over immigration, however, the religious variable maintains a rather low priority and visibility, even though it is rearranging the demographic expression and future structural organization of the churches. The social history of religion has often incorporated the fact of ethnic diversity. United States religious history in particular has looked at the conflict- and integration-relationships of ethnic minorities with religious institutions. Recent scholarship has reiterated Timothy L. Smith's thesis that the soul of an ethnic group is religion. Reciprocally, the history and growth of the United States Catholic Church can only be understood in

Rev. Silvano Tomasi, CS is Secretary of the Pontifical Council for the Pastoral Care of Immigrants.

terms of its multi-ethnic heritage, and the future, as well, of the Church will be conditioned by the ethnic factor. The fifth centenary of the evangelization of the Americas would have benefited from a deeper analysis of the impact of migrations in the way they shaped the whole continent, north and south, and gave it a Christian cultural foundation.

We can safely assume that contemporary migrations are consistent with human patterns of life throughout history and that the interaction of migration and religion, either in the establishment of new religious movements and denominations or in changing existing ones, is practically self-evident. But a qualitative difference has emerged. The geographical frontiers have all been reached; new settlements and the peopling of new regions, as in colonial times, are no longer a dominant aspect of migration. A new phenomenon appears to be the increasing pluralism of developed societies, in which the art of intercultural relations determines what type of community and solidarity will keep the planet livable.

The megatrends serve well as context for the more limited task of looking at the newest immigrants in relation to the future of our church and its mission of evangelization. In his first *ad limina* address to the United States bishops in 1988, the Holy Father observed:

> One of the great riches of the Church in the United States is the way in which she herself incarnates universality of catholicity in her ethnic makeup, taken as she is from every nation and race, people and tongue (Rev. 7:9). The Church in the United States has the advantage of being naturally disposed to live catholicity and to show solidarity with all those particular churches where her people came from originally. The ethnic contributions to the various liturgies celebrated during my visit were not mere folkloric expressions; they were rather keys opening the door to a fuller under-

standing of the ecclesial reality of the Church in the United States.

On the other hand, this ecclesial reality is seriously challenged, as John Paul II also said, because the world has arrived at the doorstep of each parish and because meeting the needs of the most recent migrants is a sign of the times that calls us to reflection and action.

In my reflection I will discuss the context and background of the American Church's response to immigrants, some key issues in the present ministry to immigrants, the critical role of the parish, and the transition from exodus to Pentecost as a theological vision for the future.

Context and Background

The history of the Catholic community clearly shows the link between religion and the immigrants' culture and mobility.

Since John Carroll's 1789 appointment as first bishop in the United States, the kaleidoscopic history of American Catholicism has developed with the inflow of immigrants. Carroll himself worried about this. He described how immigrants poured "in upon us in large numbers from the various European countries" and continuously added to Church membership, which in 1785 amounted to 23,000.

From the beginning, Catholic development in the United States would reflect an unresolved ambivalence. On the one hand Catholics tended to become associated with the dominant culture and to downplay their ethnic diversity; on the other, they manifested a strong need to project a Catholic identification with their own ethno-cultural traditions in order to allow the incorporation of newcomers and maintain their loyalty.

Bishop Carroll in 1792 faced a troubled Boston congregation and expressed the wish that "all would lay aside national distinctions and attachments and strive to form not Irish or English or French Congregations or Churches but Catholic-American Congregations and Churches." But problems related to ethnic differences persisted. French-born Ambrose Marachal (†1828), archbishop of Baltimore, petitioned Rome against "having more Irish bishops," and Irish laity and priests worked hard to eliminate all French-born bishops. The historical contradictions and concerns of accommodating immigrants is exemplified by the first American schism, when German-speaking immigrants rebelled in Philadelphia against Bishop Carroll, who had refused to give them a pastor of their language. And the same kind of concerns arose in 1920, during the first evangelization project of the newly founded Maryknoll Sisters, when they set out immediately "to work with Japanese immigrants in Seattle and Los Angeles" a year before the first group sailed for China.

Key Issues

Conflict adjustment and evangelization took place in a Church that saw itself as a beleaguered but compact minority with fairly clear theological and political positions. Today witnesses an almost complete reversal of this 200-year historical pattern. Now immigrants are incorporated into a Catholic community intent, not on making itself acceptable as an American institution and as an actor in the public arena, but on resolving a case of split personality.

Headlines have reported on the progressive-conservative polarity. Some observers have also commented on the two cultures of modern Catholicism: one Catholic culture that views religion as an institutional function preoccupied with dogma, discipline, and leadership; and the second, "far larger Catholic culture of those Catholics who focus on the meaning of everyday life and working with moral dignity in a materialistic and number-struck world

more socially and personally urgent than the institution-
ally oriented goals of the first culture."

The two identities, or split personality, the immigrants are caught between combine several of these elements but mostly are distinguished by differences in
wealth and power.

The post-immigrant Church speaks to the conscience
of the nation on peace and on economic justice for all. In
the mainstream of American life, its ethnic memory is fad-
ing and its agenda articulates well national concerns of
egalitarianism, democracy, individualism, and women's
rights. These Catholics are middle class, educated, in a
social position of leadership, and able to define what issues are priorities.

The recent masses of immigrants and refugees, on
the other hand, are mostly poor, marginal, and concerned
with survival. As the pastoral letter on *Catholic Teaching
and the United States Economy* points out, minorities,
women, and children are most affected by poverty.

For example, 38% of all Puerto Rican families — and
they are American citizens — 30% of blacks, and 26% of
all Hispanics in the United States were living in poverty
in 1987, compared to 10% of white non-Hispanics. Poverty rates for Hispanics increased between 1978 and
1987, while rates for whites and black Americans have
decreased. The number of poor Hispanics grew from 2.9
million in 1979 to 5.5 million in 1987, a 90% increase.
Poverty both of money and of English language afflicts
most other immigrants and refugees as well.

The practical consequences of this dichotomy can
easily be anticipated for pastoral and catechetical work.
There is a correlation between class and religious expression. The style of devotion and involvement in community
are different. Most United States pastoral agents among
immigrants are the product of a middle-class Church, and
their inculturation into the world of the poor is a new
experience, compared to earlier immigrants, whose
priests, sisters, and bishops came almost exclusively from

the same poor immigrant community and then moved ahead with these communities.

Thus the newest immigrants continue to show the interaction between religion and culture, but in a nation and Church undergoing rapid change in almost every area of existence.

The drama that is played out now between immigrants, the United States church, and society affects how the Church will start its journey into the 21st century.

According to a recent Gallup poll, about 28% of the 245 million Americans are Catholic, and perhaps close to one-quarter of Catholics are Hispanic. By the year 2000, observes Leon Bouvier, almost 30% of the 80 million Catholics may be Hispanic. The fertility of European-origin Catholics is below reproduction, as is the national rate. Population growth, then, can lead to a single ethnic majority as a demographic base of the Church.

The appearance of new, culturally different groups of immigrants can trigger surprising comments even within the Church. When the Irish began to appear in large numbers, bishops of English and French origin could not restrain their amazement at the behavior of the Irish. In 1833 James Whitfield, archbishop of Baltimore, commented: "Irish with a few exceptions, they could all stay at home. . . . You may say that as an Englishman I have our national prejudice against the Irish, it may be somewhat true, but the greater number of the Americans entertain similar prejudices." When the scene changed again and the Italians appeared, Bishop Becker of Wilmington wrote to Cardinal Gibbons in 1884: "It is very delicate to tell the Sovereign Pontiff how utterly faithless the specimens of his country who come here really are. Ignorant of their religion and a depth of vice little known to us yet are their prominent characteristics."

Politically capable immigrants may be seen as troublemakers; devotional immigrants as superstitious. But over time the gifts of each group have been recognized and have converged in a dynamic and continuous rejuvenation and enrichment of the nation. Diversity is an immediate consequence of immigration patterns, especially if the country's fertility rate is below reproduction.

Immigration accounts for 28% of overall population growth. We are not swamped, however, as certain rhetoric claims. If the United States population is 6 or 7% foreign-born now, it was 15% or so in 1910, and in comparison, France's population is 11%, Canada's is 16%, and Australia's is 20% foreign-born. Particular areas and cities are more affected than others. The Anglos will become a minority by the year 2000 in California if trends persist. In New York City nearly one of every four residents is foreign-born. In 1990, minorities composed 25% of the United States population and 35% of the youth cohorts.

Fairfax County, Virginia, presents an example of how the social fabric of America is touched by the presence of newcomers; 55 languages are represented among the students in the public schools. In Los Angeles, Sunday Mass is celebrated in 42 languages. The Catholic Church is experiencing in an even more acute way the demographic changes at work in our society. European-background Catholics have low fertility, comparable to the national Protestant rate, and the leading countries contributing immigrants are of a Catholic tradition: the Philippines, Mexico, Dominican Republic, Cuba, Haiti. New Catholic communities of Koreans, Chinese, and Indians have sprung up around the country. Immigration, if we take a rough estimate of its Catholic percentage, adds a new parish of 2,000–3,000 people every four days. The world has come to the door of every parish. The missions have come to us. In many cities, cross the street and you are in a different cultural world.

From the point of view of pastoral action, the rapidity of change is a major challenge. Between 1970 and 1980 New York City lost one million white Europeans, who were replaced by one million newcomers from Latin America, the Caribbean, and Asia. Immigrants are a blessing; they bring new vitality. But they also bring new problems. Es-

tablished life in the neighborhood is upset, and new culture styles are introduced. How do you incorporate these
newcomers into the community of faith?

Today, as in the past, many Americans are asking
the same question: Do the country and the Church have
a right to expect the newest immigrants to be assimilated
into our culture, or should each group be allowed or encouraged to maintain its ethnic identity and cultural heritage? The water glass represents the original host society.
Adding sugar to it will not change its appearance, though
the taste will be affected. That represents total assimilation. But adding cola will create a new mix and change
the appearance as well as the taste. That represents the
melting pot. To continue the analogy, adding oil to the
water will result in separate entities, as the oil does not
mix with the water. That represents cultural pluralism.
Finally, if the sugar, cola, and oil are kept out of the
water glass, we have cultural separatism.

The recent teaching of American bishops has moved
in the direction of pluralism. Their 1983 pastoral letter,
The Hispanic Presence, states: "Respect for culture is
rooted in the dignity of people made in God's image. The
Church shows its esteem for this dignity by working to
ensure that pluralism, not assimilation and uniformity, is
the guiding principle in the life of communities in both
the ecclesial and secular society" (no. 5). Religious and
cultural pluralism as a fact and a challenge is articulated
in *The National Catechetical Directory for Catholics in the
United States* (no. 194), in the *Statement on Cultural Pluralism* of 1980, and in other public-policy positions of the
Church.

The relationship between faith and culture is a recurring concern. The Church advocates a dynamic conserva-
tion of the immigrants' culture and religious traditions,
not assimilation, for a pluralistic integration enriches host
country, Church, and immigrants. The Church does not
build unity on culture, but on Christ and the Eucharist.
All cultures are respected, and faith cannot be identified

with any. Popular religiosity, multiculturalism, and inculturation have now moved from the limited area of migration documents to the whole Church's concern with evangelization. Mutual acceptance includes culture and race, the overcoming of the irrational fear of difference, a willingness to learn. The 1988 Vatican document on *The Church and Racism: Towards a More Fraternal Society* declares: "In the apprenticeship to difference, everything cannot be expected all at once, but the possibilities for new ways of living together and even of mutual enrichment must be considered."

The bishops, in their 1986 pastoral statement on immigrants, *Together, A New People*, took a further step in the search for an adequate answer to the question of cultural adaptation. There, the welcome of new persons and groups into the parish and the diocese is linked to the preferential option for the poor, the requirements of justice, and respect for all cultures, which are all precious but all relative since communion in diversity is built on Christ and the Eucharist.

Newcomers want self-identity, but even more a decent life for themselves and their families. The other side of evangelization, therefore, is the overcoming of marginalization and powerlessness. The acceptance of cultural differences becomes folkloric entertainment if access to life in society is blocked. "Basic justice demands the establishment of minimum levels of participation in the life of the human community for all persons" (*Pastoral Letter on Catholic Social Teaching and U.S. Economy*, no.77).

Culture and justice are the twin tracks on which immigrants' inclusion moves. The use of one's language, the unification of families, the right to asylum, and equal treatment in work are essential to the human dignity of newcomers. These issues, therefore, take on a religious dimension and demand the involvement of the Church for their achievement. The question of justice is relevant beyond the process of immigrants' incorporation, and it extends to policy in a direct way. As a community of faith, we have to challenge the old assumptions of legislation that remain anchored on "national interest."

The moral basis for an alien-admission policy in the rich countries cannot be limited to the concept of sovereignty, for the "push" factors driving immigration should enter into the evaluation discussion. In light of the encyclical *On Social Concern*, questions can be reformulated and reproposed, such as: Can closed borders be morally justified? To what extent should cultural homogeneity be maintained through immigration policies? How far can a society go in limiting the comforts and perhaps the freedom of its citizens in view of the extreme needs of individuals living elsewhere, if we accept the equal moral worth of all individuals? The richness of our Catholic tradition offers the resources for addressing the tough issues raised by the reality of interdependence. The immigrants become a parable of faith. They are transnational actors, an avant-garde that builds the world family and that teaches about, and calls for, solidarity.

The Parish's Critical Role

Acceptance and assistance to individual immigrants constitute half the service. Integration comes about from a position of strength, and the immigrant community has historically proven to be an extremely important requirement for the immigrants' transition into a new society. Providing the opportunity for a collective identity and group participation has a direct bearing on the preservation of faith among non-Christian immigrants. A review of American pastoral strategies shows that the ethnic parishes anticipated with successful American pragmatism the effectiveness of the base communities. These language parishes, 10% of all parishes in 1948, met the spiritual and political needs of European immigrants and kept them in the Church. In *Presencia Nueva*, the 1988 study of Hispanics in the archdiocese of Newark, Dr. Vidal recommends such parishes as the cornerstone of the Hispanic apostolate (p.344). The Americanizing bishops of the 1880s and 1890s, like Cardinal Gibbons, recognized the indispensable function of the ethnic parish, although they differed with the spokesmen for the Germans on how long such parishes should last. The administrative difficulties related to the aging of ethnic parishes should not hide their basic success. Perhaps now time limits should be set and old structures courageously entrusted to new immigrants in the inner city, so that the newcomers control and experience their own turf, where they freely celebrate their religious expression. In this way, they will achieve the structural basis for a community.

It is interesting that, to attract Catholic immigrants, sects and various denominations successfully use a practice generally abandoned by Catholics, who invented it. And unity in diversity can be realized not only in multicultural parishes — in themselves an ideal and often idealistic pastoral strategy — but also at a diocese-wide level around the person of the bishop, even with a variety of types of parishes. As long as the dynamics move from community to communion, the specific ways in which the parish meets the immigrants' needs seem secondary, whether personal parish, mission with the care of souls, multi-cultural parish, national parish, or chaplaincies. Nurturing the faith and communicating it to immigrants are the priorities.

Most newcomers arrive in a postmodern society from social environments still dominated by a rural and often preindustrial culture. In the cultures of developing countries, the group and the family are important; face-to-face communication and immediate expressions of religiosity are dominant. As immigrants adapt to our urban American environment, the clash of cultures and traditions touches on belief very directly. In Mexico City, long lines of women, and even men, move on their knees to show their devotion to Our Lady of Guadalupe. But you cannot transport such a scene to the National Shrine of the Immaculate Conception in Washington, DC.

The question has been raised whether, in their adjustment to middle-class American society, Catholics have simply accepted those dominant values of American life that go beyond the basic constitutional freedoms and liberties: unrestrained competition for social and economic status; consumerism and waste; and extreme individualism.

As Herberg puts it: "The prophetic spirit of the Church has been lost in a tendency to enjoy the benefits of American life while providing religious supports for the institutions which provide the benefits. This creates an uncomfortable relation of religious to a dominant culture which may constitute a challenge to the Church." The pastoral letters *The Challenge of Peace* and *Economic Justice for All* provide prophetic witness at the institutional level. The race of immigrants toward middle class needs to be placed in the context that Catholics, too, are the very culture they seek to change. Immigrants may risk moving out of their devotional religiosity, their popular religion, and leave behind the symbols and the worldviews they provided, in order to embrace a life-style — itself in need of evangelization — that middle-class parishes exhibit.

Surely this new challenge for the Church from today's immigrants calls for it to play its critical role vis-a-vis the immigrants' cultures and that of our own society, with the Gospel as the only measuring rod.

The 1988 Gallup survey of the "Unchurched American — Ten Years Later" found that 57% of Hispanics said religion was very important to them, but 44% said they attend church only once a week and 43% said they have been invited to churches other than their own. NORC, Chicago, concluded from its surveys: "Catholics of Hispanic origin in the United States are defecting to Protestant denominations at the rate of approximately 60,000 people a year. Over the past 15 years this departure from

226 \ *Silvano Tomasi, CS*

Catholicism has amounted to almost one million men and women, almost one of 10 (8%) of the Spanish Catholic population." In "Hispanic Shift of Allegiance Changes Face of U.S. Religion," a front-page article in the *New York Times* (May 14, 1989), Robert Suro wrote: "From store-front churches in urban slums to gleaming temples along suburban freeways, perhaps more than four million of the roughly 20 million Hispanic Americans now practice some form of Protestant Christianity, according to several demographic studies. And the movement away from Ca-tholicism, which traditionally claimed virtually the entire Hispanic population, has accelerated in the 1980s."

The reasons given for the shift in religious affiliation are many:

- In their religious practice those who leave were better Catholics than those who stay in the Church (abortion, Sunday church, etc).

- Immigrants find in the sects a response to their emotional, communal, and religious needs on the way to middle class.

- Immigrants find a more immediate religious expression, a mystique, an escape from anonymity, a good, simple catechesis based on the bible, cultural identity, and hope.

In the Asian and Caribbean communities the intensity of proselytism seems the same.

The brunt of the newest immigrants' impact is felt by the parish. I mentioned before the demand of community and the strategy of national parishes to act as base communities.

The "Final Report to the Bishops of the United States" by the Parish Project (1982) states that the parish in the United States "remains a critical unit of the Church's organized ministry and the most prevalent context of conversion, community, and mission for Catholics, beyond the intimacy of the family." The conclusion of *The*

American Catholic Parish: A History from 1850 to the Present is equally clear: "A key to understanding the history of American Catholicism is the parish."

De facto, many of the 19,000 American parishes are in some degree or other multicultural. A policy of inclusion would enable different ethnic groups to interact beyond mutual tolerance. Once a parish model is chosen, then appropriate planning should follow. The task of welcoming the newest immigrants and refugees cannot be delegated to a few specialized agencies and persons: the future of the total Catholic and national communities is affected.

Several practical steps can help respond to the pastoral needs of newcomers. These steps go along a continuum that ranges from the strictly spiritual to the social and political dimensions, since the object of the Church's concern is the human person in its entirety:

- Formation of parish teams to welcome pluralism and to promote the appreciation of diverse religious expressions
- Missioning permanent deacons to the ministry of welcoming newcomers to the parish
- Use of full-time paid catechists for some cultural groups without clergy or religious of their own
- Development of lay leadership to run immigrant communities of faith within the particular churches
- Sharing religious experience/stories across cultural liturgies and apostolic movements
- Making parish facilities available for immigrants' gatherings and for celebrations as a group
- Participation of immigrants in parish councils, in multicultural liturgies, and in apostolic movements
- Progressive education for immigrants who are not used to registering in a parish or giving donations in envelopes
- Providing scholarships for immigrants in Catholic schools

- Integration of parish outreach with the services provided for various refugee, elderly, and youth groups in the neighborhood

- Programs for families challenged by children Americanizing much faster than their parents

- At least initial support of alternative seminary structures for vocations from immigrant and other groups, including scholarships for immigrant seminarians

- Introducing into seminary curricula the dimensions of immigration and cultural pluralism and the teaching of the immigrants' languages

- Support of evangelization resource centers and pastoral agents for the newest arrivals

- Advocacy for fair immigration legislation and for social services

This litany of needs could be even longer. Newcomers relive the exodus experience of liberation from violence, fear, and poverty. Their dream for a promised land is the same we all share; it is the dream fulfilled at Pentecost, a feast of all peoples. Our American bishops have stated: "Welcoming new individuals and groups into the life of the parish and of the diocese becomes an exercise of incorporation that in this new historical moment calls for creativity and flexibility" (*Together, A New People*, 5,A).

If we hold to such a vision, we will not lose this opportunity to build up the Church for the year 2000 and beyond.

20.

The New Hispanic Reality

Allan Deck, SJ

IN THE 17TH AND 18TH CENTURIES THE CHURCH INITIATED an effort to evangelize China. But in the early part of the 18th century a decision from Rome eliminating what were called the Chinese Rites adversely affected this venture. China has not been significantly evangelized to date, in large measure because of this one decision.

The Church thus lost an historic opportunity to win the loyalty of the largest group of people in the world. Today the Church is smaller, the Church is less than what it could be, because of historic decisions and policies that were adopted by leadership.

We are in an analogous situation in the United States today. You and I are the beneficiaries of the policies and the vision that the leadership of the Catholic Church adopted a hundred years ago. But this American Catholic Church is being dramatically transformed before our very eyes. It is becoming Hispanic. Unfortunately, what we are doing now as a church is in no way commensurate or proportionate to the immensity of the challenge and the needs we must meet if the Church is going to be strong, vibrant, and vital in the century to come.

For the leaders in the present-day American church possess a mind-set that reflects the concerns and the points of view of middle-class, mainstream Americans. I

Rev. Allan Deck, SJ is a theologian at Loyola Marymount University and a specialist in Latin American Studies.

Catholics, but the future does not belong to them as much as to these new and still marginal people.

If we believe that we are going to retain the loyalty of these new immigrants by telling them to do what we do, to act like we do, to fit into our current institutions, then we are barking up the wrong tree. We are not going to succeed. Studies during the last 20 years about the loyalty of Hispanic Catholics to the Church indicate that things have changed dramatically. All of the reports 20–25 years ago said that at least 88% of the Hispanics were Catholic, but comparable studies today indicate that only 70% are Catholic. And non one knows how much more the number will drop. But if we don't get with it, I assure you, it will continue to drop.

I believe it's very critical to respond very soon in a much more adequate way to this enormous challenge.

If we love the Church, if we want it to be rooted in the American context, we have no choice but to discover how it might be rooted in the world of these immigrant people. They are the future of the Church in this country.

Now there are two fundamental features of an effective outreach to these immigrant groups. First, we will be successful in maintaining the loyalty of the Hispanic immigrants if we have ministers who come from their ranks, who feel like them, who think like them, who are masters of the language, who use metaphors that appeal to and move the people.

Such ministers will come only from the ranks of these people. The Association of Theological Schools (ATS) every year produces a study of people getting degrees in theology in Protestant and Catholic institutions. Virtually all schools of theology, Protestant and Catholic, are part of ATS. Its most recent report indicated that 1,200 Hispanics are studying in either Protestant or Catholic schools of theology and that, of the 1,200, 300 are in Catholic schools of theology and seminaries and 900 in Protestant schools of theology. In addition to finding ways to bring Hispanic students into Catholic institutions that would form them to become ministers, whether as priests or laity, we have to promote the development of the faculties in our seminaries and schools of theology.

I don't want to be misunderstood as putting down the quality or the efforts of our Catholic seminaries and theological centers. In many respects, we have seen growth and improvement over the past 10 years, especially in the quality of faculties.

But I feel that we do not have in place faculty people who interact sufficiently with the Hispanic students. We don't have faculty imbued with an urgent vision of the Church's present reality. Frequently they lack the cultural sensitivities, skills, and background required today, nor do they approach their areas of expertise from the perspective of the Hispanic communities. And so, our seminaries and schools of theology have tended to be dysfunctional and irrelevant in addressing the needs of the Hispanics. They are much more functional in dealing with the needs of the mainline American church, of our middle-class groups.

They are not going to become effective in meeting the needs of the Hispanics until our faculties develop. Those who teach are the most critical part of the institution, because they carry out its policies.

Administrators are important, too, of course, but I would say that the faculty is more important. They may have all the good will in the world, but if their studies, their exposure, their language skills, their cultural sensitivities have not included immersion in the cultures and language of Hispanics, they are not going to succeed. Plenty of evidence indicates that faculty are failing, because although we're taking Hispanic students into our seminaries in larger numbers right now, equally large numbers are leaving. Faculty need to develop their area of expertise from the prospective of the immigrant.

The second element fundamental to outreach is that the parish become the point of contact with Hispanic people. Most of our efforts to appeal to and win over the loyalty of the immigrant group will rise or fall depending on how capable the parish system is of relating to this group. Currently it is not able to. We had a successful national-parish system going back a hundred years, the key to the success of the Catholicism that you and I enjoy today. Indeed the Church was built on the experience of national parishes that, one way or another, provided a receptive milieu for immigrants, whatever their language and culture.

When I start talking about the national parish, and about finding in the new code of Canon Law a modality suitable for our context, the personal parish, I am met with looks of consternation and incomprehension by clergy, even by some bishops. Why? Because psychologically our priests have left behind that whole national-parish phase. Their mind-set, their psychological space is the assimilated middle-class Catholic Church to which, unfortunately, their seminary preparation usually restricted itself. But this Church is diminishing, while the Church that's growing is not being addressed. The psychology, then, of many priests is somewhere else, simply not adapted to this dramatic transformation.

Historical analogies are found in the experiences of the Congregationalist Church, the Presbyterian Church, and the Episcopalian Church from the 18th century to the 19th century. Once mainline churches accounting for most of the Christians in the United States, they turned into sideline churches in terms of membership as the Methodists and the Baptists grew. The policy of the Methodists and Baptists was to go to where the people were and bring them ministers who spoke their language, who could sit down with them, who understood what their problems were. The lesson was: Don't remain in your ivory-tower institution or in your big urban center, or wherever, but move out.

This formula placed the Methodists and the Baptists among the largest groups of Christians in this country. But the Methodists did not persist in the policy and went the way of the mainline churches — more sophisticated, more identified with the middle and upper classes — and so they lost the ability to get down with the newcomers, who were poor. The Baptists, on the other hand, never gave up on this approach, and indeed the Baptists and other evangelical and fundamentalist churches are the only American Protestant denominations that are growing.

The Catholic Church, in my judgment, will follow the same pattern. We will become like the Episcopalians if we persist in having seminaries, schools, and policies that only address the needs of the dominant, mainstream, middle-class, assimilated Catholics. We are running a great risk. I think there is plenty of historical precedent for what I am saying.

We need to work with the presbyterate. For priests are key players in almost any problem in the Church. When the priests are not on board and are not in some way supporting, nourishing, and encouraging ministry among diverse groups, we are setting ourselves up for a lot of frustration. We therefore have to work with the priests to find out how we can motivate, support, and encourage them to address this issue.

We need to promote a knowledge of parish models that work. One of our most harmful attitudes is the idea that the American Catholic Church has overcome its immigrant phase. Now we can have one big, happy family, one parish, and we'll have something for the Vietnamese, the Chinese, the Hispanics, and the English-speaking community.

In most cases, this approach doesn't work, because of the principle enunciated by Fr. Tomasi in his contribution and stated many times by sociologists: people do not integrate from a position of weakness. When you have four different groups, one of which has more background, knowledge, power, and influence than the three others, you know which group is going to dominate.

So, in our parish context we have to create an environment that makes the people feel at home, that in some

234 \ *Allan Deck, SJ*

way is like the one they are familiar with — where their language is spoken, where they have people who know them and their customs, who accept them, where the people are allowed to do things the way they are used to doing them, instead of bowing to someone taught in a seminary that had no or little regard for the customs of these people.

We have to consider many different approaches. There are, for instance, integrated parishes; national or de facto national parishes, where we only work with people of one ethnic group; parishes that are two-tracked, where you have something for one group and something for the other, somewhat like having two parishes in the same place. We need to look at the effectiveness of all these approaches and offer options, because the Hispanic group is not uniform. Some Hispanic people are at a very delicate stage of engagement with the United States. Others, like their children. are further along in being assimilated. We therefore need to have differentiated approaches to deal with this complexity. But our priests are not being assisted with viable models that might be helpful to them in reaching out.

The fourth area is Catholic education. Catholic schools were founded precisely to educate the German youth, the Czech youth, the Polish youth. But the function of the Catholic schools today, unfortunately, is not to educate Hispanic youth to the same degree.

One-fifth the students in Catholic grammar and secondary schools are Hispanic. Generally they are the most assimilated Hispanics and come from families that have been here awhile, are educated, and don't have language problems. The public schools have most of our Hispanic young people. But for some reason the Church and the schools are not feeding into higher education Hispanic people who have the skills, the background, and the inclination to assume important roles of leadership in the Hispanic Catholic community.

Large numbers of very simple people, working-class people, and even peasants who come from rural areas are in many of our parishes. But the parishes lack the committed middle-level Hispanic who is able to articulate issues and fight for the needs of the people, whether as priest or layperson, as teacher, professional, or otherwise.

Those who achieve these skills frequently have gone to Catholic schools but then have gone on to get lucrative jobs and some kind of work not in a church context. The same is true of those who have gone to public schools. Until that gap is bridged, we are not going to have an articulate Hispanic leadership in the Catholic Church. And the way we address it is critical to our future.

International

21.

Church and Mission in Latin America

Archbishop Marcos G. McGrath, CSC

WHEN WE TALK ABOUT AIDING OUR BROTHER CHRISTIANS AND all our brothers in other lands, we are in the tradition of the Church, a tradition going back to the time St. Paul first took up a collection in Corinth to support the mother church in Jerusalem.

The missionary effort of the Church is really the heart of the history of the Church, as the Church makes its presence felt alongside the thrust of civilizations and cultures. Since the Middle Ages — and now in modern times — the traditional springboard for missionary work has been Europe. European money financed the sending of personnel — monks, priests, then, in addition, religious men and women and, later still, male and female lay missionaries. A French laywoman, Pauline Jaricot, promoted more systematic ways of raising funds for the missions, and her efforts led to the creation of the Society for the Propagation of the Faith.

Europe has given us three great mission centuries in modern times: the sixteenth, the nineteenth, and the twentieth. Hilaire Belloc, the famous English Catholic author, wrote in the 1920s, "Europe is the Faith, and the Faith is Europe." Though this was not exactly so — the faith has always been ecumenical and universal — in a

---

Archbishop Marcos G. McGrath, CSC is the Archbishop of Panama.

certain sociological and political sense, and also in the expression of Church theology, it was in many ways true, just as the Church of the early centuries and early councils was Middle Eastern and North African in its problems and expressions.

Even in Vatican II, that most ecumenical of all ecumenical councils — because so many bishops were natives from all the continents of the world and because it was the first that could and did address the problems of the entire world — the principal theological forces were Middle European.

Nonetheless, the bishops and their assistants from the rest of the world, particularly from what was coming to be called the Third World, including Latin America, brought many questions and suggestions that successfully oriented the council toward a broader worldview of the Church. This development corresponded to the dramatic shift in the Church's center of gravity and missionary push during this century.

Before developing this point, it is good to feel and to stress the missionary impulse of Europe through this century. Europe's first great contribution, carrying over from the previous century, was of emigrant Catholics, priests, and funds to the newly emerging Catholic Church in far-off areas, such as Australia, but most strongly in the United States. The growth of this new and vigorous expression of Anglo-Saxon Catholicity, marked by a brogue or other strong European cultural admixtures, was impressive. Missionary, organized, and disciplined, the U.S. Catholic Church soon became the largest contributor of funds to the Propagation of the Faith and began sending its own missionary personnel to the Far East, and then to Africa and Latin America.

The missionary efforts of the European church were cut short by the Second World War. But soon after, rising from their shambles through the significant assistance of the Marshall Plan, these Catholic peoples once more turned to their missionary task, more decidedly than before. Missionaries went by the thousands to Asia, Africa, and, especially from Spain, to Latin America. The systematic collection of funds, for both the religious and the social activities of churches in the Third World, became increasingly significant. Even now, when priestly and religious vocations have declined in Europe and North America and fewer Catholic missionaries are coming to our countries, Europe continues to raise funds, sometimes in increasing amounts, and send them to us.

This aid has been most effective at a decisive moment for our churches to the south. The bishops' 1979 meeting in Puebla expressed this fact rather eloquently:

> The generous assistance in personnel and economic means which our Churches and the Latin American Bishops Council (CELAM) have received from the sister Churches of Europe and North America has contributed significantly to the evangelization effort in the entire continent. For this we express our profound thanks. The aid itself is a sign of the universal charity of the Church. The effort to guide this assistance within the plans and programs of the local Churches is, furthermore, a sign both of respect and of communion. (*Puebla Document*, no.103)

Vatican II marks a turning point in world mission. While the missionary impulse from the North continues to be strong, although recently more in the form of funds than of personnel, the scene and the actors on the stage of world mission have been shifting. These changes, especially between the Northern and Southern Hemispheres and between the First and Third Worlds, are both quantitative and qualitative.

In *The Coming of the Third Church* (England: St. Paul Publications, 1976), Walter Bühlmann brings home this quantitative change. His charts are expressive. In 1900 the majority of the world's Catholics (51.5%) resided in Europe and North America. By the year 2000, 70% of the Catholic population will reside in the Southern Hemisphere, with Latin America accounting for 592 million, Africa for 175 million, and Asia and Oceania for the remaining 80 million. These numbers make the task of helping the Church in the Southern Hemisphere increasingly more expensive and, therefore, require greater discrimination and greater concentration on specific priorities.

But I think that the qualitative changes are even more important. All parts of the world, particularly Latin America, have felt the profound impact of the Vatican Council. But its impact has not been the same all around the world. When we read articles on this 20th anniversary of the conclusion of Vatican II, we are asking many questions: Was it good? Was it bad? Would history have been better without it? In my view, for our part of the world — Latin America — the council was the greatest blessing of the 20th century. But I think we should assess its impact in different areas of the world.

Fr. Ted Hesburgh, named to the Papal Commission on Culture, has proposed that the commission convene to study the aftereffects of the council — particularly of the *Pastoral Constitution on the Church in the World Today,* which set us off on the dialogue with world culture.

The council must be evaluated continent by continent, and cultural area by cultural area, because of the great differences the Church experiences in each area of the world.

We from the South feel that the Church in Europe and North America has experienced prolonged cultural crises that have not yet been resolved. Among other effects, these have produced a crisis of identity, evidenced by the large number of priests and religious leaving their orders. In the last few years, though, there seems to be a new resolution, from which new paths will be taken.

A Historical Perspective

In Latin America the effect of the council has been aggiornamento, or renovation, in a sense that I'd like to explain by placing our Latin American church in historical perspective. We can hardly tell where we are going unless we tell how we got to where we are.

There are four periods in the development of the Church in Latin America:

(1) The first is the period of colonial conquests. The religious effort of evangelization at the very beginning of the conquests of Latin America was directed at undoing the frequent avarice and cruelty of the Conquistadores. At the close of this period, however, in the 17th and 18th centuries, the missionary effort waned, as evidenced by an acceptance of the status quo, in which the official linkage of church and state worked to the detriment of religious growth in Latin America.

(2) In the second period, the period of independence — achieved politically in Latin America particularly from 1812 to 1825 — the colonies broke off from their mother countries. This was a political, not a social and economic, break or revolution; it did not change the basic socioeconomic structure. The essentially aristocratic ruling class continued in power, and society continued to be feudal in nature. In fact, the political leaders were "sons of the Spanish and Portuguese," or criollo. The Church struggled with the political power as well, for the new heads of state wanted to control the Church, just as the Spanish colonial authorities had wanted to. The Church was determined to retain the influence in Latin America it had exercised under Spain and Portugal. A century would pass before the idea of separation of church and state became acceptable to both sides. So the 19th century is marked by a political struggle between the proclerical conservatives and the anticlerical liberals within the upper class. This decimated the

Church in Latin America, as in many countries Catholicism was persecuted by the liberals in power. Celebrating Mass could even be a capital crime. Religion became such a politicized issue that governments closed seminaries (thus preventing the formation of clergy), broke up parishes, and took away church properties. This struggle continued to the end of the century and left the Church very weakened.

(3) In the third phase, beginning in 1899 with the Council on Latin America, called by Leo XIII, a revival of the Church took place, and from 1900 to Vatican II, several significant changes ensued. Encouraged by Pius X, lay participation in church affairs increased. Responding to Leo XIII, Benedict XV, Pius XI, and Pius XII, the Church addressed social questions. Liturgy, biblical studies, and ecumenical contacts prospered in certain places. The Second Vatican Council was the culmination of, and response to, 70 years of change in the Church, strongest in Europe but also significant in Latin America.

Of the more than 2,800 bishops present at Vatican II, 750 came from Latin America. We brought few answers and many questions, and we were able to secure seats on the various commissions of the council, thus assuring Latin American input and a broader worldview.

(4) Since the council, the Church in Latin America has been trying to live as deeply as possible the double orientation of the council, which consists of 1) returning to the sources — the building up of the Church upon the Word of God, and the community living of the Gospel; and 2) going out to make the message live in the world. This double perspective is necessary. To understand our church, we have to start from the Word of God, from the Vatican Council, and from the synod documents that have followed, as well as from papal encyclicals and the whole magisterium of the

Holy See. We then need to look at the documents of the bishops' 1968 meeting in Medellin — the first continental and overall effort to apply the council to Latin America — and their 1979 meeting in Puebla in 1979. These texts are complemented by each country's local church documents. You'll find that most of our countries are carrying on efforts at what we call pastoral assemblies to determine our pastoral priorities, following the method of *Gaudium et Spes:* See, judge, and act. The Church in Latin America historically did not organize itself on a strong diocesan and parish basis, as the Church in North America did. We had organized primarily through religious congregations and their missionary areas. Episcopal conferences did not exist until about 20 years ago and are still developing, with the assistance of CELAM. As a result, we face a number of organizational challenges in order to bring about a community effort.

Priorities in Aid

1. A first priority: the aid institutions — their witness to the world

Emphasis upon the Gospel and evangelization is fundamental to this effort. For this reason, the idea of sharing and supporting is extremely important to the whole Church. The agencies and foundations of the American church represent a positive aspect of evangelical poverty, in the sense that we don't spend everything on ourselves, we share it with others. We have to live more deeply this social side to evangelical poverty. I think that by practicing such poverty through their foundations, American Catholics witness to this truth, both to themselves and others. But its influence has to spread to the secular sphere much more. There is urgent need for greater generosity in the search for a sense of community in the world. This is old talk but very apropos.

What the American church is doing must rub off on other people, on governments, because dedicated and effective foundations, governments, and international agencies are necessary if we are going to create the sense of a world effort to bring about justice for all people.

If greater generosity were poured forth in troubled areas, we would not have to be salvaging situations, as we are trying to do now. With a little forethought and much less economic investment, problems developing over the last 30 years could have been solved so much better. A State Department official asked me, "What can be done for Central America?" One suggestion I have is: Don't neglect the rest of the world the way you've neglected Central America for the last 40 years. Think of the Caribbean and/or parts of Africa. Think of what can be done now to build up a better economic, social, and political relationship with and for all these people. Within this context, we Catholics have a great role to play, for we believe, unlike Cain, that we are our brothers' keepers (Gn 4:9).

2. A second priority: help us to help ourselves

This principle is obviously fundamental in all assistance efforts, whether it is helping a child to walk, a church to grow, or a community to develop solutions to its problems.

My suggestion here is very concrete: Give financial assistance to programs that will help our churches to finance themselves. For the most part, they do not have good administrative or economic organizations, and our people do not realize sufficiently their need, their duty, and their ability to support their own church. You can help our programs of self-awareness and self-support and, by so doing, encourage more churches to try them out.

Permit me a small example. When I became archbishop of Panama in 1969, I discovered that from roughly a million Catholics the archdiocese received an annual income of less than $30,000, and it possessed no other source of income. On top of that, we had to undertake a major missionary effort to create new base and parish communities in the rural areas and especially in the new urban and suburban areas of a capital city that in 20 years grew from 250 to 750 thousand inhabitants. What to do? We were receiving some aid from abroad, which amounted to about 85% of what we had to spend for the archdiocese. We began small local campaigns for individual donations; they helped somewhat, but fell far short. A commission I had appointed suggested calling upon a United States agency experienced in raising church funds, so we wrote the U.S. Bishops' Secretariat for Latin America. They put us in touch with the agency and also financed its work with us for two years. By the end of that time, in 1975, we had launched our first annual campaign, which we had tailored from the American model to fit the peculiar circumstances and attitudes of our people. It was a success, raising over $200,000. In 1982 the seventh annual campaign raised $392,000, of which only $20,000 was spent on the campaign itself.

With these funds, which now constitute perhaps two-thirds of what the archdiocese spends on its pastoral work (one-third comes in aid from abroad), we have been able to promote energetically the evangelization of new and marginal areas; aid and support the priests, the religious sisters — there are close to a hundred in parish evangelization — and the lay catechists and delegates; finance the training programs for all these "pastoral agents"; develop departments for pastoral action in specialized areas, such as youth, family, education, social action, catechism, liturgy, and lay movements; and fund our vocational programs and seminaries, which at present are filled to overflowing.

Other dioceses are working on self-financing. Three others in Panama have taken up our program, and Brazil's episcopal conference has an annual campaign for all the dioceses. I heartily suggest that the American church bring together information on these experiences, perhaps hold a specialized seminar, together with some European

Catholic aid agencies, particularly Adveniat, to further this assistance toward self-aid.

3. A third priority: the Church's primary task is religious

In identifying the priorities for assisting the churches, we must remember the Church's prime task: bring God to the people and the people to God, through Christ, our Lord. Unless the Church does this, it cannot accomplish anything else worthwhile.

The council, in *Gaudium et spes*, has illuminating words on this subject:

> Christ, to be sure, gave His Church no proper mission in the political, economic, or social order. The purpose which he set before her is a religious one. But out of this religious mission itself comes a function, a light, and an energy which can serve to structure and consolidate the human community according to the divine law. As a matter of fact, whenever circumstances of time and place create the need, she can and indeed should initiate activities on behalf of all men. This is particularly true of activities designed for the needy, such as the works of mercy and similar undertakings. (No. 42)

This text does not deny, rather it clearly affirms, the Church's right and duty to engage in social activities of assistance to the needy and of inspiration to humane and just community organization. But it also stresses that this should come about as a result of the energies which flow from the religious mission of the Church.

Catholic funding agencies sometimes tend to spurn systematically the properly religious areas, such as seminaries, parish promotion, catechetics, pastoral training centers, etc., in favor of projects of social assistance. The German Catholics have solved the problem by setting up two official Church agencies, Misereor and Adveniat, one for the social area, the other for the religious, and they often work together on the two aspects in one and the same program.

Remember that for the Church to inspire the world, it must first exist, and your aid may often be vital to that end.

4. A fourth priority: the missionary efforts, old and new

There are areas of our continent and our Church that have always been and still are missionary, particularly among indigenous populations. They can only function, as missions, with outside help, which sometimes comes from the Propagation of the Faith or other mission societies. Often the funds can be earmarked for specific projects.

A new mission area has formed throughout Latin America because of the qualitative changes I have mentioned. The impoverishment of many rural areas, the large numbers flocking to the cities and swelling them at phenomenal rates, largely through inner-city and peripheral slum dwellings, produce growing sectors of our society that suffer from both economic and spiritual anomia, that is, a lack of identity, a lack of support, a disorientation in the shifting sands of national problems.

The Church has to be a prime mover in raising consciousness on the vital and integral needs of these peoples. But, once again, to do so effectively, the Church must be present, through and in the people themselves. This means a conscious, persistent, and faithful effort and program to train pastoral agents in each area and community, the promotion of the community itself, and assistance in building up its parish centers, churches, parish houses, etc., modestly and in evangelical poverty, through which that presence, fundamentally religious and thereby also strongly social, is made more dynamic and effective.

We have many needs in this missionary evangelization, which is both communal (building up church base groups) and liberating (freeing from sin, freeing up for strong social efforts to overcome community needs, injustices, and conflicts). Some of these needs: support for priests, sisters, and lay pastoral agents, especially in the initial stages of raising community; support for their training, for training centers and programs; support, or at least seed money, for building church centers, temples, and parish houses in the poorest areas.

Such assistance often speeds up by five or ten years the bringing together of a community in and about a parish. Like all help, but with particular stress here, this aid should be given with the agreement of the local bishop, so that it will fit well into the evangelization of the whole diocese.

5. A fifth priority: ministerial and formation programs

The promotion and development of local vocations is vital for all our churches. But it is even more critical for some of our churches, which are only now emerging from a chronic lack of local vocations and an excessive dependence upon pastoral agents from abroad.

I refer here to all local vocations in the Church: lay, religious, and priestly. Our experience is increasingly clear: the promotion and strengthening of lay vocations and their active responsibilities in the Church, particularly among the young, is the prime source and cause of the encouraging increase in priestly and religious vocations in many, if not most, Latin American countries.

Assistance to training programs and to lay movements, both spiritual and apostolic — for example, for catechists and professors of religion — therefore provides a twofold benefit to our churches. The council's call to one common sanctity and commitment in and for the Church in the world today has greatly narrowed the gap between the laity and the religious or priest.

Assistance to seminaries, their installation and operation, has once more become a vital necessity. These, like the priesthood, are generally no longer the isolated realities they were in the past. Other groups in the Church often use their facilities, and the seminary training includes more contact with the pastoral activity in all sectors of the Church. The seminaries are also becoming in many areas the locus of "continued education and formation" programs for the clergy and, when possible, also for the religious and laity.

6. A sixth priority: the Church and social change

The pope, on his recent visit to Central America, insisted very strongly and frequently on the Church's role in promoting the necessary social changes in our area. I have deliberately left this point to the end for two reasons: first, to stress the fact, as the pope has often done, that the Church must be religious if it is to give at all, religiously or socially; and second, to emphasize that many private agencies, Catholic, Protestant, and ecumenical, are financing in our part of the world social groups and programs advocating and promoting policies and activities hostile to the very spiritual and social values the Church defends. This support often results from a snap visit, a chance contact, a friend on the spot — and a great lack of understanding of the basic spiritual and ideological forces at stake. At times the groups being financed by religious bodies from abroad are, in effect, in more or less hostile relationship to the Church, especially in Central America. They should by all means be very aware of the social needs and address them, but with an ear attentive to the guidance of the local church. We are intent upon making our "preferential option for the poor," announced in Puebla, a reality for our churches in each country. Help us to do so.

This sixth norm or priority leads to my conclusion. When you are going to assist or finance a project, try to do it with as much awareness of what is going on in the local church as you can possibly discern. Resist, however, the temptation to spend large sums on staff and other overhead. Develop your contacts with the local church, visit from time to time, exchange information with it and with the fellow funding agencies. It is both humorous and discouraging to discover, at times, groups in our countries that are being funded by Catholic agencies from abroad, unbeknownst to the local pastors, and whose activities are sometimes equally unknown to those who are funding them. There are even cases where such groups are highly divisive on the local scene. There is so much to be done. Let's try to do it together.

22.

Setting Priorities for the Church:
A View from Africa

Bishop Peter K. Sarpong

WE OF THE AFRICAN CHURCH WOULD LIKE TO EVOLVE A theology founded on the African reality. We are convinced that if we stick to the Western type of theology, we cannot touch the hearts of our simple people and we shall continue to be removed from the grass roots, talking over the heads of the faithful. Our other main interest is to make the Church and her theology speak to the African in his existential condition.

I am a Church leader. In any case, I am supposed to be! As such, I must promote the kingdom of Christ among my people in Ghana. He has said in no uncertain terms that his kingdom is for the poor. He has entrusted the care of the downtrodden, the powerless, the dispossessed, the deprived, the marginalized, the sick, the hungry, the poor . . . to the Church. I strive to demonstrate my full awareness of this in some meaningful manner. I have made it a policy to visit an average of two villages in my diocese every weekend. In those villages, what I see contradicts the human dignity that the Gospel preaches. There is squalor, superstition, general distress, and suffering.

I want to do something to console my people. But what can I do in real, practical terms? My utter helplessness in the face of situations calling for my intervention is

Bishop Peter K. Sarpong is the Bishop of Kumasi, Ghana.

my greatest agony. My anguish increases with the realization that much of the hardship to which the masses of people are subjected is caused by educated leaders, many of whom have passed through the portals of Catholic schools. It is their perpetration of the social crimes of bribery and corruption, extortion, nepotism, black-marketing, smuggling, and hoarding that has in large measure caused the political and economic chaos that has resulted in the total lack of the most basic human needs: drugs, water, educational materials, food, safety, clothing, housing, transportation. What is even worse, crimes such as abortion, armed robbery, and assassination, which were unheard of in the "good old days," have now become the order of the day. Add to these the many repressive measures instituted against the people in the blessed name of national security, and the picture is gloomy indeed.

With more than 50 independent nations, Africa is a vast, heterogenous land with a bewildering variety of ethnic groups, cultures, and occupations. But what has been outlined above for Ghana can, without much exaggeration, be multiplied several times over the continent.

To be sure, the Church appears to be gaining a foothold in Africa. On Sundays churches are filled to capacity; church societies flourish; converts are made easily; the African clergy and religious are fast increasing in number. For many outside Africa, these are signs that the future of the Church is in Africa. I have my doubts. The relevance of the Church is being questioned by many enlightened elements in large cities like Lagos, Accra, Nairobi, and Kinshasa.

The Church does not appear to be speaking to the ordinary African. She does not have the same grip on the African that the traditional religion had. She appears to have become a status symbol; the faith of many is only skin-deep. In times of crisis many Christians do not hesitate to fall back on their traditional magico-ritualistic devices for assistance. The worst in tribalism manifests itself with alarming frequency. A witchcraft mentality persists, and many outmoded customs prevail.

Several factors account for this situation. The Church is only 100 years old in sub-Saharan Africa. Forty-two percent of Africans are Moslems (145 million), while 30 percent (104 million) still follow the traditional religion. In 1980 the population of Africa was 468,765,000, of which only 12.6 percent (59,141,000) were Catholics. Clearly, Catholics in Africa are living in a predominantly non-Catholic environment. This factor, coupled with obnoxious customs that die hard, is bound to have an adverse effect on their faith and its practice.

The divergences among African countries present a very interesting picture. The major seminary in Enugu, Nigeria, is numerically the largest in the world. The 6 million Catholics of this giant country, however, represent only 6 percent of the total population. Zaire's 12.5 million Catholics form 44.5 percent of the population, but in absolute terms it tops the list of African countries in number of Catholics. With 0.1 percent, 0.2 percent, and 0.3 percent respectively, Somalia, Niger, and Tunisia have proportionately the lowest numbers of Catholics. The biggest concentration of Catholics is found in the Seychelles (93.4 percent of 66,000 inhabitants), the Cape Verde Islands (91.8 percent of 320,000), and Reunion (91.4 percent of 490,000 inhabitants). In Ghana Catholics form between 12 percent and 15 percent in a population of between 12 million and 14 million.

The hierarchies of Africa have been taking shape since 1950. Many countries, like Ghana, have an all-African hierarchy. Several indigenous religious congregations have been founded and are flourishing. Some, like the Immaculate Heart of Nigeria, have become pontifical and missionary, sending personnel to other parts of Africa.

In 1978 there were two patriarchates, 52 archdioceses, 288 dioceses, one prelature, one abbacy nullius, two apostolic administrations, apostolic vicariates, 11 apostolic prefectures, and two patriarchal vicariates. Africans in charge of the ecclesiastical territories included 44 archbishops, 181 bishops, five administrators, 14 auxiliary bishops, and 12 cardinals. One of the cardinals is presently in charge of the Papal Commission on Justice and Peace in the Roman Curia.

Problems

I can single out only a few of the many problems facing the Church in Africa:

1. Marriage: Over the centuries, Africa's has been a polygamous society, in which men have felt it their right to marry as many women as they can afford to. There were good reasons for this in the past, but the advent of Christianity has introduced a clash of interests. What does a pastor do with a polygamous man who is living happily with his wives, has several children with them, and would like to be a Christian? Is it Christian to ask him to drive away the wives? Who then looks after the children? And so on. What about a woman who is married to a polygamous man and would like to be converted? Should the polygamous state of her husband be an obstacle to her receiving the grace of God?

2. Capitalism: Unfair competition generated by liberal capitalism has done a lot of harm to Africa. Every African nation has a very few people who are fabulously rich, while the rest are living a subhuman existence. Not only do the poor lack the necessities of life, but even the little that some may have is taken away from them by their greedy, unscrupulous, powerful compatriots. These "masters" are found in business, in politics, in education — everywhere. The gap between the very wealthy 2 percent and the deprived 98 percent is widening all the time. Nobody condemns wealth acquired honestly, but when one adverts to the fact that 90 percent of the wealthy in Africa came by their pos-

sessions through objectionable and illegal means,
then it becomes clear that the Church in Africa has a
formidable, unenviable task to perform. The situation
disillusions many Church members and causes many
to leave the Church, especially when they realize that
these extortionists are often prominent members of
the Church. There is no gainsaying that sheer cupid-
ity and avarice are the primary disastrous current destroying the African church.

3. Socialism: Many Africans, repudiating the greed and
selfishness exhibited by their brothers and sisters, see
the salvation of Africa in the adoption of such ideologies as scientific socialism and Maoism. A cursory
look at the African political and economic scene leaves
one in no doubt that Africa is a very fertile ground for
any ideology that promises Africans heaven on earth.
Communists are hardly the angels they pretend to be.
Their motivation is well known. But the fact remains
that a hungry man is a desperate, angry man. A person struggling to exist will accept anything that gives
him hope of survival, and if anyone comes along with
promises of blessings that the old system has failed to
provide, it is natural that the new structure, whatever
it is, will at least be given a chance. This is what is
happening in Africa today.

As a result of this materialistic outlook on life, which
flows from these two currents, the African political
arena has been very turbulent. More than 20 African
nations have experienced military coups within as
many years. Civilian politicians are either incompetent
or corrupt. Their mismanagement of the affairs of
state gives the armed forces the alibi for considering it
their duty and their right to "rescue" their nations by
force of arms. Soldiers are not trained in the art of
statesmanship. So they invariably end up by worsen-
ing an already extremely bad or deteriorating situ-

ation. Intractable old problems are, in the process, exacerbated, and new ones created.

4. Islam: It is a Koranic doctrine that Islam must conquer the whole world, and Africa is its number one target. Islam will not rest on its oars until it has achieved its aim.

It adopts attitudes and practices appropriate to different situations. In the northern part of Africa, Islam has no problem; it is the national religion everywhere, and other religions are merely tolerated. In Nigeria Moslems are most powerful, and they exhibit their might in every way. When the constitution of Nigeria was being drawn up, militant Moslems agitated for Islamic laws and Shariah courts so that there would be two legal systems: one inspired by the British law system and the other established on the principles of the Koran. While the Moslem majority has not gained the upper hand to the same extent as their brothers and sisters in, say, Egypt and Libya, they are very much on the offensive. When the pope visited Islamic northern Nigeria last year, he received a very cold welcome and could not even give his prepared speech. In Ghana, where they are in the minority and their influence is minimal, Moslems must needs be less vocal, but the intensity of their activity, albeit covert, is not thereby lessened; it is a matter of strategy.

Many events in Africa can be attributed to the enthusiasm of Moslems for their monotheistic religion. We cannot talk about the Church in Africa in isolation from the tremendous influence of Islam.

Wherever possible, we try to avoid open confrontation and initiate dialogue. For our primary schools in Ghana, for example, we have produced textbooks on religious instructions that are acceptable to Protestants, Catholics, and Moslems. Some Catholics find it difficult to see how we can obviate the danger of watering down our Catholic doctrine. But the danger is only illusory, for the body of the textbooks deals solely with the issues of common concern, like the existence of God, justice, and so on. Matters of sectarian and denominational interest are treated in the appendices, where each group can choose the material about itself. This is, however, a very unique and isolated situation. In general, the bishops who have to deal with Moslems tell us that they operate in an atmosphere of open or concealed antagonism and hostility.

5. Sects: These are religious movements and churches of entirely African origin. They have been called pentecostal churches, healing churches, clap churches, spiritual churches, faith churches, and so on. These churches number in the thousands in each African country. Sundkler, in his book *Prophetism in South Africa*, has identified some 5,000 of these sects in one country. Basing themselves on the Bible, they call themselves Christian and mix Christian ideas and practices with traditional religious beliefs and ritual. The spectrum ranges from those that are very biblical to those whose nature is such that it is very difficult to ascertain whether or not they believe in the Bible. All of them are noted for their lack of theological sophistication and grounding. But this is where their enormous attraction to the simple African lies. They play on the emotions of their disciples, utilizing the magical mentality of the African to the full. Ministers take a keen interest in each individual worshiper and try to help him in the concrete world of his daily life. The worship sessions of the sects are very lively; devotees sing, dance, make merry, and approach God in a very human, African way.

It is noteworthy that the membership of the sects is largely drawn from the mainline churches, particularly the Methodist Church, but also the Catholic, Presbyterian, and Anglican churches. Some members of the established churches abandon their allegiance altogether to become members of these new ones. Others adopt the new churches while retaining their membership of the old churches. In Kumasi, hundreds of Catholics will attend Mass on Sunday and, immediately after, rush to the sect to pray! One wonders what they thought they were doing at Mass if not praying.

The Catholic Church in Africa has much to learn from these sects, even if most of their founders are demonstrably frauds. They make their followers feel they are human beings. Their worship is not dreary; it is not something to be gone through quickly and forgotten about. Indeed, normally their Sunday services last anywhere from four to eight hours. In a way, the sects are a kind of rebellion against the old churches, whose liturgy is fashioned on European sentiments and fails to impress the African.

If we are serious about evangelizing Africans, then we can ill afford to ignore the African culture in our efforts. After all, it has produced such great saints as Cyprian, Augustine, Anthony, Perpetua, Felicity. These pillars of the Church were successful because they employed the African idiom effectively. Had they not restricted their activity to the urban areas, the African church would never have been swept aside by the might of Islam.

Responses

In light of these forces and of our common commitment to the cause of Christ, the Christian churches in Africa try as much as possible to work in an ecumenical atmosphere. We have an ecumenical association of African theologians based in Cameroon. Our main aim is to join forces and let Christ lead us. Our interest lies in two main areas. First, we would like to evolve a theology founded on the African reality. We are convinced that if we stick to the Western type of theology, which is rooted to a large extent in Aristotelian philosophy transformed by Thomism, at least in the Catholic Church, we cannot touch the hearts of our simple people. We shall continue to be removed from the grass roots and to talk over the heads of the faithful.

Africans believe in the most salient aspects of the Catholic faith. A study of our cultural soil reveals that it was prepared by God for the reception of the Christian seed: the seed of love, of compassion, of unwavering faith in, and total reliance on, God.

So, one of the main interests of this association is to utilize what Pope Paul VI described as "the African genius," that is, African concepts and categories, in presenting the faith and inculcating the morality of the Christian religion in the African.

Our other main interest is to try to make the Church and her theology speak to the African in his existential condition. The African has been at the receiving end of injustices all throughout history. Has the word of God any consoling and assuring message for the vast majority of Africans languishing under the callous grip of ignorance, hunger, poverty, disease, oppression, and destitution?

So far, the Africans' faith is not deep enough to sustain them; it has not solidified because it is only obliquely related to their life. At worship the African is naturally spontaneous and addresses himself to his shame, his barrenness, and his illness. He misses all this when he attends the Roman Mass, where the priest reads a prepared prayer whose relevance to the individual may not be immediately obvious.

Our association publishes the *Bulletin of African Theology*, a quarterly geared toward achieving these objectives.

The mainline churches of Africa have an umbrella organization, the All-Africa Conference of Churches, whose headquarters are in Nairobi, Kenya. We, the Catholic bishops, have our counterpart, the Symposium of Episcopal Conferences of Africa and Madagascar, with its secretariat in Accra, Ghana.

Each section of Africa, north, east, central, west and south, has a regional association. The Association of Member Episcopal Conferences of East Africa (AMECEA) is based in Nairobi. In the West, we have the Association of Episcopal Conferences of Anglophone West Africa (AECAWA), headquartered in Liberia, and there is another grouping for the French-speaking West African bishops. The General Assembly of AECAWA takes place once every three years in a different city. There is another grouping for the French-speaking West African bishops. Each regional group discusses problems common to its region in order to find solutions.

On the academic level, the Church has four institutions of Advanced Ecclesiastical Studies. Until recently we were sending all our students to Europe and America for specialization. I now have two priests and four seminarians in the United States, two seminarians in Rome, one priest each in England, Ireland, and Germany, and so on. I myself had to go to Rome and Oxford for my specialized studies in theology and social anthropology. The current policy aims at trying as far as possible to let our priests and religious specialize in the environment to which they are going to apply their knowledge in the future. To this end we have established institutes of higher learning in Nairobi, Kenya, for English-speaking East Africans; in Port Harcourt, Nigeria, for English-speaking West Africa; in Abidjan, the Ivory Coast, for French-speaking West Africa; and in Kinshasa, Zaire, for French-speaking Central Africa.

Our perennial problems — and they are very severe — are the dearth of funds to run these institutes and the shortage of personnel to teach in them. Not infrequently the odds are almost insuperable. Yet the necessity of these institutes for the consolidation of the Church in Africa is incontrovertible.

In spite of her minority status, the Church is one of the formidable forces in Africa, enjoying a tremendous influence everywhere; the bishops' conferences and the bishops are respected and relied upon. The Ghanaian hierarchy has had to issue statements on national matters as a matter of routine, to the delight and admiration of all. The Church in Africa has always been in the vanguard of education, and without her the educational situation in Africa today would be lamentable. The Church has placed comparable emphasis on health care, both curative and preventative. In Ghana we have more hospitals than the government, all sited in remote areas, where the need is greatest. The Church has achieved much in the area of social welfare also. It has spearheaded the introduction of credit unions all over the continent. Indeed, in these areas the Church is so successful that even in hostile Islamic surroundings she is acknowledged and sometimes envied as the champion of progress and development. And the Church has produced some of the preeminent politicians of Africa, for example, the great Léopold Senghor of Senegal, Houphouey-Buoigne of the Ivory Coast, Mobutu Sese Seko of Zaire, Kwame Nkrumah of Ghana, and Julius Nyerere of Tanzania. Hence, few though the members of the Church in Africa are, one cannot imagine what the African continent would be like or how it would look without her.

The Church has been able to accomplish all this by forming outstanding laymen and laywomen who stand shoulder to shoulder with anyone in the universal Church. In material terms, the African church is very poor, and in terms of the number of priests, religious, and monks, it is handicapped. We have therefore been constrained to adapt ourselves to our poor situation and have had to rely extensively on dedicated laymen and laywomen. It has even been suggested that but for societies and organizations run by the laity, the Church would have been obliterated from the face of Africa ere long. In the cathedral parish of Kumasi alone, there are more than 40 different associations of men and women, girls and boys, manifesting their faith by performing various commendable works.

It was lay converts who penetrated the interior of Africa to spread the faith. In the absence of priests from our villages, it is lay people who conduct services on Sunday, give instructions, and, in fact, deputize for the priest in everything except hearing confessions and saying Mass. Some dioceses of Africa, to underscore the key role that the laity play in the Church, have instituted special ministries for them.

The indispensable contribution of the laity in Africa to the Church's activities did not commence with Vatican II. Right from the beginning, our forefathers, knowing our inadequacies in several areas, but mainly in terms of ordained priests, wisely learned to make use of the layperson. When, therefore, Vatican II came out with a decree on the laity, its instructions inevitably fell short of what we had been doing. After all, as far back as the 1880s, the laity in Africa had distinguished themselves so heroically that some of them were canonized in the 1960s as the martyrs of Uganda. There are millions more African lay saints than can ever be given such universal recognition.

So the Church has come to stay in Africa, despite the indisputable obstacles. Her impact is great and widespread; but much still remains to be accomplished. If we bask in the sunshine of false hope and unfounded optimism, we shall be overtaken by events. The time of mass conversions of so-called pagans is past and gone. The early missionaries did their best, and, indeed, one is at wit's end to comprehend how they could do so much in those deplorable and cruel circumstances. They had to walk on foot for miles on end through the inhospitable jungles of Africa, sleeping in forests and facing daily the menace of deadly diseases such as malaria, yellow fever, and smallpox. Most of them lasted a few days, others a few months; only a small number enjoyed the pleasure of evangelizing for a few years before being struck dead by disease, the venom of some dreadful creature, or human foe. Yet they remained undaunted.

Even though the conditions in which the early missionaries worked have changed for the better, the present-day indigenous clergy and missionaries have no less an arduous task to perform. They are working in countries that are independent, countries with definite political and economic stances that are not always in the best interest of Christianity or even humanity. They are not dealing with illiterates, but find themselves face to face with people who may be better educated and more intelligent than themselves. They perpetually risk the danger of being slandered and denigrated. They have to know how to adapt themselves without in any way compromising the Gospel of the Lord. It is not easy.

Our Needs

It is here that we need the help of the older churches. We need their help in evolving theologies that suit us. We look up to the older churches to tell us what they did or are doing to offset the effects of crude materialism, which has invaded us through liberal capitalism and atheistic socialism. We look to them to find out how we can make our societies really Christian. We, of course, are aware that the old churches have their own problems. They have to deal with crime, laissez-faire attitudes, irreligion, sexual promiscuity, and permissiveness, to name a few vices negating the Christian cause. But we appeal to the old churches to feel with us, to come to our aid by way of good will, of financial aid, and of assistance in the form of equipment, personnel, and, most importantly, prayers.

We require your brotherly assistance to break the vicious circle of hunger, disease, and poverty. Because people are hungry they become sick. Because they are ill they cannot work, and so they are poor. Because they are poor they cannot get enough to eat, and so they are hungry; and we are back to square one. You may start with any of the trinity of human evils, and the story is the same. The three in turn breed ignorance and superstition of the worst type. But this is surely not as God intended things to be. It is fundamental to our faith that God created man in his own image, and we cannot conceive God as rugged, ignorant, destitute, wretched, uncouth, needy, deprived.

Here the rigid dichotomy between evangelization and human development, the sacred and the profane, spirit and matter, becomes artificial. We must seek to improve the lot of and liberate the whole man, body and soul, mind and spirit, both the tangible and the intangible in him. Man is man precisely because he is a composite of all these, a homogenous unit that cannot be truncated and dismembered without destroying its very essence. Man must not be treated piecemeal, but approached holistically. The catastrophic economic plight of the African affects his spiritual life.

For several reasons, the religious function of the Church in Africa must go hand in hand with a genuine effort at improving socioeconomic conditions for the masses of the people, or else her credibility and influence will be shattered to pieces.

But when all is said and done, man's wretchedness must be blamed squarely on sin. Pride, greed, and selfishness account for all the inhumanities and atrocities, hardships and distress that have become our daily bread in Africa. We need God. Only he can restore us to our pristine state of sanctity, justice, love, and peace. We must help one another to refrain from taking our inspiration from, and depending on, human beings. Let us go back to God, and all our problems will be obliterated.

264 \ *Bishop Peter K. Sarpong*

So, I think one top priority for the Church in Africa is the formation of youth who will show unflinching loyalty and total commitment to the noble cause of Christ. We believe that to secure a future for the Church, we must get hold of the young man and the young woman now. We therefore have such associations as the Catholic Youth Association, Young Christian Students, Young Christian Women, Pax Romana, the Aquinas Society, the Catholic Youngsters Club, the Movement of Catholic Intellectuals, Catholic Graduates for Action, and others, all of which, with varying degrees of intensity, are bursting with vitality. If you happen to receive requests for help from any of them, do please assist in the name of the good Lord. Only a devoted Catholic spirit holds a future for the Church in Africa.

I would like to stress here the need for exchanges of visits. Once you have been to an African country and seen things for yourself, you will never be the same again. Stereotypes of Africans as either innocent souls or diabolical savages will be discarded. Africans are neither angels nor devils; they are human beings, like all other persons, capable of the vilest actions and at the same time the most noble deeds. The African can be as immoral as the Italian, as holy as the Italian. He can be as sinful as the Irishman and as saintly as the Irishman. He can be as selfish as the American and as generous as the American. He can be as cruel as the Russian and as gentle as the Russian. He can be as murderous as the German and as kind as the German. He can be as hypocritical as the Englishman and as honest as the Englishman. In brief, in his behavior the African is an Italian, an Irishman, an American, a Russian, a German, and an Englishman — a human being.

I therefore have the temerity to suggest that a group such as yours occasionally organize exchanges of students and young people between African countries and yours. In 1976 I was invited to send a group of young students, 50 in all, to Holland. A group of young Dutch

boys and girls made a reciprocal visit to Ghana the following year. The two visits have achieved much more than
any talks or other types of education could ever do.

I led another group of 20 young singers, drummers,
and dancers to Germany for three weeks. The advantage
to both the Germans who saw or met us and to us is
incalculable. Such exchanges, financed by the older
churches, go on frequently among our Protestant breth-
ren.

American dioceses and parishes could take a further
step and adopt dioceses and parishes in Africa as their
sister dioceses or parishes. I think they call this practice
twinning or partnership. Much could be learned about
one another through letters, exchange of magazines,
talks, and other ways. I also humbly submit that it would
go a long way to enhance the universality of the Church if
priests and bishops from America could go on holidays to
Africa to live with their brothers and sisters there, work
with them, experience their problems, and share their
joys for a month or so.

On major international issues like apartheid and co-
lonialism, we expect our older churches to face up to the
reality and speak out for the truth. Sadly, rather often in
Africa the credibility of the Church is dealt a deadly blow
by the action of people and governments of countries that
have the reputation for being Christian. Church leadership in many an African country has often been extremely
embarrassed by such actions. We need to be aware of
each others' problems; we need to be sensitive to each
others' plights. It is surely because you are convinced of
this that you have asked me to come all the way from
Ghana via Europe to address you for 30 to 60 minutes.
You have done this at considerable sacrifice and expense
to yourselves. You have shown love and demonstrated
that it is absolutely essential that we stand together under the banner of Christ. Love and unity are just what we
want and need in Africa. No state can be higher.

You have helped us a lot by sending us money, drugs, equipment, and personnel. Without your foundations and others in Europe, Canada, and Australia, we could hardly do anything either in the purely pastoral area or in socioeconomic development. On behalf of my brother and sister Africans, I register our sincere gratitude and appreciation for your Christian sensitivity. In your own way you are missionaries. I can assure you that missionaries can never be redundant anywhere in Africa. If their motivation is, as it should be, love, then love can never be defeated. It is love that has prompted you to invite me to share with you some of our concerns and some of our triumphs. I have done my best to give you a bird's-eye view of the situation in Africa. It could never be said to be a complete description. In fact I have only scratched the surface, just indicating the major points deserving attention. My hope is that I have not wasted your time. If I have, forgive your brother. For the rest, let me assure you that together with you and in union with our brothers and sisters elsewhere in the world, through the powerful intercession of the Blessed Virgin Mary, Mother of God and our Mother, we shall relentlessly seek to preach, establish, promote, and spread the kingdom of Christ.

In this way we set for ourselves the only task of the Church in Africa: to replace hatred with love, let violence give way to peace, overcome sin with righteousness, make injustice succumb to equity, chase away falsehood with truth, dispel ignorance with wisdom, wipe out superstition with the light of Christ, subject domination and repression to true freedom and liberty, and thus restore the battered humanity of the Africans to its God-given dignity. In the last analysis, this is the only priority worth setting, to the confusion of the devil, for the salvation of souls, and to the greater glory of God.